GENDER, AGEING AND LONGER WORKING LIVES

Cross-national perspectives

Edited by
Áine Ní Léime, Debra Street, Sarah Vickerstaff,
Clary Krekula and Wendy Loretto

First published in Great Britain in 2017 by

Policy Press
University of Bristol
1-9 Old Park Hill
Bristol
BS2 8BB
UK
t: +44 (0)117 954 5940
pp-info@bristol.ac.uk
www.policypress.co.uk

North America office:
Policy Press
c/o The University of Chicago Press
1427 East 60th Street
Chicago, IL 60637, USA
t: +1 773 702 7700
f: +1 773-702-9756
sales@press.uchicago.edu
www.press.uchicago.edu

© Policy Press 2017

British Library Cataloguing in Publication Data
A catalogue record for this book is available from the British Library

Library of Congress Cataloging-in-Publication Data
A catalog record for this book has been requested

ISBN 978-1-4473-2511-6 hardcover
ISBN 978-1-4473-2514-7 ePub
ISBN 978-1-4473-2515-4 Mobi
ISBN 978-1-4473-2513-0 epdf

The right of Áine Ní Léime, Debra Street, Sarah Vickerstaff, Clary Krekula and Wendy Loretto to be identified as editors of this work has been asserted by them in accordance with the Copyright, Designs and Patents Act 1988.

Cover design by Policy Press
Front cover image: Shutterstock
Printed and bound in Great Britain by CPI Group (UK) Ltd, Croydon, CR0 4YY
Policy Press uses environmentally responsible print partners

Contents

List of tables and figures   v
List of abbreviations   vii
Notes on contributors   ix
Acknowledgements   xii
Series editors' preface   xii

Part One: Gendering later life work: Empirical, theoretical and policy issues   **1**

one   The empirical landscape of extended working lives   3
    Debra Street

two   Theoretical and conceptual issues in the extending working lives agenda   27
    Clary Krekula and Sarah Vickerstaff

three   Gender perspectives on extended working life policies   53
    Áine Ní Léime and Wendy Loretto

Part Two: Extended working life in seven OECD countries   **77**

four   The Australian empirical landscape of extended working lives: a gender perspective   79
    Elizabeth Brooke

five   Extended working lives in Germany from a gender and life-course perspective: a country in policy transition   99
    Anna Hokema

six   Extended working life, gender and precarious work in Ireland   117
    Áine Ní Léime, Nata Duvvury and Caroline Finn

seven   Ageing and older workers in Portugal: a gender-sensitive approach   137
    Sara Falcão Casaca and Heloísa Perista

eight   Sweden: an extended working life policy that overlooks gender considerations   157
    Clary Krekula, Lars-Gunnar Engström and Aida Alvinius

nine   The United Kingdom – a new moral imperative: live longer, work longer   175
    Sarah Vickerstaff and Wendy Loretto

ten   Is 70 the new 60? Extending American women's and men's working lives   193
    Debra Street and Joanne Tompkins

Part Three: Conclusion   **217**

eleven   Gendered and extended work: research and policy needs   219
for work in later life
Sarah Vickerstaff, Debra Street, Áine Ní Léime and
Clary Krekula

Index   243

List of tables and figures

Tables

1.1	Life expectancy at birth by gender (1975, 1995, 2015, estimated)	7
1.2	Percentage of national populations aged 65+	8
1.3	Dependency ratios (2015, estimated)	8
1.4	Labour force participation rates, by gender and age (2013)	11
1.5	Gender pay and pension gaps	12
1.6	Average effective retirement ages, by gender (1995–2012)	13
1.7	Older workers' experiences (2003, 2007, 2013)	15
1.8	Ratio of women's to men's share of care work (2014)	16
1.9	Time use for women and men aged 15–64 (various years)	16
1.10	Full-time/part-time older worker employment (%), by gender, age and country (2013)	17
1.11	Involuntary part-time employment	19
3.1	Policy dimensions	
3.2	Changes to state pension age/normal retirement age	65
3.3	Policies to encourage flexible working around retirement age	65
3.4	Policies for work and (adult) family care (2010)	68
3.5	Policies for work and childcare: paid maternity leave (weeks), April 2015	69
5.1	Labour force participation rates of age group 55–69 in Germany (%) (1985–2015)	106
6.1	Contract type and hours of work in Ireland, by year and sex	126
6.2	Gender gap (%) in mean annual employee cash income (€), by age group	127
6.3	Health conditions of older employed workers, by age and sex	128
7.1	Distinctive patterns of employment in Portugal (2014)	147
7.2	Patterns of vulnerability in the labour market in Portugal and the EU28 (2014)	148
9.1	Percentage of men and women age 50+ in employment in the UK, by age band (2004–16)	176

Figures

1.1	Year at which 50% of women aged 15–64 were in the labour force	10
4.1	Female employment over age 55, by industry (1995–2015)	88
10.1	Annual labour force participation rate of Americans aged 55 and older, by age (1975–2015)	196
10.2	Median weekly earnings for full-time work, by age and gender (2014)	198
10.3	Access to retirement income for men and women aged 65 years and older, for largest race and ethnic groups (2011)	199
10.4	Percentage of men and women aged 65 and older receiving income from each source	199

List of abbreviations

ABS	Australian Bureau of Statistics
ATP System	Supplementary Pension System (Sweden)
CIG	Commission for Citizenship and Gender Equality
CPI	Consumer Price Index
DB	Defined benefit
DC	Defined contribution
DSP	Disability Support Pensions (Benefits)
DWP	Department for Work and Pensions
EC	European Commission
ENEA	National Strategy for Active Ageing
ESA	Employment Support Allowance
EWL	Extended working lives
FMLA	Family and Medical Leave Act
GDP	Gross domestic product
GDR	German Federal Republic
HILDA	Household, Income and Labour Dynamics in Australia Survey
IB	Incapacity Benefit
IGR	Intergenerational report
IRA	Individual Retirement Account
ISF	Synthetic General Fertility Index
LFP	Labour force participation
LTU	Long-term unemployment
MTAWE	Male total average weekly earnings
NGO	Non-governmental organisation
NRA	Normal retirement age
NWCI	National Women's Council of Ireland
OECD	Organisation for Economic Co-operation and Development
PAYG	Pay-as-you-go principles
RSI	Minimum Income Benefit
SCP	State contributory pension
SCSEP	Senior Community Service Employment Program
SNP	State non-contributory pension
SPA	State pension age
SS	Social Security
STP	Single-Tier Pension
TILDA	The Irish Longitudinal Study of Ageing

| WASPI | Women Against State Pension Inequalities |
| WLB | Work–life balance |

Notes on contributors

Aida Alvinius, PhD, is a researcher in sociology at the Swedish Defence University's Leadership Centre in Karlstad. Her research has focused on leadership during demanding conditions. She has published within the field of organisation, leadership and emotion management.

Elizabeth Brooke, Adjunct Professor, Swinburne University, has been researching the effects of the ageing global population on workforce demographics, policies and practices since the 1990s. As former Director of the Business, Work and Ageing Centre, Swinburne University, her publications include Australian research into the economic and social contributions of older workers and innovative models of aged care workforce development. She is currently co-authoring a book on women's retirement transitions.

Nata Duvvury is senior lecturer and co-Director of the Global Women's Studies Centre, National University of Ireland, Galway. Her research interests include older women workers' access to pensions, gendered impacts of recession and austerity, and precarious employment and older workers. She has published a number of research articles and reports and several book chapters. She is actively involved in several networks, including Board member of the Research Stream on Gender, Labour and Welfare State of the European Sociological Association.

Lars-Gunnar Engström has a PhD in public health and is a senior lecturer in social work at Karlstad University, Sweden. Her primary research interests are sickness and social insurance, health, and gender in an extended working life.

Sara Falcão Casaca, PhD, is a sociologist and Senior Associate Professor at Sociology at ISEG (The School of Economics and Management), University of Lisbon. Sara is a Full Researcher at the Research Centre in Economic and Organisational Sociology (SOCIUS-CSG), where she has coordinated and participated in research projects mainly focused on gender, the labour market and organisations. These have also been main topics of her publications. She has been providing expert advisory support on public policies related to gender and non-discrimination issues for national and international public agencies.

Caroline Finn completed a PhD at the National University of Ireland Galway in 2016 on gender and poverty, analysing EU–SILC data. Her research interests include intra-household economic inequality and gender relations, poverty and older people, and gendered impacts of economic recession. She has co-authored several journal articles and research reports, including one on *Deprivation and its measurement in later life* (2012) and a position paper, 'The effects of austerity on older people in Ireland', for Active Retirement Ireland in 2014.

Anna Hokema is a research associate at the Research Center on Inequality and Social Policy (SOCIUM), University of Bremen, Germany. She is a sociologist and holds a PhD from the Bremen International Graduate School of Social Sciences. Her research focuses on ageing and the labour market, gender, and qualitative research methods. Her most recent publication (with S. Scherger) is 'Working pensioners in Germany and the UK: quantitative and qualitative evidence on gender, marital status, and the reasons for working', *Journal of Population Ageing* (2016), 9, 91–111.

Clary Krekula, PhD, is an Associate Professor in Sociology at Karlstad University. Her research has focused on a gender perspective on age and ageing. Her publications also include work on critical age studies and organisational ageing.

Wendy Loretto is Dean of the University of Edinburgh Business School, and Professor of Organisational Behaviour. Her main research field is age and employment, with a particular focus on changes in employees' and employers' attitudes and practices in extending working lives. She is especially interested in the ways in which gender and age interact to affect work and retirement experiences. She has several publications in these areas.

Áine Ní Léime is on Year 3 of a Marie Sklodowska Curie International Outgoing Research Fellowship at Case Western Reserve University at Cleveland, Ohio, conducting a qualitative, internationally comparative research project exploring the gender implications of extended working life policy in the US and Ireland. Her publications are in the areas of gender, ageing and employment.

Heloísa Perista, PhD, is a sociologist and senior researcher at CESIS (Centro de Estudos para a Intervenção Social [Centre for Studies for Social Intervention]). Equality of women and men in the labour market is a particular focus of her research themes and publications. She has been involved in a large variety of projects and in several European Union networks, such as the EC Network of Experts on the Situation of Women in the Labour Market and the European Observatory on Working Conditions (EWCO/Eurofound). She also has a long record of work as an expert consultant and a trainer on gender equality.

Debra Street is Professor and Chair of the Department of Sociology at the State University of New York (SUNY) at Buffalo. A Fellow of the Gerontological Society of America, an elected member of the US National Academy of Social Insurance, and recipient of the CISP 2016 Award for Outstanding Contributions to International Education, Street has authored over 70 articles, chapters and research reports focused on health and income security over the life course.

Joanne Tompkins is a PhD student in Sociology at the State University of New York (SUNY) at Buffalo, specialising in ageing, the life course and medical sociology, particularly how social factors influence end-of-life planning.

Sarah Vickerstaff is Professor of Work and Employment at the University of Kent, UK. Her research interests are in the changes to the relationship between paid work and the life course, in particular, at the beginning and end of working life. She has published widely in peer-reviewed journals, books and reports on these topics and on gender and older workers.

Acknowledgements

Áine Ní Léime wishes to acknowledge the Marie Sklodowska Curie International Outgoing Fellowship, funded by the European Union's Framework Programme 7, which provided funding that facilitated her to engage in policy analysis.

The editors wish to acknowledge Joanne Tompkins for her excellent, efficient and timely work in checking references and ensuring conformity with Policy Press guidelines.

The editors wish to acknowledge the Irish Research Council's New Foundations Scholarship in 2014, which facilitated discussion of the initial idea for the book.

COST Action IS1409 also provided opportunities for the editors to meet and discuss the work in progress.

Series editors' preface

Chris Phillipson (University of Manchester, UK),
Toni Calasanti (Virginia Tech, USA) and
Thomas Scharf (Newcastle University, UK)

As the global older population continues to expand, new issues and concerns arise for consideration by academics, policy makers and health and social care professionals worldwide. Ageing in a Global Context is a series of books, published by Policy Press in association with the British Society of Gerontology, which aims to influence and transform debates in what has become a fast-moving field in research and policy. The series seeks to achieve this in three main ways. First, the series is publishing books which rethink key questions shaping debates in the study of ageing. This has become especially important given the restructuring of welfare states, alongside the complex nature of population change, both of these elements opening up the need to explore themes which go beyond traditional perspectives in social gerontology. Second, the series represents a response to the impact of globalisation and related processes, these contributing to the erosion of the national boundaries which originally framed the study of ageing. From this has come the emergence of issues explored in various contributions to the series, for example: the impact of transnational migration, cultural diversity, new types of inequality, and contrasting themes relating to ageing in rural and urban areas. Third, a key concern of the series is to explore inter-disciplinary connections in gerontology. Contributions provide a critical assessment of the disciplinary boundaries and territories influencing the study of ageing, creating in the process new perspectives and approaches relevant to the 21st century.

Against this background, we are especially pleased that one of the early books in the series addresses a range of concerns relating to gender, ageing and extended working lives. The book's editors, Áine Ní Léime, Debra Street, Sarah Vickerstaff, Clary Krekula and Wendy Loretto, have played a key role in raising awareness of the complex issues that arise for women and men when countries adopt policies aimed at encouraging longer working lives. Taken together, the various chapters, guided by an insightful cross-national comparative framework, make a major contribution to theoretical and empirical understandings of this changing emphasis of public policy. The book will be essential reading for academics, non-governmental organisations, and policy makers who share an interest in ageing.

Part One:
Gendering later life work: empirical, theoretical and policy issues

ONE

The empirical landscape of extended working lives

Debra Street

Introduction

Populations everywhere are ageing, but especially so in affluent countries. People are living longer and reaching older ages healthier and less frail than at any other time in human history. The combination of unprecedented longevity and the growing size of aged populations makes it obvious that state pension systems have become expensive components of modern welfare states. In most countries, politicians and policymakers are pursuing neoliberal policies to limit state interventions into social welfare in general, and to minimise, where possible, the growth of pension costs in particular. These complex social, economic and political circumstances are all part of the empirical landscape of extended working lives.

The sheer magnitude of demographic change seems, unavoidably, to pose some challenges for traditional public defined contribution pension systems, which are typically the costliest social policy tranche in most affluent countries. Although productivity increases since the mid-20th century created the capacity for nations to first expand, and then sustain, their welfare states, the changing ratio between young and older citizens undeniably puts the issue of the responsiveness of pension systems into public discourse. Alongside the policy influences associated with population ageing, current political preferences for welfare state restructuring (Pierson, 2001; Gilbert, 2002), the re-individualisation of risk (O'Rand, 2011) and neoliberal ideologies (Hacker, 2006) work together to create a seemingly irrefutable logic: people *must* extend their working lives and delay retirement. From a public policy perspective, the argument is often that individuals must wait longer to retire because their fellow citizens cannot contribute enough revenue to keep public pension promises. From a neoliberal ideological perspective, the state should stop nannying individuals by offering traditional pensions. Instead, individuals should be able to choose pension arrangements that they prefer and be more responsible for financing their own retirements, a process of re-individualising risk (see O'Rand, 2011). From a human capital perspective, and particularly in the context of proportionately smaller working-aged populations, another claim is that older workers have scarce human capital that employers *need*, and that failing to use older workers would be both irrational and inefficient (Weller, 2007). Furthermore, if the popular culture pundits have it right that '70 is the new 50' (Byham, 2007), individuals themselves may not only *want* to extend their working lives, but also benefit from it beyond earning wages (see, eg, the vast and growing literature on 'successful' ageing and its productive/active variants). Macro-level circumstances (demographic change, policy actions and ideological stances) combined with meso-level processes (evolving labour markets, firms coping with a projected shortages of workers) and claims that individuals want to work to older ages make initiatives designed to encourage workers to delay retirement and extend working lives widespread and seemingly inevitable.

This chapter sets the stage and complicates the seemingly simple *facts* that provide the overarching rationale for extending working lives everywhere by presenting the empirical patterns of real-world experiences for current older workers in the countries (Australia, Germany, Ireland, Portugal, Sweden, the UK and the US) analysed in greater detail in this book. Consequently, this chapter presents population-level data for each country (where available) to document the characteristics of populations, older workers and national labour markets. The empirical landscape presented here also provides a foundation on which the chapter authors build. For the *facts* to be fully considered, Krekula and Vickerstaff argue convincingly (in Chapter Two) that understanding requires problematising the life courses of both older people and ageing workers. This stance is amplified in Chapter Three, where Ní Léime and Loretto turn a feminist political-economy lens that is sensitive to life-course issues on policies associated with extended working lives. Becoming acquainted with the empirical landscapes of these countries can also help readers better understand similarities and differences experienced internationally, challenging the simplistic idea that extended working life could ever be a straightforward enterprise or a one-size-fits-all solution that would work everywhere. Populations are ageing. Pension systems are under pressure. However, exhorting individuals to stay in work to later ages or merely shifting retirement ages upwards, in the absence of thoughtful policies and practices that make work pay for older workers and their families, will accomplish little more than consigning a large subset of precariously employed older workers to low-wage, low-quality employment (Lain, 2012) and redistributing an even heavier burden of risk to some of the most vulnerable older citizens in each country (Ní Léime and Street, 2016). Understanding the foundation for the 'must work longer' claim starts with considering some of the empirical realities of ageing populations and older workers early in the 21st century.

Simple problems, simple solutions?

Must all or most workers in affluent countries remain in employment to older ages? A widespread conviction seems to be 'yes', and that the challenges of ageing populations and expensive pensions systems can be met by that straightforward and inevitable solution. Future workers must simply work longer than workers currently do (see Vickerstaff, 2010). The assumption is that individuals will be willing and able to remain in employment and take some pressure off state pension systems by doing so. As straightforward as that seems, such a simplified stance masks an incredibly complex set of multi-level interactions within country-specific labour markets, and a stunning lack of awareness of the interconnectedness of global trends, national economies, social policies and family lives. Even if extending work is a feasible strategy for some workers, making it a successful strategy for most workers can only be effective if policy changes are managed carefully and include initiatives that can support the many older workers whose risks and vulnerabilities are already well documented and understood. The first complicating factor is that national labour markets operate in a globalised economy: jobs are not available on demand (Brady et al, 2005). Further, labour markets are comprised of structured inequalities: classed and gendered workers and inadequate and unevenly distributed employment opportunities. The second complexity involves normative expectations that employed women are still held most responsible for unpaid care work (Ginn et al, 2001; Bianchi and Wight, 2010; Bianchi, 2011). Exacerbating that issue is the rapid change in the private sphere of family forms and intimate social relations (Bianchi, 2011). The third complexity is the reality of stagnant wages (Saez and Zucman, 2016) and the inability of many workers to save for their own retirements (Helman et al, 2015), even while currently employed. Expecting public pension system respite in such circumstances is a bleak prospect. A fourth complicating factor is in the jobs sector itself, populated as it is with reluctant employers (Johnson, 2007; Roscigno et al, 2007) or, in many places, few to no appropriate available jobs for older workers at all. There are many more. However, each of these complications is nested, for each country, within the additional complexities of national economies and cultures.

Other underlying assumptions to the uncritical advocacy of extending working lives are equally problematic: that older workers choose to retire, rather than face unemployment, underemployment or redundancy; that older workers can easily remain employed or find appropriate alternative employment when jobs are lost; that older workers' health and level of physical function are sufficient for the jobs that are available; that workers' non-age-related characteristics will be no impediment to employment; and that older workers' jobs will be good enough, that is, appropriate to their training, skills and abilities and offering enough hours and pay to promote financial security as working lives are extended in tandem with retirement age increases. Downplayed in such exhortations are many of the disconnects associated with: the spatial realities of skill-matching in an increasingly globalised labour market; predictable differences in the health statuses and functional capacities of some older workers; the persisting gender gaps in pay and normative expectations for unpaid work; and the pervasive ageism that contributes to the reluctance of many employers to retain, retrain and/or hire older workers.

Live longer, work longer

It would be naive to assume that the national pension systems first developed in the early 20th century to provide retirement income for male industrial workers would necessarily be up to the task of meeting the retirement needs of 21st-century citizens. After all, both the proportion of the population old enough to be eligible for pensions and the expected duration of receiving pensions were much lower in the early to mid-20th century, when national state pension systems were widely implemented and matured (Street and Desai, 2016), compared to the opening decades of the 21st century. The human triumph of increased longevity has multiplicative effects that worry policymakers. First, because people are living longer, individuals who retire can expect to receive pension benefits for much longer periods than the architects of 20th-century pension systems anticipated. For example, in the early years of US Social Security (enacted in 1935), average life expectancy in the US was only 61, the number of years a typical Social Security recipient was expected to receive his pension was only a few years (Moon and Mulvey, 1996) and 6.9% of the US population was 65 or older. Similar interactions between the size of the older population and more years of life expectancy from 65 onwards have occurred in all affluent countries. As Table 1.1 shows, even in the past few decades, women's and men's life expectancies have increased in all the countries analysed in this book.

Table 1.1: Life expectancy at birth by gender (1975, 1995, 2015 estimated)

	Women			Men		
	1975	1995	2015	1975	1995	2015
Australia	76.2	80.8	84.7	69.2	75.0	79.7
Germany	74.5	79.9	83.0	68.2	73.3	78.3
Ireland	–	78.3	83.1	–	72.8	78.4
Portugal	72.1	79.0	82.6	64.6	71.7	75.9
Sweden	78.1	81.7	84.0	72.2	76.2	80.1
UK	–	79.3	82.8	–	74.0	78.4
US	76.6	78.9	82.0	68.8	72.5	77.3

Note: Life expectancy at birth: How long, on average, a newborn can expect to live if current death rates do not change.
Source: For 1975 and 1995, data from http://stats.oecd.org (Health Status–Life Expectancy); for 2015, data from CIA (various years).

Beyond individuals living longer lives, the entire age structure of national populations has changed, from relatively young to ageing and older. The size of the aged population – the proportion of citizens old enough to have been traditionally entitled to public pensions – is relatively larger than at any time in human history and is still growing (see Table 1.2). Given that public pensions were designed and expanded in the early to mid-20th century, it is no surprise that a refrain first heard in the 1980s (Street and Quadagno, 1993), and that reverberates in even more policy circles now, is 'too many, too expensive'.

Nearly every affluent country has a public pension system designed to provide stable income in old age after individuals withdraw from paid employment, institutionalising retirement and bestowing what John Myles (1989) called a citizen's right 'to stop work before wearing out'. Pension systems were designed by policymakers who took into account the economic, labour market, family structures and social conditions of their times. One circumstance that informed early pension policymaking was the age structure of national populations, that is, the proportion of 'working-age' adults (conventionally defined as those individuals between the ages of 15 and 64) to the much smaller proportion of 'elderly' (65 and older) citizens. In pay-as-you-go defined benefit pension systems, the dominant approach to 20th-century pension funding, workers' contributions (earmarked contributions or other tax revenue) funded the state pensions for retirees.

Table 1.2: Percentage of national populations aged 65+

	1995	2000	2005	2010	2015
Australia	11	12	12.9	13.5	15.5
Germany	16	16	18.9	20.3	21.5
Ireland	12	12.3	11.5	12	12.6
Portugal	–	15	17.1	17.6	18.9
Sweden	17	18	17.4	18.8	19.9
UK	16	16	15.8	16.2	17.7
US	13	12.6	12.4	12.8	14.8

Source: Data for 1995, 2000, 2005, 2010 and 2015 from CIA (various years).

The balance between the size of the working-age and older populations has shifted over time. One measure of that is the dependency ratio (the proportion of children under 15 and adults 65 and older – presumed not to be employed – to adults aged 15–64), a shorthand way of representing different age groups in the population. According to its proponents, the dependency ratio reflects the 'burden' carried by citizens in working-age groups to sustain resources for 'non-productive' components of the population. The old-age dependency ratio is one statistic used to justify raising ages for pension eligibility and extending work. Table 1.3 shows estimates of total, youth and elderly dependency ratios for 2015.

Table 1.3: Dependency ratios (2015, estimated)

	Total	Youth	Elderly
Australia	50.9	28.2	22.7
Germany	51.8	19.6	32.2
Ireland	53.7	33.5	20.2
Portugal	53.5	21.6	31.9
Sweden	59.3	27.5	31.8
UK	55.1	27.6	27.6
US	50.9	28.6	22.3

Source: Data for 2015 from CIA (various years).

Dependency ratios reduce human social relationships to their lowest economic denominator. Dependency ratios do not consider investments or legacies, only value for 'independent' citizens assigned as earning power through employment. Other socially valuable activities, because they are not monetised as employment is, are beyond the scope of dependency ratios. Neither is the skewed distribution of wealth taken into account. Consequently, there are obvious problems with uncritically using dependency ratios to understand the possible implications of national age structures for labour forces – ranging from erroneous assumptions that many 15 year olds are routinely employed, or that most 15–64 year olds adults are employed but most 65 year olds are not, to the inability for dependency ratios to take unpaid and essential but non-monetised care work into account. Another flaw in dependency ratios is the fact that productivity increases have, at least until now, permitted fewer workers to support larger non-employed segments of the population in mostly non-problematic ways. It is not that dependency ratios are useless or unimportant for providing insights for policymakers about challenges confronting pension regimes; they serve as reminders of the shifting age structure of populations. However, dependency ratios used uncritically can be very misleading. Like so many other measures that are asserted confidently as the justification for undifferentiated appeals to extend working lives, dependency ratios taken out of context do little to inform policymakers about the finer-grained circumstances of dependency, or about which groups of older workers stand to benefit most from extended work or are most vulnerable to suffer in the face of such demands.

Although dependency ratios focus on these issues, proportionately fewer working-aged citizens, increased longevity and more pensioners are not the only population-level changes that bear on working lives. Recall that public pension systems were designed mainly to meet male industrial workers' retirement income needs. Yet, women's labour force participation has transformed labour markets around the world, reaching unprecedented levels by the beginning of the 21st century (Bianchi, 2011). Figure 1.1 shows, for each of the countries analysed in this book, the year that half of all adult women became labour force participants. Differences in the timing of women's increased labour force participation reflect national economic conditions and policy regimes.

The diversity of life experiences among older people have led critical and feminist gerontologists to problematise the notion of the presumed 'ungendered' and 'unclassed' worker for decades (Philipson and Walker, 1987; Arber and Ginn, 1991; Minkler and Estes, 1999; Calasanti

Figure 1.1: Year at which 50% of women aged 15–64 were in the labour force

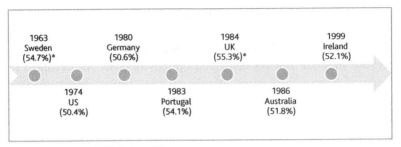

Note: * Data not available before this year.
Source: http://stats.oecd.org

and Slevin, 2001; Ginn et al, 2001; Orloff, 2009), and that stance is further explicated in the chapters that follow. National welfare regimes, labour markets and pension systems designed with breadwinning men and homemaking women as their underlying rationale have been disadvantageous for women's later-life financial security (Ginn et al, 2001). Sometimes, recognition that existing policies and pension systems poorly serve the later-life income needs of women or other vulnerable workers has provided an impetus for progressive policy changes that ameliorate disadvantage. Yet, interactions among pension structures, other social policies and labour market practices often punish women workers for doing what is socially necessary – childbearing – and normatively expected – providing unpaid child and elder care, preferably while also employed. Policies that do or do not support parenthood, make allowances for the provision of child and eldercare, or provide support for income maintenance are all implicated in women's and men's rates of employment over the life course and their financial circumstances in later life.

The contemporary older workers portrayed in Table 1.4 started their working lives during a period when manufacturing jobs were still widely available, where (in most countries) employment and occupational opportunities were more limited than they are for women today, and where (with the exception of Sweden) few 'family-friendly' policies were in place. These factors, the structure of public pension systems and cultural differences in expectations for women's and men's employment are reflected in the higher rates of labour force participation by older men than women in all seven countries. Counter-intuitively, the differences between women's and men's labour force participation are least in both the most 'family-friendly' Sweden and the least 'family-friendly' neoliberal US. One country encourages and supports women's employment while minimising income and status differences, while the other expects and necessitates women's work so that families can make ends meet.

Table 1.4: Labour force participation rates, by gender and age (2013)

	Women					Men				
	50–54	55–59	60–64	55–64	65+	50–54	55–59	60–64	55–64	65+
Australia	77.0	65.3	45.1	55.8	8.0	87.2	80.8	62.5	72.2	16.9
Germany	82.3	74.8	45.4	60.7	3.6	91.4	85.8	61.7	74.4	7.7
Ireland	66.0	58.2	34.5	47.0	5.0	87.0	76.3	56.4	66.9	14.5
Portugal	76.7	59.1	34.0	46.9	8.3	88.4	75.6	48.9	62.7	20.5
Sweden	88.0	82.4	64.7	73.5	11.1	91.8	89.5	74.1	81.8	18.8
UK	80.7	71.1	38.4	55.1	6.8	88.7	81.4	58.7	70.4	13.3
US	73.0	67.2	50.0	59.2	14.9	83.9	78.0	60.5	70.0	23.5

Note: The labour force participation rate is the labour force divided by the total working-age population.
Source: http://stats.oecd.org (Labour Force Statistics by Sex and Age Indicators).

Despite increasing and extensive labour force participation, the tension between public and private expectations in women's life courses mean that their earnings and later-life financial security have not, so far, kept pace with men's. Gender pay gaps (see Waldfogel, 1997; Bettio et al, 2013; D'Addio, 2015) are present in all of the countries considered in this book, and women's retirement income is, to a large extent, the product of both lifetime average lower earnings and pension systems designed for men's life courses (Ginn et al, 2001; Bettio et al, 2013; D'Addio, 2015), as shown in Table 1.5. Women experience lower rates of pay, on average, than men throughout their working lives; the disadvantage that women experience in terms of income is exacerbated in later life, as evidenced by an even larger gender gap in pensions.

While some countries have made gender-sensitive and family-friendly adjustments to public pensions, women still fare worse than men in terms of later-life income. The advantage of greater life expectancy for women is often accompanied by more years in poverty in later life. Table 1.5 documents the gender gap in pensions, an outcome that reflects the accumulation of women's disadvantages experienced during the prime income-earning years, due to both time out of paid work and a persistent gender gap in wages. Even in Sweden, with its social-democratic approach to social policy, women's pensions were worth nearly 30% less than Swedish men's; in the UK, the gender gap in pensions was nearly 40%, while it was even greater in Germany. If women in the future continue to experience working lives more similar to men's, the gender gap in wages may further diminish. However, the normative expectation of women's unpaid caring, which often requires periods of no or reduced employment, shows no evidence of abating, meaning that the large gender gap in pensions is likely to persist into the future.

Table 1.5: Gender pay and pension gaps

	Gender pay gap (2013)	Gender pension gap (2011)
Australia	18.0	n/a
Germany	13.4	44.8
Ireland	12.8	34.8
Portugal	16.7	31.5
Sweden	15.1[a]	29.4
UK	17.4	39.6
US	17.5	34.9[b]

Notes: [a] Swedish data from 2012; [b] US data from 2010.
Source: For the 2013 gender pay gap, data from OECD Stat (www.oecd.org/gender/data/genderwagegap.htm); for the 2011 gender pension gap, data from D'Addio (2015) (no data available for Australia).

In most wealthy countries, men's labour force participation at older ages declined in the last decades of the 20th century as most men chose to retire at or near the age of eligibility for partial or full public pensions. However, the rising age of eligibility for state pensions in many countries and the contraction of individualised retirement savings in the aftermath of the Great Recession (2008–09), when the world seemed on the verge of economic collapse, have contributed to many men choosing or trying to stay in employment to older ages. For women, patterns of labour force withdrawal are somewhat different. Women historically retired at younger ages than men, in part, due to lower state pension ages for women (most of which have since been equalised) (see Chapter Three) and as an outcome of couples' joint retirement decision-making (a result of women's propensity to have older spouses) (Moen et al, 2001; Ekerdt, 2010). As the data in Table 1.6 show, women still typically retire at younger ages than men, except in the US and the UK. The dominant trend for older women has been to remain employed to later ages, and at least since the 1990s, later retirement has also been the trend for men.

Table 1.6: Average effective retirement ages, by gender (1995–2012)

	Women					Men				
	1995	2000	2005	2010	2012	1995	2000	2005	2010	2012
Australia	59.5	59.7	61.4	63.2	62.9	62.3	62.0	63.7	65.1	64.9
Germany	59.0[a]	60.3	60.7	61.2	61.6	60.3[a]	61.0	61.8	62.0	62.1
Ireland	64.5	66.0	65.3	63.8	62.6	63.2	65.2	64.9	63.4	64.6
Portugal	62.3	62.5	66.1	64.6	66.4	63.4	65.1	66.3	66.5	68.4
Sweden	61.8	62.3	62.4	63.9	64.2	62.7	63.7	65.1	65.7	66.1
UK	60.7	60.9	61.4	61.9	63.2	62.0	62.4	63.3	64.1	63.7
US	63.6	63.5	63.2	65.3	65.0	64.2	64.7	64.6	65.5	65.0

Note: [a] Data for 1996.
Source: Organisation for Economic Co-operation Development (OECD) estimates based on national labour force surveys, EU Labour Force Survey and national censuses.

The aftermath of the Great Recession has influenced efforts to extend working lives, although more from the perspective of workers' lived experiences than through any progressive policy initiative. Many workers who had planned to retire younger but who could choose to remain employed did so in an effort to stabilise their financial security when housing and equities markets plummeted. For other older workers, the combination of devalued retirement savings coupled with job loss in their immediate pre-retirement years was an individual economic catastrophe that rippled its way through national economies (Munnell and Rutledge, 2013; for country-specific discussions, see also CESifo, 2015). Research shows that older workers who lose jobs often face downward employment mobility (Hirsch et al, 2000), as many did during the Great Recession. Losing a job and being able to find only lower-paid or less secure employment doubly disadvantaged some victims of the Great Recession. For such workers, attempting to extend working lives was a necessity, not a choice. Older workers have struggled to become re-employed, enduring longer spells of unemployment than their younger counterparts (see Table 1.7). Aside from US, where the economy recovered somewhat more quickly than most other countries, post-recession spells of long-term unemployment (a year or longer) have plagued older jobseekers. Among the challenges in the skills-based post-industrial economies covered in this volume is that current older workers often have relatively low levels of tertiary education, lacking the usual credentials for 'knowledge economy' jobs. Further, although training is often touted as the solution to employment problems (Behaghel et al, 2011), job-related training for older workers is rare. Even in Sweden and the UK, where training schemes are extensive, older workers receive much less training than their younger counterparts. Training is often touted by proponents of extending working lives as the solution to the older worker job–skills mismatch that undermines employability, but the data in Table 1.7 show that training is a relatively rare experience for contemporary older workers, and less readily available to them compared to younger workers.

Of course, capacity to work at older ages is not solely a function of job openings, retirement choices, training and education, or unemployment rates; it must also take into account differences across subgroups of older workers arising from their own health status and functional abilities, on the one hand, and the need for individuals (usually women) to provide unpaid care for family members whose age, health or frailty demands it, on the other (Calasanti and Slevin, 2001; Ginn et al, 2001). Although longevity and the health status of older persons has, on average, improved in recent decades, there remain large subgroups of older workers whose caring responsibilities, or their own health and functional abilities, make it difficult to remain in usual employment, or to be employed at all.

Balancing work and families

Even in countries with the most egalitarian social policies for supporting family needs – such as Sweden, where family-friendly policies are more prevalent than in most other nations – women still do substantially more unpaid work on average than men. Of course, different data sources measure the gender differences in unpaid work in different ways. For example, the Organisation for Economic Co-operation Development (OECD) Gender, Institutions and Development Database (see Table 1.8) calculates a ratio of women's to men's shares of unpaid care work.

The OECD time use data measures unpaid work in a somewhat different way. Regardless of country considered, the OECD time use data shown in Table 1.9 indicate that men were more engaged in the formal economy because they spend more minutes, on average, each weekday working for pay (and in leisure pursuits) compared to women. In contrast, women spent more time in unpaid work (and personal care). Except for Sweden, where men and women spend nearly identical amounts of time working, for all other countries, women spent more minutes per average day in work (paid plus unpaid) than did men. Women's disproportionate risk of low income in old age is not because they do not work enough. Rather, it is a result of failing to have sufficient, or sufficiently paid, employment or because they are unlucky enough to live in a country that fails to provide compensatory

Table 1.7: Older workers' experiences (2003, 2007, 2013)

	Australia			Germany			Ireland			Portugal			Sweden			United Kingdom			Unites States		
	2003	2007	2013	2003	2007	2013	2003	2007	2013	2003	2007	2013	2003	2007	2013	2003	2007	2013	2003	2007	2013
Employment																					
Employment rate, 55–64 (% of the age group)	50.3	56.5	61.5	39.0	51.3	63.5	49.4	54.2	50.9	51.7	51.0	46.9	69.0	70.1	73.7	55.4	57.3	59.7	59.9	61.8	60.9
of which, 55–59	60.2	66.4	70.3	60.1	66.7	75.9	57.3	61.7	59.9	59.5	59.0	57.4	78.2	79.8	81.7	67.4	68.9	72.5	68.4	69.7	68.6
of which, 60–64	37.2	44.8	51.5	22.6	32.9	49.9	39.2	45.3	40.8	42.8	42.0	35.8	56.9	60.7	65.8	39.9	44.6	46.1	48.9	51.7	52.1
Gender gap in employment, 55–64 (ratio men/women)	1.54	1.39	1.28	1.53	1.37	1.21	1.94	1.70	1.36	1.46	1.33	1.31	1.06	1.09	1.09	1.40	1.35	1.26	1.20	1.19	1.17
Employment rate, 65–69 (% of the age group)	14.1	20.2	26.0	5.5	7.1	12.6	14.4	18.5	15.8	27.4	27.0	20.3	13.0	14.7	18.7	13.4	15.2	20.4	26.2	28.7	30.3
Job quality																					
Incidence of part-time work, 55–64 (% of total employment)	25.0	24.3	24.4	22.9	24.0	24.5	24.5	26.3	30.9	17.2	16.6	16.7	16.6	16.4	12.3	29.4	28.3	27.7	11.7	10.8	9.5
Incidence of temporary work, 55–64 (% employees)	4.6	6.1	6.5	4.2	4.5	3.8	2.8	5.1	6.6	10.7	10.6	9.6	6.0	7.1	6.2	5.4	5.0	5.2	3.7	3.3	–
Incidence of self-employment, 55–64 (% of total employment)	22.4	18.9	15.7	18.3	16.7	14.4	21.8	20.5	21.3	46.1	42.3	32.1	13.8	14.0	13.5	18.9	18.6	19.5	–	–	–
Full-time[a] earnings, 55–64 relative to 25–54 (ratio)	0.96	0.97	1.02	1.06	1.07	1.08	1.04	1.16	1.02	1.16	1.38	1.33	1.07	1.10	1.10	0.92	0.95	0.97	1.09	1.08	1.15
Unemployment																					
Unemployment rate, 55–64 (% of the labour force)	3.8	2.7	3.8	9.7	10.3	5.8	2.1	2.3	10.7	4.3	6.5	13.7	4.8	3.9	5.1	3.3	3.3	4.7	4.1	3.1	5.3
Incidence of long-term[b] unemployment, 55+ (% of total unemployment)	43.2	30.5	34.0	66.5	76.9	63.0	45.4	42.4	74.2	54.5	67.9	74.6	38.6	27.8	31.0	36.3	35.4	47.7	18.7	14.3	34.7
Neither employed nor completely retired, 55–64 (% of the age group)	–							3.3	10.0				5.3	4.8	6.2						
Employability																					
Share of 55–64 with tertiary education[c] (% of age group)	26.9	29.4	35.2	26.5	26.1	29.3	19.8	20.3	27.3	7.9	8.0	12.0	27.2	27.9	30.6	25.5	29.7	34.4	40.4	42.0	45.3
Participation in training[d] 55–64																					
Absolute (% of all employed in the age group)	–	–		2.9	4.2	4.3	6.2	3.8	2.8	0.6	0.8	4.0	12.6	12.3	19.1	15.4	14.6	12.1	–	–	–
Relative to employed persons aged 25–54 (ratio)	–	–		0.63	0.69	0.67	0.77	0.64	0.74	0.24	0.54	0.52	0.80	0.82	0.81	0.66	0.68	0.76	–	–	–

Notes: [a] Mean gross weekly earnings, 2001, 2007 and 2011; [b] unemployed for more than one year. [c] 2005, 2007, 2012. [d] Job-related training during the last month, 2004, 2007 and 2012.

Source: OECD estimations from national labour force surveys, EU Labour Force Survey, the OECD Earnings Distribution database and the OECD Education database.

policies that acknowledge women's undervalued contributions with regard to the socially essential but entirely unpaid work that many women provide.

Table 1.8: Ratio of women's to men's share of care work (2014)

Country	Unpaid care work
Australia	1.81
Germany	1.79
Ireland	2.29
Portugal	4.25
Sweden	1.49
UK	1.85
US	1.61

Note: Female-to-male ratio of time devoted to unpaid care work.
Source: OECD Gender, Institutions and Development Database 2014 (GID-DB).

Table 1.9: Time use for women and men aged 15–64 (various years)

OECD activity categories	Women						
	Australia 2006	Germany 2001–02	Ireland 2005	Portugal 1999	Sweden 2010	UK 2005	US 2010
Paid work or study	172	181	197	231	269	197	242
Unpaid work	311	269	296	328	207	258	248
Total hours worked	483	450	493	559	476	455	490
Personal care	666	656	629	674	617	598	648
Leisure	269	326	290	200	272	339	269
Other	22	9	28	7	76	48	32
Men							
OECD activity categories	Australia 2006	Germany 2001–02	Ireland 2005	Portugal 1999	Sweden 2010	UK 2005	US 2010
Paid work or study	304	282	344	372	322	297	308
Unpaid work	172	164	129	96	154	141	161
Total hours worked	476	446	473	468	476	438	469
Personal care	649	636	602	677	573	574	627
Leisure	297	351	341	289	314	382	315
Other	18	8	23	5	77	46	29
Total hours worked	1440	1441	1439	1439	1440	1440	1440

Source: OECD Time Use Study.

One strategy that many unpaid carers use to balance their need for income with the need to provide care is to be employed part time. Over half of all carers are employed, and the patterns of persistent gendered difference in unpaid caring (along with other factors, such as pension structure and labour market conditions) are reflected in the patterns of full-time and part-time workers among men and women, as shown in Table 1.10. Not all of the part-time work is due to the demands of caring. Some older workers choose to reduce hours of employment to ease the transition from work to retirement, others are underemployed in that part-time work is all that they can find. In all countries, older women are more likely than men to be in part-time rather than full-time employment. Among women who remain employed after age 65, the US is clearly the outlier. Two thirds of American women aged 65+ who are employed work full time, compared to only about one in five in Germany. Compared to men in all the other countries in this volume except Ireland and the US, higher percentages of American women aged 65+ work full time. Even in the US, the pattern of later-life work is higher proportions of full-time work among men than women.

Table 1.10: Full-time/part-time older worker employment (%), by gender, age and country (2013)

	Women full time					Women part time				
	50–54	55–59	60–64	55–64	65+	50–54	55–59	60–64	55–64	65+
Australia	68.0	64.7	55.5	61.2	39.2	32.0	35.3	44.5	38.8	60.8
Germany	60.5	59.9	54.1	57.8	19.1	39.5	40.1	45.9	42.2	80.9
Ireland	57.7	56.7	43.8	52.4	30.7	42.3	43.3	56.2	47.6	69.3
Portugal	86.4	83.2	73.4	79.7	37.6	13.6	16.8	26.6	20.3	62.4
Sweden	88.7	87.3	80.2	84.1	28.5	11.3	12.7	19.8	15.9	71.5
UK	66.4	62.6	44.6	56.5	22.2	33.6	37.4	55.4	43.5	77.8
US	88.9	88.3	83.3	86.4	67.5	11.1	11.7	16.7	13.6	32.5
	Men full time					Men part time				
	50–54	55–59	60–64	55–64	65+	50–54	55–59	60–64	55–64	65+
Australia	93.3	89.9	82.9	87.1	59.8	6.7	10.1	17.1	12.9	40.2
Germany	94.6	93.3	86.6	90.7	38.2	5.4	6.7	13.4	9.3	61.8
Ireland	89.5	85.5	80.0	83.4	68.3	10.5	14.5	20.0	16.6	31.7
Portugal	95.3	90.3	80.2	86.5	42.4	4.7	9.7	19.8	13.5	57.6
Sweden	95.4	93.8	87.3	90.9	39.8	4.6	6.2	12.7	9.1	60.2
UK	93.0	89.4	79.8	85.6	49.2	7.0	10.6	20.2	14.4	50.8
US	97.2	96.1	92.4	94.6	77.3	2.8	3.9	7.6	5.4	22.7

Note: Common definition of full time and part time: full time = 30+ hours/week; part time = less than 30 hours/week.
Source: http://stats.oecd.org (Labour–Labour Force Statistics–Full-time Part-time employment–Incidence of FTPT employment–common definition).

Reasons for these gendered differences in older workers' employment are discussed in greater detail in the country-specific chapters.

Extended employment, whether full time or part time, in some well-compensated jobs and rewarding career paths doubtless appeals to many older workers who have good jobs and who are among the employed 'elite' in intrinsically rewarding, highly paid, highly skilled jobs with good occupational benefits. In contrast, for some older workers, pay cheques are earned through wear and tear on their bodies from physically demanding work. Other jobs are low skilled, routinised and non-autonomous employment, and they are usually poorly compensated. Such demanding and unrewarding jobs could hardly be expected to inspire a desire to extend working life, especially if retirement is perceived as a feasible alternative. Even a job that seems absolutely necessary to keep may become increasingly difficult to maintain for many older workers, especially women, due to competing demands within families. The neoliberal turn that has individualised pension risk has also shrunk public assistance for social care in many countries (Grootegoed and Van Dijk, 2012; but see Campbell et al, 2010) and seems to ensure that many contemporary older women will be unable to remain as full-time employed at the same time as they need income from jobs. After all, someone must care for ageing parents, frail spouses and young or disabled children. As women continue to outlive men, more and more older women workers confront similar challenges to their earlier and current women counterparts: how to balance work and family and how to manage to remain employed while still being 'good' workers/wives/mothers/daughters/daughters-in-law who routinely provide a disproportionate amount of unpaid care work within families.

Working longer, but in which kinds of jobs?

Even leaving aside supply-side issues, such as the specific characteristics of individual workers, or finding a solution to the unpaid care dilemma that so many older women face, there remains the problem of which jobs, exactly, will be readily available for older workers. Will there be demand? Changes in labour markets have been rapid, sometimes occurring at almost blistering speeds, as industrial employment (and the high incomes and good benefits that such jobs often provided) largely evaporated from the most affluent countries in the waning decades of the 20th century as globalisation sent manufacturing jobs to cheaper labour markets in less developed countries. Nothing has really filled the employment vacuum created by these lost industrial jobs, and many older workers are likely disproportionately clustered in dying industries. Wealthy economies are increasingly characterised by bifurcated labour markets, with secure professional employment in the knowledge sector for the well educated, and increasingly widespread insecure, precarious, low-paid, substandard jobs throughout much of the service sector. Some professional occupations that were formerly secure are also becoming precarious with respect to tenure and insecure conditions of employment. The Great Recession did not cause this pattern of bifurcated employment, but it reinforced and sped up the processes well under way (Kollmeyer, 2009).

The notion of extended working life as a way to take pressure off public pension systems seems to imply the need for full-time employment. Yet, as Table 1.10 showed, older women are far less likely to be employed full time than their male counterparts, a pattern that also reflects trends among younger workers. Some part-time work among older women reflects their choices – a preference for part-time work to preserve time for another valued activity. For individuals 'easing' into retirement, part-time bridge jobs that offer such flexibility may be highly prized (Loretto et al, 2005) for both men and women. For others, part-time employment is what workers have settled for, rather than what they want in terms of employment.

When older women work part time involuntarily, it may be partly due to the inability to find full-time work, but also due to substantial caring responsibilities, including care for grandchildren (Harrington Meyer, 2014) and ageing parents and partners (Calasanti and Slevin, 2001; Ginn et al, 2001). It is also possible that women who 'choose' to

Table 1.11: Involuntary part-time employment

	Women			Men		
	15–24	25–54	55+	15–24	25–54	55+
Australia	35.8	29.0	17.0	38.2	57.6	25.1
Germany	9.4	11.7	12.3	8.3	27.8	10.3
Ireland	26.6	27.6	25.2	31.9	53.8	37.4
Portugal	47.9	58.0	21.2	44.6	49.0	6.8
Sweden	30.8	27.2	7.0	33.3	31.7	5.1
UK	22.4	12.5	7.9	26.7	42.1	11.3
US	11.0	11.8	7.0	12.8	19.3	7.1

Note: Cannot find full-time work/would prefer more hours, as a percentage of part-time employment.
Source: http://stats.oecd.org (Labour Force Statistics) and https://data.oecd.org (Jobs–Employment).

work part time because caring interferes with full-time employment may not interpret that part-time work as involuntary. There is no consistently gendered pattern of involuntary part-time work observable in the data presented in Table 1.11, nor is it possible to discern why any individuals would regard themselves as involuntarily part-time workers. Some older workers cannot find full-time work and doubtless want more income. Other older workers having caring responsibilities which mean that while they would prefer more hours, caring responsibilities interfere with increasing hours of work.

Some older workers who are employed part time may perceive themselves as having more options than younger workers and feel pulled towards retirement, or, as Roscigno et al (2007) suggest, older workers may be pushed to retirement due to discrimination in the workplace. Alternatively, difficulty in finding suitable employment at older ages may be attributable to the discretion of hiring managers who are ageist (consciously or not) and whose hiring decisions are biased against older workers (Roscigno et al, 2007).

Extending working lives depends on available job openings that older workers are qualified to fill and who employers want to hire, an insight documented over a quarter-century ago (OECD, 1990). In developed countries, the growing incidence of high-skilled occupations is an optimistic trend for highly educated segments of working populations. However, accompanying the 'good job' hopes is a major challenge presented by the 'hollowing out' of medium-skilled jobs. Those medium-skilled jobs were good jobs during mass employment in the 20th century, often manufacturing jobs that provided good wages and pensions for most workers. While such middle-income jobs are declining in wealthy countries, they are being (partly) replaced by growth in low-skill, low-wage jobs (ILO, 2015). The evidence pertaining to future employment prospects for all workers points to the increasing bifurcation of labour markets into good and bad jobs. This, in turn, suggests that extending working lives in affluent countries may become even more difficult for large segments of older populations in the future, with more workers of all ages (including older workers) funnelled into low-wage and increasingly precarious jobs (Lain, 2012; ILO, 2015). In some cases, retraining may improve job prospects for older workers, but many employers are reluctant to attempt to train older workers (Behaghel et al, 2011), and available data suggest that this happens rarely in any case. There is no way to know whether the low level of training that current older workers experience, shown in Table 1.8, is due to the reluctance of workers themselves to be trained, or whether employers simply do not offer it to older workers (Loretto and White, 2006; Martin et al, 2014). Despite empirical evidence that older workers are as capable of learning new skills as younger workers, and that older workers are often regarded as more committed to and dependable on the job than younger workers (Roscigno et al, 2007), ageism in the workplace – especially among management and human resources ranks, but even among older workers themselves – undermines older workers' chances of even being considered for jobs that require retraining or new skills acquisition (Conen et al, 2012; Martin et al, 2014).

Ageism manifests in hiring, training and retention decisions (Johnson, 2007). At particular risk, at least in the US, are precisely those 'middle status' workers – not dominantly those in the professions, nor those in less attractive unskilled and service jobs. Rather, age discrimination is most often legally proved in skilled and semi-skilled positions (Roscigno et al, 2007) – the very types of jobs on which many older workers would need to depend for extended working lives to 'work'. Moreover, as problematic as ageism is for older workers in general, women face even more severe barriers to employment as older workers (Duncan and Loretto, 2004; Roscigno et al, 2007). They experience the double disadvantage of the intersection between sexism and ageism because social age differs for women and men, with women becoming 'socially older' than men at the same ages (Calisanti et al, 2006; England and McClintock, 2009). Of course, it is not only women who face multiple disadvantages as older workers; the vulnerabilities include age's intersections with low-skilled individuals, minority racial/ethnic groups, immigration status, individuals in poor health or with functional limitations, and those with lower levels of education, who face multiple disadvantages in trying to compete for, or hang onto, jobs in their later years.

Conclusion

Throughout the affluent countries of the world, assertions that working lives must be extended are ubiquitous. However, the persuasiveness of such arguments must take into account the unique contexts of each nation's particular demographic structure, political system, economic prospects, pension/welfare state regime and labour market practices. The empirical landscape for all the countries documented in this volume sets the stage for their shared challenges of meeting the needs for populations of all ages, coping with the aftermath of the shock of the 2008 global financial crisis and the drumbeat of neoliberal ideological opposition to current social welfare arrangements. What shapes the policy topography of each country are country-specific circumstances, the national labour market and employment prospects for older women and men, whose work is shaped by varied political economies and distinctive employment opportunities. Researchers and policymakers alike know that women's working lives – both paid and unpaid – differ from men's. Women earn less than men for equivalent jobs, are more likely to work part time, are more likely to take a career break to bear and care for children, and are more likely to provide unpaid care for disabled adult children and frail older family members. Further, when age enters the employment picture, it is not just older workers who present policy challenges. Youth unemployment, too, is a large and growing problem – in fact, questions persist about the availability of adequate employment for all citizens, regardless of age (ILO, 2015). Identifying a particular demographic group, such as pre-retirees, as the singular problem or culprit is not the most effective way to design workable social policies to support or encourage extended working lives since many labour market challenges are global and not necessarily age-specific in scope. Extending working lives is, at best, a single possible approach for some workers in response to just one of myriad employment and policy challenges. As the subsequent chapters will demonstrate, taking gender into account is essential; otherwise, policies designed to extend working life will worsen women's current later-life disadvantages, whether in terms of burdens of care or later-life poverty.

On its face, dramatic changes in life expectancy and the proportions of national populations above state retirement age do seem to imply that extended work and postponed retirement ages are a straightforward fix for income adequacy in later life – but only when that landscape is viewed from a great distance. The real contours of successful policies for extending working lives require much more nuance than has been exhibited to date. The theoretical questions brought to bear on the issue of the gendered implications of extending working lives, as Krekula and Vickerstaff argue so convincingly in Chapter Two, are essential for sensitising policymakers and stakeholders to the complexities of policy design in ways that dignify and respect older workers. After all, there are no such ungendered, unclassed, unhealthed individuals as implied by assertions that there really is no choice, citizens everywhere 'must work longer'. Supportive policies across the life course are critically important to the experiences of older workers and their potential for extending working lives, as Ní Léime and Loretto demonstrate in Chapter Three. Not every policy initiative has been friendly or adaptive for creating adequate potential for extending working lives.

Rarely are policies and practices that recognise the inescapable need to balance family needs and employment demands planned in a cohesive or integrated way. Nor are the varied needs and aspirations of older women and men who are now being urged to remain employed to later ages adequately addressed, as the following chapters in this volume demonstrate.

References

Arber, S. and Ginn, J. (1991) *Gender and later life*, Thousand Oaks, CA: Sage Publications.

Behaghel, L., Caroli, E. and Roger, M. (2011) Age biased technical and organisational change, training and employment prospects of older workers, Discussion Paper Series Forschungsinstitut zur Zukunft der Arbeit, No. 5544. Available at: http://nbn-resolving.de/urn:nbn:de:101:1-201104133632

Bettio, F., Tinios, P. and Betti, G. (2013) The gender gap in pensions in the EU, European Commission.

Bianchi, S.M. (2011) Family change and time allocation in American families, *The Annals of the American Academy of Political and Social Science, Work, Family, and Workplace Flexibility* 638, 21–44.

Bianchi, S.M. and Wight, V. (2010) The long reach of the job: employment and time for family life, in K. Christensen and B. Schneider (eds) *Workplace flexibility: Realigning 20th century jobs to 21st century workers*, Ithaca, NY: Cornell University Press.

Brady, D., Seeleib-Kaiser, M. and Beckfield, J. (2005) Economic globalization and the welfare state in affluent democracies, 1975–2001, *American Sociological Review*, 70(6), 921–48.

Byham, W.C. (2007) 70: the new 50 – retirement management: retaining the energy and expertise of experienced employees, Development Dimensions International.

Calasanti, T.M. and Slevin, K.F. (2001) *Gender, social inequalities, and aging*, Walnut Creek, CA: Alta Mira Press.

Calasanti, T., Slevin, K.F. and King, N. (2006) Ageism and feminism: from 'et cetera' to center, *NWSA Journal*, 18(1), 13–30.

Campbell, J.C., Ikegami, N. and Gibson, M.J. (2010) Lessons from public long-term care insurance in Germany and Japan, *Health Affairs*, 29(1), 87–95.

CESifo (Ifo Institute, Center for Economic Studies) (2015) DICE Forum: pensions and the financial crisis, DICE Report, various authors, 13(2), 1–49. Available at: http://www.cesifogroup.de/ifoHome/presse/Pressemitteilungen/Pressemitteilungen-Archiv/2015/Q3/pm_20150807-DICE-Report-2-2015.html

CIA (Central Intelligence Agency) (various years) World factbook.

Conen, W.S., Henkens, K. and Schippers, J. (2012) Employers' attitudes and actions towards the extension of working lives in Europe, *International Journal of Manpower*, 33(6), 648–65.

D'Addio, A. (2015) New OECD data and analysis revealing the wide gap in pension benefits between men and women, OECD Gender Portal, Gender Equality. Available at: http://www.oecd.org/gender/data/newoecddataandanalysisrevealingthe widegapinpensionbenefitsbetweenmenandwomen.htm

Duncan, C. and Loretto, W. (2004) Never the right age? Gender and age-based discrimination in employment, *Gender, Work and Organization*, 11(1), 95–115.

Ekerdt, D.J. (2010) Frontiers of research on work and retirement, *The Journals of Gerontology Series B: Psychological Sciences and Social Sciences*, 65(1), 69–80.

England, P. and McClintock, E.A. (2009) The gendered double standard of aging in US marriage markets, *Population and Development Review*, 35(4), 797–816.

Gilbert, N. (2002) *Transformation of the welfare state: The silent surrender of public responsibility*, New York, NY: Oxford University Press.

Ginn, J., Street, D. and Arber, S. (eds) (2001) *Women, work and pensions: International issues and prospects*, Buckingham: Open University Press.

Grootegoed, E. and Van Duk, D. (2012) The return of the family? Welfare state retrenchment and client autonomy in long term care, *Journal of Social Policy*, 41(4), 677–94.

Hacker, J.S. (2006) *The great risk shift: The assault on American jobs, families, health care and retirement and how you can fight back*, Oxford: Oxford University Press.

Harrington Meyer, M. (2014) *Grandmothers at work: Juggling families and jobs*, New York, NY: New York University Press.

Helman, R., Copeland, C. and VanDerhei, J. (2015) The 2015 retirement confidence survey: having a retirement savings plan a key factor in Americans' retirement confidence, Issue Brief #415, Employee Benefit Research Institute.

Hirsch, B.T., Macpherson, D.A. and Hardy, M.A. (2000) Occupational age structure and access for older workers, *Industrial and Labor Relations Review*, 53(3), 401–18.

ILO (International Labour Office) (2015) *World employment and social outlook: Trends 2015*, ILO: Geneva.

Johnson, R.W. (2007) *Managerial attitudes towards older workers: A review of the evidence*, Washington, DC: Urban Institute.

Kollmeyer, C. (2009) Explaining deindustrialization: how affluence, productivity growth, and globalization diminish manufacturing employment, *American Journal of Sociology*, 114(6), 1644–74.

Lain, D. (2012) Working past 65 in the UK and the USA: segregation into 'Lopaq' occupations? *Work, Employment and Society*, 26(1), 78–94.

Loretto, W. and White, P. (2006) Employers' attitudes, practices and policies towards older workers, *Human Resource Management Journal*, 16(3), 313–30.

Loretto, W., Vickerstaff, S. and Wright, P. (2005) Older workers and options for flexible work, Equal Opportunities Commission.

Martin, G., Dyock, D., Billett, S. and Johnson, G. (2014) In the name of meritocracy: managers' perceptions of policies and practices for training of older workers, *Ageing and Society*, 34(6), 992–1018.

Minkler, M. and Estes, C.L. (eds) (1999) *Critical gerontology: Perspectives from political and moral economy*, Amityville, NY: Baywood.

Moen, P., Kim, J.E. and Hofmeister, H. (2001) Couples' work/ retirement transitions, gender, and marital quality, *Social Psychology Quarterly*, 64(1), 55–71.

Moon, M. and Mulvey, J. (1996) *Entitlements and the elderly: Protecting promises, recognizing reality*, Washington, DC: Urban Institute Press.

Munnell, A.H. and Rutledge, M.S. (2013) The effects of the great recession on the retirement security of older workers, *The ANNALS of the American Academy of Political and Social Science*, 650(1): 124–42.

Myles, J. (1989) *Old age and the welfare state*, Lawrence, KS: University of Kansas Press.

Ní Léime Á and Street, D. (2016) Genderblind policies for extending working life: Women's disadvantage in Ireland and the United States, *Critical Social Policy*, DOI: 10.1177/0261018316666211. Available at: csp.sagepub.com

OECD (Organisation for Economic Co-operation and Development) (1990) Displacement and job loss: the workers concerned, *Employment Outlook*, 43–75.

OECD (Organisation for Economic Co-operation and Development) (various years) Labour force statistics online. Available at: http://www.oecd.org/std/labour-stats/

O'Rand, A. (2011) 2010 SSS presidential address: the devolution of risk and the changing life course in the United States, *Social Forces*, 90(1), 1–16.

Orloff, A.S. (2009) Gendering the comparative analysis of welfare states: an unfinished agenda, *Sociological Theory*, 27(3), 317–43.

Phillipson, C. and Walker, A. (1987) The case for a critical gerontology, in S. Di Gregorio (ed) *Social gerontology: New directions*, London: Croom Helm, pp 1–15.

Pierson, P. (ed) (2001) *The new politics of the welfare state*, Oxford: Oxford University Press.

Roscigno, V.J., Mong, S., Byron, R. and Tester, G. (2007) Age discrimination, social closure and employment, *Social Forces*, 86(1), 313–34.

Saez, E. and Zucman, G. (2016) Wealth inequality in the United States since 1913: evidence from capitalized income tax data, *Quarterly Journal of Economics*, 131(2), 519–78.

Street, D. and Desai, S. (2016) The US old age welfare state: social security, supplemental security income, Medicare, Medicaid, in M. Harrington Meyer and E. Daniele (eds) *Gerontology: Changes, challenges, and solutions*, Santa Barbara, CA: Praeger, 83–110.

Street, D. and Quadagno, J. (1993) The state, the elderly and the intergenerational contract: toward a new political economy of aging, in K.W. Schaie and W.A. Achenbaum (eds) *Societal impact on aging: Historical perspectives*, New York, NY: Springer, pp 130–50.

Vickerstaff, S. (2010) Older workers: the 'unavoidable obligation' of extending our working lives?, *Sociology Compass*, 4(10), 869–79.

Waldfogel, J. (1997) The effect of children on women's wages, *American Sociological Review*, 62(2), 209–17.

Weller, S.A. (2007) Discrimination, labour markets, and the labour market prospects of older workers: what can a legal case teach us?, *Work, Employment and Society*, 21(3), 417–37.

TWO

Theoretical and conceptual issues in the extending working lives agenda

Clary Krekula and Sarah Vickerstaff

Introduction

Governments across the Global North are facing the reality of ageing populations and ageing workforces. These demographic changes have resulted in a debate that, to a great extent, has described the ageing population as a challenge to welfare provision and benefits. The reasoning is that the tax base is shrinking as the majority of older workers leave the labour market too early, often before state pension age. The focus of debate and policy development for extending working life has therefore mainly been based on economic perspectives. This is different from, for example, the comprehensive and long-running political debate on the need for increased labour market participation among women, which argues that women's participation in working life is a matter of democracy, justice and improving the way in which the competence and resources in society are utilised, rather than as just an economic necessity (see, eg, Hernes, 1987). It is also clear that the debate on older people's extended participation in working life is not based on a social movement, such as the one putting forward demands for job opportunities for women. Rather, it is an issue raised and motivated largely by groups other than older workers themselves.

While the rates of older worker labour market participation vary considerably across countries (as discussed in Chapter One), there is a common response among international, European and national authorities that extending working lives by encouraging people to work for longer and delay retirement is a necessity for the foreseeable future (OECD, 2006, 2011; Munnell and Sass, 2008; Magnus, 2009; Vickerstaff, 2010). Further, a new era is needed in which assumptions about the desirability and acceptability of early retirement, which had become embedded in the later part of the 20th century, are replaced by a new willingness to work longer. A common national policy response to this scenario has been to propose or to raise the ages at which people are eligible to take their state pension, hoping thereby to nudge people to delay retirement (for a full discussion of policy responses, see Chapter Three).

The policy debate about extending working lives has, to a great extent, characterised older people as the problem. It is their patterns of participation in working life and decisions on retirement that are the focus, and, as such, the debate has depended on the use of categorical stereotypes. For example, one UK government document lamented the fact that too many people are 'leaving work prematurely', describing 'unplanned exit from the labour market' as having potentially 'catastrophic' consequences for individuals, business and society as a whole (DWP, 2014: 3). A similar example is the Swedish investigation of retirement age (SOU, 2013: 25), which described current retirement patterns as 'a relic of the past which leads to a waste of human capital' and is 'outdated' (SOU, 2013: 24), claiming that 'older workers choose early retirement because they do not fully understand the consequences it has on their private economy in the long term' (SOU, 2013: 167). In these two examples, older workers' behaviour is described as selfish, catastrophic or stupid.

The narrow economic basis of such arguments and the problematic representation of older workers underestimate the real complexity of the issue: to understand what is happening with older workers requires an analysis that moves between individual circumstances, business demand and organisation, and wider social and political policy. There is now a burgeoning international literature on older workers and growing research activity in a number of different disciplines. The bulk of this research, however, has concentrated on individuals and why they leave the labour market, and often on a particular facet of the individual's situation such as health or financial status. Knowledge about extending working life may develop incrementally, but a broader perspective is required. A review of literature in 11 countries made a plea for a more complex approach, pointing to 'multilevel interacting influences of society, work and the individual, the processual character of retirement, the dynamism of relevant factors, framework conditions and regulatory changes, and not least the heterogeneity of the older working population' (Hasselhorn and Apt, 2015: 12).

This line of reasoning points to the need for different kinds of empirical analysis, but, even more crucially, for more sophisticated theoretical foundations. This chapter seeks to provide a more encompassing framework for the discussion of extending working lives in the rest of the volume by identifying central limitations in the current debate and embedding the discussion in current changes in society that affect working life. Using this as a starting point, the theoretical developments that are needed to understand the range and complexity of situations and experiences facing older workers are outlined. As a first step, limitations in the debate on extending working life are discussed and necessary research perspectives are identified. This illustrates that the debate on extending working life: (1) tends to reduce the phenomenon to a matter of individual choices; (2) is based on a homogeneous view of older workers; (3) depicts it as an issue isolated from current social changes in society and working life' and (4) is based on a simplified view of work. As a second step, these perspectives are looked at in greater depth to emphasise research issues that may contribute to a deeper problematisation of gender and extending working life.

A narrow focus on individuals

Policy and research on extending working lives have tended to focus on individuals. Expressed differently, policy discourse about the desirability of extending working lives frequently assumes that the target of policy changes is a generic individualised 'adult worker' (Lewis, 2002, 2007). For example, policy discourse in the UK has frequently presented the older worker as failing to understand the health and financial benefits of extending their working lives and the consequences of not saving enough for a comfortable retirement. With that framing, the task of government becomes to:

> help everyone to take responsibility for their retirement income, to move away from the idea of a cliff-edge retirement that is inevitable at a given age, and ensure they plan for a retirement that is based on personal circumstance and choice. (DWP, 2014: 4)

For many governments, the focus is on trying to persuade individuals to make 'better' decisions and decide to delay retirement (see, eg, Chapters Seven and Nine).

Descriptions of extending working life as a simple matter of older worker's individual choice are contradicted by empirical research. There is comprehensive evidence which illustrates that older people experience discrimination in working life (Loretto et al, 2000; Garstka et al, 2005; Nelson, 2005; Gee et al, 2007), that older workers and jobseekers try to counteract discrimination by developing strategies to present themselves as younger (Hurd Clarke and Griffin, 2008; Berger, 2009), that older people experience discrimination in the recruitment process (Benedick et al, 1996; Benedick et al, 1999; Neumark, 2009), that unsubstantiated beliefs that older workers do not stay long enough or the 'age coding' of work tasks are used to argue against hiring older people (Krekula, 2011), that people over the age of 50–55 are often forced or talked into early retirement (Eurolink Age, 1993), and that employers usually prefer employees in their 30s (Kalavar, 2001).

The term 'older workers' has been used for different age groups, for example, middle age to older ages (Walker et al, 2007), from ages around 40 (Ainsworth and Hardy, 2004) or for people over the age of 50 (Loretto and White, 2006; Lewis and Walker, 2011). Regardless of the specific age used, older workers are discursively described as having a different and largely unattractive identity (Riach, 2009) and positioned as marginal (Fevre, 2011) within work organisations. Put together, this research show that older people's conditions in working life are surrounded by discriminating and excluding practices, and that their participation is in no way a simple matter of individual choices.

Theoretical problematisation of inequality also underscores the difficult aspects of depicting older people's participation in working life as an exclusively individual matter. In direct contrast to the individual focus, Tilly (1998) argues that significant differences in people's advantages are not about individual qualities, but rather correspond to categorical differences such as old/young, woman/man, rich/poor. Even when the categorisation is based on apparent biological markers, they are dependent on comprehensive social organisation. Inequality, he argues, is created when categorisations are used to solve organisational problems; in other words, when they are institutionalised. Schwalbe (2008) follows the same line of argument: that inequality is not something that just happens on its own. Rather, inequality is a performance, it is created by the way people think and act. He joins Tilly and highlights the structure of categorisation and challenges the simple notion that people are different because of what they do, but rather that they are categorised unequally based on age, background, gender and so on, which has profound institutional implications beyond individual behaviour or choice.

Researchers who study age also emphasise the importance of moving beyond mere descriptions of age categories to focus instead on the processes where they are applied. Bodily (1994) argues that the core of ageism is the notion that different ages can be related to delimiting qualities and actions. Using the concept of 'age coding', Krekula (2009: 8) presents a similar line of argument, defining age coding as 'practices of distinction that are based on and preserve representations of actions, phenomena and characteristics as associated with and applicable to demarcated ages'. She emphasises that age coding is an amalgam of practices that can be used in different situations to legitimise, negotiate and regulate resources, as a resource in interactions, and to create age-based norms and deviance. Writing age codings into regulatory documents and rules, and then inscribing those rules into institutional practices, upholds normative assumptions about age and structures hierarchical age relations. The research approaches outlined earlier point to some of the simplifications that exist in the individualisation of the issue of extending working lives, and point to the need to add a power perspective to the analyses.

The limiting homogeneous narration of the category 'older people'

This narrative of individual choices and decisions also presents older workers as de-gendered, de-classed individuals, shorn of their individual biographies and social contexts. The experiences of many (and in current conditions of economic precarity, perhaps increasingly the majority) are neglected and misunderstood. There is a need to problematise these homogeneous categorisations of older people and older workers, respectively.

The homogeneous representation of older people in the debate on extending working lives runs counter to the extensive research which shows that the propensity to leave the labour market before state pension age, retire gradually or return to work after retirement is strongly correlated with a range of social factors that are classed and gendered (Banks et al, 2008). For example, ill-health (a major factor in early labour market withdrawal) typically has a steep social gradient, with lower social classes suffering more limiting health conditions at earlier ages (Marmot et al, 2010). Research on the UK and the USA demonstrates clearly that it is the poorest groups in society who are least likely to extend their working lives (Lain, 2011, 2016). Differences in labour market careers between women and men persist into older age, affecting the propensity to continue working, as does marital status (Lain and Vickerstaff, 2015). The frequent exhortation to delay retirement, save more and make 'better' choices neglects the reality that the family, health, labour market and pension positions of people aged 50+ are a complex mixture of disadvantages and advantages built up over the life course, and which may have enduring consequences that cannot easily be reordered at the end of working life. A life-course perspective on older workers is obviously critical to understanding the realities they confront. Complicating individual life courses is the fact that people are typically part of dynamic social groups – families and other social networks – their lives are linked to others. Consequently, aspirations, ideas and decisions are made not in isolation, but often as part of family structures. Understanding older workers requires an awareness of the long-run effects of linked lives and sometimes the unexpected shocks, such as ill-health or divorce, which can fracture long-run expectations and plans.

Another example of differentiation among older workers is in research that illustrates how caring for older relatives affects people's labour market participation. Research has illustrated a notable negative impact of caring on labour force participation by older carers and also identified caring responsibilities as a barrier to the employment of older workers. For example, in one study, difficulties in arranging working hours and the lack of alternative disability care arrangements were described as the most commonly experienced barriers to finding employment (Gray et al, 2008). Swedish studies have also shown that providing extensive care for a close relative affects women's working lives far more than men's working lives, and that women aged over 55 who are providing extensive care for a close relative are excluded from the labour market to a much greater extent than other women (see Chapter Eight).

The comprehensive research that shows variations in older people's propensity to work indicates that the differentiation of older people's opportunities to work for longer requires consideration of other social categorisations than just age. Indeed, differences among people become greater as they age (Bal and Jansen, 2015) as the accumulation of experiences, skills and health issues over the life course makes older people increasingly different from each other. Thus, several life domains – class, gender, race, sexuality, health and location – and not just age, intersect to affect people's situations.

A feminist gerontology, as outlined by Calasanti (2004), makes a point beyond simply arguing that a more diverse range of individuals need to be considered, suggesting instead that researchers focus on 'the relational character' of inequalities that adhere to age, gender, race and class, for example. As Yuval-Davis (2006) puts it, different social divisions are intermeshed in a 'grid of power relations' that operates at individual and institutional levels. This requires an understanding of the ways in which different forms of discrimination and disadvantage interact and intersect. Within discrimination and diversity studies, the concept of gendered ageism is beginning to become a focus of research. The theoretical debates about how to understand gendered ageism focus, in particular, on whether the experience and impacts of age on employment simply add to other already-existing patterns of advantage and disadvantage to create double or multiple jeopardies or whether it is necessary to conceptualise age and gender as intersecting and creating distinct categories: 'The effect of multiple categories in producing work–life outcomes is not additive but interactive, producing outcomes qualitatively different from the simple addition of the effects of different categories combined' (Özbilgin et al, 2011: 188). The argument here is that neither age nor gender is a fixed category with a simple meaning.

Overall, the reasoning outlined earlier illustrates the need for an intersectional approach which recognises that age and gender, among other categorisations, will interact in different ways at different times in people's lives. This also points towards the need for a life-course perspective to understand the current and likely future experiences of older workers.

Interactive societal processes that affect the debate on an extended working life

The individual focus of the debate has also meant that it has treated the issue of extending working life as a phenomenon disconnected from surrounding society and trends. However, neither the debate nor the ageing population are phenomena that take place in a vacuum. They are happening in the context of social changes both in society and within labour organisations that affect and contribute to the understanding both of ageing and of older workers and extended working lives. In this section, the implementation of an extended working life is placed in a wider societal and organisational context in order to anchor the discussion in current social trends.

Many researchers have used the concept 'new economy' to describe the comprehensive changes that have taken and are taking place in society and working life (Sennett, 1999; Beck, 2005; Standing, 2011), where new and rapidly changing information and communication technologies increase interconnectedness between countries, and contribute to a widening of social divisions. The development is characterised by a rapidly increasing selection of reproducible goods and by a rapidly expanding service sector. Along with an increased polarisation of the labour market, this has contributed to increasing inequality between groups of employees, countries and regions (Quah, 2003; Rubery, 2015). Perrons (2005) argues that employment segregation and the low market valuation of care and reproductive work have resulted in widening class inequalities, which are gendered. However, while this perspective illustrates how changes affect the experience of gender within labour organisations and contribute to broadening inequalities between women, so far, it has only been used to a limited extent to problematise how this affects labour market demand for older workers more generally. In a period of continuing austerity, these assumptions fail to give an adequate picture or understanding of the realities of extending working lives. There are therefore reasons to discuss precarity, as well as the rapid change as such, and the impact on older workers.

Standing (2011) describes the precariat as the growing group in the labour market with insecure working conditions who lack basic rights and have few opportunities to develop their careers. An increased international access to labour and changed working conditions, with a rapid increase in temporary jobs and part-time employment, are described as examples of underlying processes. According to Standing, around a quarter of the adult population could be expected to belong to the precariat and thus lead a life characterised by insecure employment, leading to anger, worry and alienation. Lorey (2015) illustrates the spread of precarisation by claiming that it now constitutes a rule. Social insecurity is, she argues, a form of neoliberal governance. Globally speaking, it has been said that the public sector is transforming into a zone for the precariat and women have taken up a disproportionately large section of precarious jobs, although there are significant variations from country to country.

The ageing population is also described as an instigating factor in the growth of the precariat since older workers, according to Standing (2011), make up a growing source of cheap labour. His line of argument has certain empirical support from studies showing that many older people want part-time jobs (Lain, Vickerstaff & Shukla, 2015). Although the reasons why older workers may 'choose' part-time work are various, the degree of genuine 'choice' might be overstated for someone whose health is compromised and cannot manage full-time work or for someone who is juggling care demands with paid employment. Part-time work may also disguise some underemployment of older workers who would like to work full time if such work was available. Standing (2011) states that older workers form a group with a high risk of ending up in the precariat; he argues that governments can hardly find a better way to keep older people in working life, and perhaps even get them to resist retirement, than facilitating their entrance into the precariat. However, in line with, for example, Lynch

(2012), he emphasises differences between older people working part time after retirement, where some use their income to pay for 'that little extra something', while others are dependent on their wage to make ends meet.

Despite the explicit connection that has been made between the growth of the precariat and the ageing population, and the identification of older workers' position as particularly risky, the emphasis on these phenomena in the extending working lives debate is insufficient. As has been observed (Krekula and Heikkien, 2014), we do not always have the concepts and language to adequately highlight the processes that are unfolding. For example, the exclusion of older people from working life has mainly been looked at as a matter of discrimination, while the same processes among younger people are discussed in terms of (youth) unemployment. This has had the effect of limiting research looking at unemployment among older people, which is an important missing factor in the debate on extending working lives.

The contemporary societal changes in populations and labour markets are not only far-reaching; they are also happening very rapidly. A rich social-scientific discussion describes this increasing acceleration of societal processes as characteristic of contemporary society (Giddens, 1991; Beck, 1992; Rosa and Scheurman, 2008). This social acceleration (Rosa and Scheurman, 2008) brings expectations of constantly increasing productivity through tighter time frames. It contributes to accelerated technical development and social change, as well as an increased pace of life. According to Rosa and Scheurman (2008), this acceleration has undermined decision-makers' ability to predict events and to really be able to plan. The consequences are organisational actions that focus on finding the best possible temporary solutions rather than strategising for longer-term objectives. Today, workers must often settle for short-term adjustments to meet the constant changes, whereas before, individuals could work with a more predictable vision for the future. This increasing flexibilisation and fragmentation of labour, as Rubery (2015) has called it, is accompanied by the neoliberal project of deregulation in an attempt to make labour markets more open to competition. The outcome of the extent and speed of change in the context of austerity has been that decisions on the implementation of an extended working life are not even based on adequate knowledge about ageing or on the integration of knowledge about gender in current circumstances. There is a tendency to create policies that are based on immediate and short-term pressures.

In short, the arguments outlined earlier illustrate the importance of viewing older people's labour market participation in a wider perspective – one that connects analyses of current processes in society and labour organisations to the influences of rapid social change. The list of relevant processes can be made longer than the one presented earlier and critical analyses of policies on extending working lives should contribute to identifying such current processes, as well as their consequences insofar as researchers and policymakers can make predictions about the future.

A simplified view of work

The arguments for the need to extend people's working lives are also premised on a narrow conception of work as referring only to paid employment. A number of writers have made the observation that in early discussions of the implications of ageing populations, the World Health Organization's (WHO) original conception of active ageing (WHO, 2002), for example, not only involved paid employment, but was very much about healthy ageing. Increasingly, however, active ageing has come to be seen in policy discourse as referring to delaying retirement and working for longer; a shift from active to productive ageing in the narrow sense of employment (Moulaert and Biggs, 2013; Ray, 2014).

This fails to understand or take into account the range of other work that older members of society are doing, most notably, caring, volunteering and other community service of various sorts. The emphasis on paid employment also fails to take seriously the relationship between paid and unpaid work, which we know has the effect of rendering invisible household labour, primarily undertaken by women. Feminist scholarship on the boundaries and interactions between unpaid and paid work have been missing from many discussions of older workers, despite being vital for understanding the opportunities and constraints that older workers face.

A narrow focus on paid employment misses the point that labour market participation is often predicated upon domestic and intergenerational divisions of labour: women work in the home to facilitate men's employment and grandparents may look after grandchildren to enable their own children to maintain paid work. With an ageing population and a shrinking prime-age labour force, everyone is agreed that there will be increasing pressures on services to care for the elderly and that families may well be expected to do more. This raises the very real question of who will do the caring if older women are working in the labour market in greater numbers and to older ages. In the absence of good-quality accessible childcare, the urge to encourage younger women to be in paid employment as an untapped resource similarly puts pressure on older family members to step in and help out. Ennals and Hilsen (2011) have described older workers as the 'jam in the sandwich', often still with responsibilities for their own children as well as elderly relatives.

To consider realistically the opportunities and constraints on older worker labour market participation, it is necessary to understand and factor in the relationships between paid and unpaid work, especially in the context of other pressures, such as pressure on health and social care spending in an ageing society.

Four steps towards a new research agenda

Earlier, some of the limitations that surround the current debate on extending working life have been illustrated. It has been argued that a deeper understanding should start off from a contextualisation of the debate and be based on analyses with new theoretical approaches. In this section, the arguments about these theoretical approaches are developed. It is argued that a new research agenda needs to be based on four steps: (1) the need for a power perspective with potential to shed light on age-based inequality; (2) the need for an intersectional perspective and a masculinity perspective that challenges the homogeneous descriptions of older workers; (3) a feminist understanding of work; and (4) a life-course perspective that provides a framework linking the previous three.

Perspective on age and power

It was argued earlier that there is a need for a power perspective for an in-depth emphasis on gender and extending working life. Age as a power relation has been problematised within several research fields, with different scope and concepts. Ageism is so far the most established concept, although it is not a uniform concept. Ageism often alludes to prejudices, stereotypes and attitudes (see, eg, Butler, 1969) while many also add discrimination (see, eg, Palmore, 1999, 2001; Wilkinson and Ferraro, 2002); a third understanding presents ageism as an ideology and thus puts forward underlying power relations in a more explicit way (Bytheway, 1995). In the debate about who ageism is aimed at, or who suffers from its effects, some researchers consider it to be a phenomenon aimed mainly at older people (Kalish, 1979; Butler, 1980; Palmore, 2001), while others speak of all discrimination based on age and argue that it can be aimed at both younger and older age groups (see, eg, Bytheway, 1995; Palmore, 1999).

The concept of ageism has been criticised. A first concern is that it focuses on the expression of the phenomenon, which leads to questions about which terminologies are seen as ageist and what the concept refers to. This could render the concept mainly descriptive, with only limited analytical utility. A second limitation is an imagined homogeneous age category conceptualised as prone to ageism, which ignores the big differences that exist within older people as a group. Contemporary research on different types of power relations, as well as ageism, has also focused on the differences that exist within large categorisations based on, for example, age and gender. Since this complexity is not highlighted with the concept of ageism in its original form, researchers have respecified the concept by adding a gender perspective. The concept of gendered ageism has frequently been defined as a double jeopardy where two interacting power systems lead to an increased vulnerability (Itzin and Phillipson, 1995; Walker, 1998; Handy and Davy, 2007; Barrett and Naiman-Sessions, 2016). It is also conceptualised as discriminating practices (Jyrkinen, 2013) and as consisting of differentiating practices that put demarcated age groups in a marginalised position (Krekula et al, 2017). Using the concept, researchers have, for example, shown that women of all ages in working life experience ageism based on their appearance and sexuality to a greater extent than men (Duncan and Loretto, 2004; Granleese and Sayer, 2006; Clarke and Griffin, 2008). A third criticism claims that the concept has been limited in the way age has been problematised as a basis of inequality, which limits the possibilities to achieve change since it does not highlight or uncover the reasons behind older people's subordinate position in society (Krekula et al, 2017).

A relevant research approach – critical age studies – connects age research with theories of power by presupposing that age is an organising principle, a power order and something that is done (Krekula and Johansson, 2016). Here, the concept pair 'unmarked age–marked age' is used to problematise the relational connection between a tacit age normality, the unmarked age, and the age positions that are turned into its divergence by prefixes and names, the marked age. The concept pair makes it possible to analyse how the normative age varies according to context and how it receives a hegemonic character.

Age is thus described as a power relation that constructs age categories and puts them in a hierarchical relation to one another, which results in groups of individuals being systematically disadvantaged, marginalised and discriminated against due to their age. In essence, this marginalisation is based on the definition power of the unmarked age (Krekula and Johansson, 2016).

The concept pair 'unmarked age–marked age' helps to highlight the age normality that characterises different work settings, and the consequences of this. The variation between age normality in work contexts can be seen in studies showing that while employees just under the age of 40 are considered to be too old by the telemarketing industry, they are seen as too young to gain status within parts of academia (Krekula, 2011) and as the core of age normality among Swedish firemen (Krekula, 2012). From this perspective, characterisations describing older workers as flawed and problematic – as much of the debate on extended working life now does – can generally be understood as an expression of the processes of marking older ages in the workplace. This research approach points to the advantages of adding analyses of how unmarked age and marked age are constructed in different workplaces and the consequences of these constructions for women and men under varied working conditions and for their abilities to work longer.

The perspectives of intersectionality and masculinity

It is argued here that the homogeneous description of older workers needs to be problematised and the categorisations need to be diversified in order to show how precarity affects groups of older people in an extended working life. This approach can also be seen as a strategy to counteract the neoliberal reduction of social life to an interaction between individual social entrepreneurs, which hides conditions that lead to structural inequality (Bilge, 2013). In this section, two perspectives are discussed that can contribute to an approach that embraces rather simplifies complexity: an intersectional perspective and a masculinity perspective.

The concept of intersectionality was coined by Kimberlé Crenshaw (1989), who introduced it to demonstrate the marginalisation of black women in both anti-discrimination legislation and feminist and anti-racist theories. Since then, it has gained international ground within many fields, not least within gender studies. It has also turned into an approach that includes more and more phenomena, for example, social identity, power relations and discursive structures. Today, the term 'intersectionality' usually refers to an overall description of a theoretical approach which emphasises that power relations cannot be understood separately, but should be understood as dynamic interactions between intertwined axes of power, and that social locations are epistemically significant (Yuval-Davis, 2006; May, 2014); it has developed into a major analytical tool. Intersectionality can thus be defined in different ways. It can, for example, be described as a method and a disposition that is rooted in black feminism and critical race theory (Carbado et al, 2013), a perspective to analyse 'subjects' experiences of both identity and oppression' (Nash, 2008: 2), and as the interaction of 'multiple identities and experiences of subordination' (Davis, 2008: 68). However, the approach has to a more limited extent been applied to research with a 'majority-inclusive approach', where social categories are not treated exclusively by focusing on subordered positions (Staunæs, 2003: 102). From a critical postcolonial perspective, it has been argued that feminist researchers have transformed the original postcolonial critique of hegemonic feminism into an 'objective' gender approach and have thus created an idea that racialised women's experiences of structural oppression cannot be used as a starting point for theorisation (Bilge, 2013). Without the intention to neglect its genealogy, it is argued here that the intersectional approach, with these two frameworks on intersectionality, has an important role to play in the debate on extending working life.

Based on analyses of how ideas of intersecting social positions have been used for political, legal and policy purposes, Yuval-Davis (2006) declares that the question of whether to interpret the intersectionality of social divisions as a constitutive or as an additive process is central. According to her, however, at the centre of the debate is separation or conflation of the different analytical levels where the intersectionality takes place, rather than just a debate on the relationship between the divisions themselves. Prins (2006) distinguishes between the concepts of constructionist intersectionality and systemic intersectionality. These approaches differ with regards to the way they theorise power and emerging subjectivity, and thereby in the degree of agency that people can exert. The systemic approach departs from an understanding of the human subject as primarily constituted by systems of domination and marginalisation. Regarding constructionists, on the other hand, becoming a subject does not merely mean becoming subordinated to a structure. Based on this, it is suggested here that intersectionality provides an analytic approach to different conditions within the larger collective of older workers, who are otherwise undifferentiated in the debate on extending working life.

While a gender perspective on extending working life looks at the relational perspectives of the categorisations of women and men, as well as the consequences of their construction as a dichotomous pair, masculinity studies focus on relations within categorisations of men and how these construct gendered power relations. The relation between masculinity constructions and gender relations becomes especially apparent in Connell's (2005) discussion on hegemonic masculinity as a normative practice for men that subordinates both women and non-hegemonic groups of men. Hegemonic masculinity is described as the masculinity that can be found among men with power and status (Kimmel, 1994), which to a great extent associates it with being strong, successful and independent. Despite the fact that hegemonic masculinity has a normative and contextualised character, it is not homogeneous; instead, it is more accurate to speak of local hegemonic masculinities (Connell and Messerschmidt, 2005). The diversity of masculinities also appears in the fact that some masculinities, such as equality masculinity (Messerschmidt, 2012) and Scandinavian masculinity (Christensen and Qvotrup, 2014), are more in favour of gender equality than others. Multiple masculinities can also be seen in the differentiation between orthodox and inclusive masculinity, where orthodox masculinity rests upon the exclusion of anything that is regarded as feminine, while these aspects are integrated into the inclusionary form (Anderson, 2012).

Workplaces are central to the organisation of masculinities (Collinson and Hearn, 2004). Therefore, masculinity as a concept can contribute to an exploration of how notions of masculinity relate to (inhibiting) assumptions of older workers, both women and men, and also to the identification of normative practices and the consequences of them for older workers.

A feminist perspective on work

This section briefly explores how to understand work and, in particular, how feminist scholarship on the boundaries and interactions between unpaid and paid work have been missing from many discussions of older workers, despite being vital for understanding the opportunities and constraints that older workers face. It is argued here that gender has an impact on older workers' experiences and the differential retirement transitions of women and men. It emphasises the significance of the domestic domain and care, and illustrates the need for a gender perspective.

Gender studies have demonstrated that women's and men's opportunities to take part in paid employment at any age depend on gender regimes and how caring responsibilities are divided within the family (Harkness, 2008; Loretto and Vickerstaff, 2013). There is widespread horizontal gender segregation in the labour market with the sex-typing of jobs into female or male jobs, although there may be cultural variations in whether a job is seen as traditionally female or male (Williams et al, 2013) and vertical segregation, with women over-represented in lower-level jobs in occupational hierarchies. Jobs may also be segregated by race and other social characteristics into what Acker (2006) has termed 'inequality regimes' in organisations, reinforcing the importance of an intersectional approach.

Domestic labour such as housekeeping and looking after children and other dependants are everywhere traditionally seen as natural activities for women and thus rendered invisible and outside the scope of what is popularly seen as 'work', although global care chains are changing the distribution of such work between women, with career women in the Global North increasingly coming to rely on the paid labour of working-class or migrant women to look after the home while they work. The impact of caring on employment for many women may thread through the life course, including not only looking after children well into their teenage years and beyond, but also as they get older caring for elderly relatives, ailing spouses and grandchildren. The result, depending upon prevailing child- and elder-care systems, is that women are more likely to interrupt work or work part-time to accommodate caring needs in their family or are otherwise constrained to take employment that will fit in with domestic duties. The impact of care work on women's employment trajectories has most typically been examined in relation to younger women and childcare but, as has been commented, 'Centering on old people also would transform our study of carework' (Calasanti et al, 2006: 22).

As the individual country chapters to follow demonstrate, the debate on extended working lives is taking place at the same time as welfare state retrenchment, including cuts being made to public elder care in many countries. This has resulted in the need for increased informal care given by older women and men. There is a need to conceptualise care for older people simultaneously with any discussions of extended working life to fully understand the realities of older workers' situations. A feminist understanding of the relationship between paid and non-paid work is critical to this, as is bringing the household into our understanding of later-life work trajectories (Vickerstaff, 2015).

A life-course perspective

A focus on the relationship between employment and domestic work also reinforces the need to factor in an understanding of the long-run development and effects of lived lives. A life-course perspective has become increasingly common in the literature on ageing and in attempts to understand the life and work experiences of current older cohorts. While there is no single approach to life-course analysis (Motel-Klingebiel, 2015) and researchers tend to veer towards either a 'personological' or an 'institutional' approach (Dannefer and Settersten, 2010), the potential of a life-course approach is its capacity to connect individual biography, or individual time, with historical events, or social time (Phillipson, 2013: 35–8; Motel-Klingebiel, 2015: 31). This necessitates a concentration on the differentiation of and within individual trajectories and age groups and cohorts, as well as recognition of the complexity of current social trends.

With respect to the extending working lives agenda, rapid change is a feature of contemporary life, which means that some of the age-patterned certainties of the past, such as cohorts of men all retiring around the age of 65, are no longer so clear-cut. As Moen (2003: 269–91) has argued, under current social, political and economic conditions, it may make sense to think of a new phase of life: 'midcourse' – the period towards the end of paid working life and before older old age or the fourth age from the late 70s onwards. The risks that older workers now face, in the context of changing national labour markets and the global challenges of rapid social change, need to be understood and analysed in the context of life courses that reflect the cumulative effects of the experiences and events throughout lives, which shape opportunity structures and individuals' own defined aspirations and expectations. A life-course approach serves as a reminder not to fall into the trap of imagining that chronology somehow renders similar people of the same age all the same: 'the life course perspective entails that older might be more heterogeneous' (Komp and Johansson, 2015: 6). It necessitates an understanding of how inequalities are made and reproduced across the life course and how individuals at different times will find themselves at the intersection of cross-cutting disadvantages.

A sense of the life course also emphasises that individuals do not live and act in isolation; rather, 'lives are lived interdependently' (Elder et al, 2003: 13), and with respect to experiences of paid work, 'careers are not solo passages but are parts of linked lives' (Heinz, 2003: 186). As Moen (2011: 87) has put it, the emphasis on individuals:

> reifies the tendency of societies, states, employers, and scholars to think about, develop policies around, and study workers as individuals, not as family members. And yet most workers are married (or partnered), and most in the USA and Europe are part of dual-earner households.

This requires an analysis that is sensitive to the long run of people's lives and the impacts that disruptions such as unexpected ill-health, redundancy, marital breakdown and/or historical moments, such as recessionary periods, can have on the paths that people are trying to take. It underlines the fact that willingness and ability to extend a working life is formed not just in the economic sphere, but through the intersection of the many facets of our lives. A life-course perspective requires a consideration of the linkages between life domains and reinforces the point that paid work can never be wholly detached from other kinds of work, such as unpaid care work, domestic labour and emotional work in the family.

Conclusion

This chapter has looked critically at how older workers and extended working lives have been conceptualised and has argued for a feminist political-economy approach that recognises the complexity of issues facing older workers and the many differences between them. It has brought the concept of power back into the analysis to reinforce the point that access to a comfortable retirement and the ability to choose it is not just a matter of personal disposition or planning, but an outcome of socially constructed and reproduced inequalities and of the neoliberal economy. The neoliberal turn towards what Rubery (2015: 641) has characterised as the three Ds (deregulation, decollectivisation and depoliticisation) of the employment relation is evident in many of the policy initiatives outlined in the individual country chapters to follow. The push by governments to reduce early retirement and extend working lives is occurring against a backdrop of austerity and welfare state retrenchment and cannot meaningfully be understood or separated from this background.

Chapter Three charts how current policies aimed at extending working lives have been framed within existing power relations and, as such, in many cases, serve to reproduce and reinforce existing inequalities. The chapters on individual countries take up this framework to assess the extent to which the reality on the ground mirrors the concerns explored here and the ways in which debates and policy developments are mitigating or reinforcing inequalities in access to the possibilities of an extended working life.

References

Acker, J. (2006) Inequality regimes: gender, class and race, *Organizations, Gender and Society*, 20(4), 441–64.

Ainsworth, S. and Hardy, C. (2004) Critical discourse analysis and identity: why bother?, *Critical Discourse Studies*, 1, 225–59.

Anderson, E. (2012) *Inclusive masculinity. The changing nature of masculinities*, London: Routledge.

Bal, M. P. and Jansen, P.G.W. (2015) Idiosyncratic deals for older workers: increased heterogeneity among older workers enhance the need for I-deals, in M.P. Bal, D.T.A.M. Kooiji and D.M. Rousseau (eds) *Aging workers and the employee-employer relationship*, Heidelberg: Springer, pp 129–44.

Banks, J., Tetlow, G. and Wakefield, M. (2008) *Asset ownership, portfolios and retirement saving arrangements: Past trends and prospects for the future*, London: FSA.

Barrett, A.E. and Naiman-Sessions, M. (2016) 'It's our turn to play': performance of girlhood as a collective response to gendered ageism, *Ageing and Society*, 36(4), 764–84.

Beck, U. (1992) *Risk society. Towards a new modernity*, London: Sage Publications.

Beck, U. (2005) *Power in the global age: A new global political economy*, Cambridge: Policy Press.

Benedick, M., Jr, Jackson, C.W. and Romero, J.H. (1996) Employment discrimination against older workers: an experimental study of hiring practices, *Journal of Aging & Social Policy*, 8, 25–46.

Benedick, M., Jr, Brown, L.E. and Wall, K. (1999) No foot in the door: an experimental study of employment discrimination against older workers, *Journal of Aging & Social Policy*, 10, 5–23.

Berger, E.D. (2009) Managing age discrimination: an examination of the techniques used when seeking employment, *The Gerontologist*, 49 (3), 317–32.

Bilge, S. (2013) Intersectionality undone. Saving intersectionality from feminist intersectionality studies, *Du Bois Review: Social Science Research on Race*, 10(2), 405–24.

Bodily, C.L. (1994) Ageism and the deployments of 'age', in T.R. Sarbin and J.I. Kitsuse (eds) *Constructing the social*, London: Sage, pp 174–94.

Butler, R.N. (1969) Age-ism: another form of bigotry, *The Gerontologist*, 9, 243–6.

Butler, R.N. (1980) Ageism: a foreword, *Journal of Social Issues*, 36(2), 8–11.

Bytheway, B. (1995) *Ageism*, Buckingham: Open University Press.

Calasanti, T. (2004) Feminist gerontology and old men, *Journal of Gerontology: Social Sciences*, 59B(6), S305–S315.

Calasanti, T.M., Slevin, K.F. and King, N. (2006) Ageism and feminism: from 'et cetera' to center, *NWSA Journal*, 18(1), 13–30.

Carbado, D.W., Crenshaw, K.W., Mays, V.M. and Toblinson, B. (2013) Intersectionality. Mapping the movements of a theory, *Du Bois Review: Social Science Research on Race*, 10(2), 303–12.

Christensen, A.D. and Qvotrup, S. (2014) Combining hegemonic masculinity and intersectionality, *NORMA: International Journal for Masculinity Studies*, 9(1), 60–75.

Clarke, L.H and Griffin, M. (2008) Visible and invisible ageing: beauty work as a response to ageism, *Ageing & Society*, 28(5), 653–74.

Collinson, D.L. and Hearn, J. (2004) Men and masculinities in work, organisations and management, in M.S. Kimmel, J. Hearns and R.W. Connell (eds) *Handbook of studies on men & masculinities*, London: Sage Publications.

Connell, R.W. (2005) *Masculinities* (2nd edn), Los Angeles, CA: University of California Press.

Connell, R.W. and Messerschmidt, J.W. (2005) Hegemonic masculinity. Rethinking the concept, *Gender and Society*, 19, 829–59.

Crenshaw, K. (1989) Demarginalising the intersection of race and sex: a black feminist critique of antidiscrimination doctrine, *University of Chicago Legal Forum*, pp 139–68.

Dannefer, D. and Settersten, R.A. (2010) The study of the life course: implications for social gerontology, in D. Dannefer and C. Phillipson (eds) *The SAGE Handbook of social gerontology*, Thousand Oaks, CA: Sage, pp 3–19.

Davis, K. (2008) Intersectionality as buzzword, *Feminist Theory*, 9(1), 67–85.

Duncan, C. and Loretto, W. (2004) Never the right age? Gender and age-based discrimination in employment, *Gender, Work & Organization*, 11, 95–115.

DWP (Department for Work and Pensions) (2014) *Fuller working lives – a framework for action*, London: DWP.

Elder, G.H., Johnson, M.K. and Crosnoe, R. (2003) The emergence and development of life course theory, in J.T. Mortimer and Shanahan, M.J. (eds) *Handbook of the life course*, New York, NY: Springer, pp 3–19.

Ennals, R. and Hilsen, A.I. (2011) Older workers: the jam in the sandwich, in R. Ennals and R.H. Saloman (eds) *Older workers in a sustainable society*, Frankfurt am Main: Peter Lang, pp 245–52.

Eurolink Age (1993) *Age discrimination against older workers in the European Community*, London: Eurolink Age.

Fevre, R. (2011) Still on the scrapheap? The meaning and characteristics of unemployment in prosperous welfare states, *Work, Employment and Society*, 25, 1–9.

Garstka, T.A., Hummert, M.L. and Branscombe, N.R. (2005) Perceiving age discrimination in response to intergenerational inequity, *Journal of Social Issue*, 61(2), 321–42.

Gee, G., Pavalko, E.K. and Long, J.S. (2007) Age, cohort and perceived age discrimination: using the life course to assess self-reported age discrimination, *Social Forces*, 86(1), 265–90.

Giddens, A. (1991) *Modernity and self-identity*, New Jersey, NJ: Blackwell Publishers.

Granleese, J. and Sayer, G. (2006) Gendered ageism and 'lookism': a triple jeopardy for female academics, *Gender in Management: An International Journal*, 21(6), 500–17.

Gray, M., Edwards, B. and Zmijewksi, N. (2008) Caring and women's labour market participation, *Family Matters*, 78, 28–35.

Handy, J. and Davy, D. (2007) Gendered ageism: older women's experiences of employment agency practices, *Asia Pacific Journal of Human Resources*, 1, 85–99.

Harkness, S. (2008) The household division of labour: changes in families' allocation of paid and unpaid work, in J. Scott, S. Dex and H. Joshi (eds) *Women and employment: Changing lives and new challenges*, Cheltenham: Edward Elgar, pp 234–67.

Hasselhorn, H.M. and Apt, W. (2015) Understanding employment participation of older workers: creating a knowledge base for future labour market challenges, Research Report, Federal Ministry of Labour and Social Affairs (BMAS) and Federal Institute for Occupational Safety and Health (BAuA), Berlin. Available at: http://www.jp-demographic.eu/about/fast-track-projects/understanding-employment

Heinz, W.R. (2003) From work trajectories to negotiated careers, in J.T. Mortimer and M.J. Shanahan (eds) *Handbook of the life course*, New York, NY: Springer, pp 185–204.

Hernes, H. (1987) *Women and the welfare state, essays in state feminism*, Oslo: Universitetsforlaget.

Hurd Clarke L. and Griffin, M. (2008) Visible and invisible ageing: beauty work as a response to ageism, *Ageing and Society*, 28, 653–74.

Itzin, C. and Phillipson, C. (1995) Gendered ageism: a double jeopardy for women in organisations, in C. Itzin and C. Phillipson (eds) *Gender, culture and organisational change: Putting theory into practice*, London: Routledge, pp 84–94.

Jyrkinen, M. (2013) Women managers, careers and gendered ageism, *Scandinavian Journal of Management*, 30(2), 175–85.

Kalavar, J.M. (2001) Examining ageism: do male and female college students differ?, *Educational Gerontology*, 27(6), 779–811.

Kalish, R.A. (1979) The new ageism and the failure models: a polemic, *The Gerontologist*, 19(4), 398–402.

Kimmel, M.S. (1994) Masculinity as homophobia: fear, shame, and silence in the construction of gender identity, in H. Brod and M. Kaufman (eds) *Theorizing masculinities*, Thousand Oaks, CA: SAGE Publications, pp 119–41.

Komp, K. and Johansson, S. (2015) Introduction, in K. Komp and S. Johansson (eds) *Population ageing from a lifecourse perspective*, Bristol: Policy Press, pp 1–12.

Krekula, C. (2009) Age coding: on age-based practices of distinction, *International Journal of Ageing and Later Life*, 4(2), 7–31. Available at: http://www.ep.liu.se/ej/ijal/

Krekula, C. (2011) *Åldersdiskriminering i svenskt arbetsliv. Om ålderskodningar och myter som skapar ojämlikhet* [Age discrimination in Swedish working life. On age codings and myths that create inequality], official report from the Ombudsman for Discrimination. Stockholm: Diskrimineringsombudsmannen.

Krekula, C. (2012) Attityder till fysisk styrka: Om kvinnor, äldre brandmän och självupplevda begränsningar [Attitudes towards physical strength: on women, older firefighters and personally experienced limitations], in L.G. Engström, L. Jakobsen and C. Krekula (eds) *Jämställdhet, mångfald och svenska räddningstjänster. Om föreställningar och förändringsviljor* [*Equality, diversity and the Swedish emergency services. On conceptions and willingness to change*], Karlstad: Karlstad University Press, pp 71–80.

Krekula, C. and Heikkien, S. (2014) Med fokus på ålder som organiserande princip [With a focus on age as an organizing principle], *Sociologisk Forskning*, 2, 5–14.

Krekula, C. and Johansson, B. (2016) En introduktion till kritiska åldersstudier [Introduction to critical age studies], in C. Krekula and B. Johansson (eds) *Kritiska* åldersstudier [*Critical age studies*], Lund: Gleerups förlag.

Krekula, C., Nikander, P. and Wilinska, M. (2017) Gendered ageism, in L. Ayalon and C. Tesch-Roemer (eds) *Current perspectives on ageism: A multi-disciplinary approach*, New York, NY: Springer Publisher.

Lain, D. (2011) Helping the poorest help themselves? Encouraging employment past 65 in England and the USA, *Journal of Social Policy*, 40(3), 493–512.

Lain, D. (2016) *Reconstructing retirement: Work and welfare in the UK and USA*, Bristol: The Policy Press.

Lain, D. and Vickerstaff, S. (2015) *National report: United Kingdom*, Berlin: Federal Ministry of Labour and Social Affairs (BMAS) and Federal Institute for Occupational Safety and Health. Available at: http://www.jp-demographic.eu/wp-content/uploads/2015/07/UK-National-Report.pdf

Lewis, J. (2002) Gender and welfare state change, *European Societies*, 4(4), 331–57.

Lewis, J. (2007) Gender, ageing and the 'new social settlement': the importance of developing a holistic approach to care policies, *Current Sociology*, 55(2), 271–86.

Lewis, K. and Walker, E.A. (2011) Self-employment: policy panacea for an ageing population?, *Small Enterprise Research*, 18, 143–51.

Loretto, W. and Vickerstaff, S. (2013) The domestic and gendered context for retirement, *Human Relations*, 66(1), 65–86.

Loretto, W. and White, P. (2006) Employment of older workers: employers' attitudes, policies and practices, *Human Resource Management Journal*, 16, 313–30.

Loretto, W., Duncan, C. and White, P.J. (2000) Ageism and employment: controversies, ambiguities and younger people's perceptions, *Ageing & Society*, 20, 279–302.

Lorey, I. (2015) *State of insecurity. Government of the precarious*, London: Verso.

Lynch, C. (2012) *Retirement on the line. Age, work, and value in an American factory*, London: Cornell University Press.

Magnus, G. (2009) *The age of aging*, Singapore: John Wiley and Sons.

Marmot, M., Allen, J., Goldblatt, P., Boyce, T., McNeish, D., Grady, M. and Geddes, I. (2010) *Fair society, healthy lives: The Marmot review, strategic review of health inequalities in England post 2010*, London: Department of Health.

May, V.M. (2014) Speaking into the void? Intersectionality critiques and epistemic backlash, *Hypatia*, 29(1), 94–112.

Messerschmidt, J.W. (2012) Engendering gendered knowledge: assessing academic appropriation of hegemonic masculinity, *Men and Masculinities*, 15, 56–76.

Moen, P. (2003) Midcourse: Navigating retirement and a new life stage, in J.T. Mortimer and M.J. Shanahan (eds) *Handbook of the life course*, New York, NY: Springer, pp 269–91.

Moen, P. (2011) From 'work family' to the 'gendered life course' and 'fit': five challenges to the field, *Community, Work and Family*, 14, 1, 81–96.

Motel-Klingebiel, A. (2015) A lifecourse scholar's view: lifecourses crystallise in demographic structures, in K. Komp and S. Johansson (eds) *Population ageing from a lifecourse perspective*, Bristol: The Policy Press, pp 29–42.

Moulaert, T. and Biggs, S. (2013) International and European policy on work and retirement: reinventing critical perspectives on active ageing and mature subjectivity, *Human Relations*, 66(3), 22–41.

Munnell, A.H. and Sass, S.A. (2008) *Working longer: The solution to the retirement income challenge*, Washington, DC: The Brookings Institution.

Nash, J.C. (2008) Re-thinking intersectionality, *Feminist review*, 89, 1–15.

Nelson, T.D. (2005) Ageism: prejudice against our feared future self, *Journal of Social Issues*, 61(2), 207–21.

Neumark, D. (2009) The Age Discrimination in Employment Act and the challenge of population aging, *Research on Aging*, 31(1), 41–68.

OECD (Organisation for Economic Co-operation and Development) (2006) *Live longer work longer*, Paris: OECD.

OECD (2011) *Pensions at a glance*, Paris: OECD.

Özbilgin, M., Beauregard, T.A., Tatli, A. and Bell, M.P. (2011) Work–life, diversity and intersectionality: a critical review and research agenda, *International Journal of Management Reviews*, 13(2), 177–98.

Palmore, E.B. (1999) *Ageism: Negative and positive*, New York, NY: Springer Publishing Company.

Palmore, E.B. (2001) The ageism survey: first findings, *The Gerontologist*, 41(5), 572–5.

Perrons, D. (2005) Gender mainstreaming and gender equality in the new (market) economy: an analysis of contradictions, *Social Politics: International Studies in Gender, State and Society*, 12(3), 389–411.

Phillipson, C. (2013) *Ageing*, Cambridge: Polity Press.

Prins, B. (2006) Narrative accounts of origins: a blind spot in the intersectional approach?, *European Journal of Women's Studies*, 13(3), 277–90.

Quah, D. (2003) Digital goods and the new economy, Centre for Economic Performance, Discussion paper No. 563, London School of Economics, London. Available at: http://econ.lse.ac.uk/staff/dquah/p/dp-0212hbne-2pp.pdf

Ray, M. (2014) Critical perspectives on social work with older people, in J. Baars, A. Dohmen, A. Grenier and C. Phillipson (eds) *Ageing, meaning and social structure*, Bristol: The Policy Press, pp 139–56.

Riach, K. (2009) Managing 'difference': understanding age diversity in practice, *Human Resource Management Journal*, 19, 319–35.

Rosa, H. and Scheurman, W.E. (eds) (2008) *High–speed society: Social acceleration, power and modernity*, Philadelphia, PA: The Pennsylvania State University Press.

Rubery, J. (2015) Change at work: feminisation, flexibilisation, fragmentation and financialisation, *Employee Relations*, 37(6), 633–44.

Schwalbe, M. (2008) *Rigging the game. How inequality is reproduced in everyday life*, Oxford: Oxford University Press.

Sennett, R. (1999) Growth and failure: the new political economy and its culture, in M. Featherstone and S. Lash (eds) *Spaces of culture: City, nation, world*, London: Sage, pp 14–26.

SOU (Statens Offentliga Utredningar [Official Reports of the Swedish Government]) (2013) *Åtgärder för ett längre arbetsliv* [Measures for an extended working life], final report by the Government Commission for Longer Working Life and Retirement Age, Stockholm. Available at: http://www.regeringen.se/contentassets/0ce6fa7c55654f15b760 c27d5d95062d/atgarder-for-ett-langre-arbetsliv-sou-201325---hela-dokumentet

Standing, G. (2011) *The precariat. The new dangerous class*, London: Bloomsbury Academic.

Staunæs, D. (2003) Where have all the subjects gone? Bringing together the concept of intersectionality and subjectification, *NORA*, 2(11), 101–10.

Tilly, C. (1998) *Durable inequality*, Berkeley and Los Angeles, CA: University of California Press.

Vickerstaff, S. (2010) Older workers: the 'unavoidable obligation' of extending our working lives?, *Sociology Compass*, 4(10), 869–79.

Vickerstaff, S. (2015) Domain: domestic and household factors, in H.M. Hasselhorn and W. Apt (eds) *Understanding employment participation of older workers: Creating a knowledge base for future labour market challenges*, Berlin: Federal Ministry of Labour and Social Affairs (BMAS) and Federal Institute for Occupational Safety and Health (BAuA). Available at: http://www.jp-demographic.eu/about/fast-track-projects/understanding-employment

Walker, A. (1998) Age and employment, *Australasian Journal on Ageing*, 17(1): 99–103.

Walker, H., Grant, D., Meadows, M. & Cook, I. (2007) Women's experiences and perceptions of age discrimination in employment: implications for research and policy, *Social Policy & Society*, 6, 37–48.

WHO (World Health Organization) (2002) *Active ageing: A policy framework*, Geneva: WHO.

Wilkinson, J.A. and Ferraro, K.F. (2002) Thirty years of ageism research, in T.D. Nelson (ed) *Ageism: Stereotyping and prejudice against older persons*, Cambridge, MA: MIT Press, pp 339–58.

Williams, S., Bardley, H., Devadason, R. and Erickson, M. (2013) *Globalization at work*, Cambridge: Polity Press.

Yuval-Davis, N. (2006) Intersectionality and feminist politics, *European Journal of Women's Studies*, 13(3), 193–209.

THREE

Gender perspectives on extended working life policies

Áine Ní Léime and Wendy Loretto

Introduction

Policies designed to extend working lives have been actively promoted to national governments by international organisations such as the European Union (EU) and the Organisation for Economic Co-operation and Development (OECD) (OECD, 2006; European Commission, 2009, 2012). The extended working life policy approach has received a further impetus from the advent of the global financial crisis and the neoliberal policies that have typically been recommended and/or adopted to deal with its effects (Foster, 2012a). This chapter provides a critical overview, discussing the features of extended working life policies that have been recommended in recent years as the appropriate response to demographic ageing and associated concerns about the costs of pension provision and health care.

As discussed in Chapter Two, critics from feminist political economy of ageing and life-course perspectives note that extended working life policies have been introduced without adequate consideration of the differential impacts that they may have on women and men given their typically different work–life trajectories that are deeply gendered (Dewilde, 2012; Ginn and MacIntyre, 2013; Foster, 2012b, 2014). Among the problems identified with the uncritical adoption of extended working life policies is that they are primarily promoted with the narrowly focused objective of reducing future pension costs (Foster, 2014). However, most pension systems were designed for a male breadwinner model of family life and, as such, did not acknowledge the unpaid caring work usually done by women, which reduced their ability to qualify for or contribute to pensions (Ginn et al, 2001). Current reforms, which advocate the privatisation and individualisation of pensions – linking pensions more closely to earnings and requiring more contributions – are likely to result in increased gender inequality in pension outcomes. This is because women still typically have more interrupted work histories, earn less and are less able to contribute to private and/or occupational pensions (see Chapter One).

Insights from life–course scholars suggest thinking even more broadly, beyond pensions, by considering other aspects of working life, such as the impact of historical family-friendly employment policies that affected women earlier in their lives and current family-friendly and flexible employment policies for older workers approaching retirement (Ginn, 2003; Dewilde, 2012). A feminist political economy of ageing perspective highlights the need to consider gendered societal norms related to caring, conditions in the economy and related employment policies at all phases of the life course for a full assessment of the impact of work and pension reforms (Ginn et al, 2001; Ní Léime et al, 2015).

This chapter documents international policy developments and provides a gender critique of retirement, employment and pension policies. By providing a comparative overview of the policies across the seven countries covered in the book (Australia, Ireland, Germany, Portugal, Sweden, the UK and the US), we assess the degree to which the individual countries' extended working life policies have adopted the agenda set out by the OECD and the EU. Policies we consider include: those designed to extend working life, including raising the state pension age; changes in the duration of pension contribution requirements; the move from defined benefits to defined contribution pensions; policies related to caring for vulnerable members of the population; policies enabling flexible working; and anti-age discrimination measures.

We draw on a framework developed in 2001 by Ginn, Street and Arber, to assess whether pension policies are likely to be women-friendly or adverse (Ginn et al, 2001). The authors of the country chapters use the framework outlined in Table 3.1 to expand this discussion and assess the degree to which gender and other intersecting issues such as health, caring, class and/or membership of minority communities have or have not been taken into account in designing and implementing policies extending working life.

Authors of country chapters also consider whether any account has been taken of the various types of occupations in which people are engaged and of the degree to which employment is secure or precarious. A preliminary review of the literature suggests that in many countries, there has been little specific consideration of the gender effects of extended working life, for example, few policymakers appear to have engaged in gender mainstreaming (examining the gender impacts of introducing policies) (Foster, 2014).

Table 3.1: Policy dimensions

Retirement	Employment	Pension
• Age of state pension age entitlement • Mandatory/normal retirement age • Tax rules on working and drawing a pension • State pension deferral	• Discrimination legislation • Collective agreements on age/retirement • Access to flexible working • Current and past parental, maternity/paternity leave	• Contribution requirements • Changes to state pensions • Defined benefit to defined contributions • New occupational pensions • Credits for time spent caring

International policy actors and extended working life

For the past two decades, international policy bodies such as the OECD and the EU have urged national governments to adopt policies designed to extend working life, partly in response to demographic ageing (European Commission, 2009; OECD, 2006, 2013a). Such policies include both pension reforms and employment policies. For example, the influential OECD (2006) report *Live longer, work longer* encouraged people to remain longer in employment. The report recommended that states introduce employment policies to strengthen financial incentives to continue working, tackle barriers from employers, combat age discrimination and improve the employability of older workers, along with a variety of pension system reforms. The OECD has used various soft-governance mechanisms to promote this policy agenda, including publishing country-specific follow-up reviews that identify whether or not countries have complied with their recommendations (OECD, 2013a). The European Commission, using 'Active Ageing' as a framework, has also encouraged countries to extend working life (European Commission, 2009, 2012). In 2007, the European Commission adopted Council Directive 2000/78/EC, which directs member states to make unequal treatment by age in employment, recruitment and training illegal. It introduced a target of 50% employment rates for those aged between 55 and 64 years of age by 2010 in the EU at the Stockholm Council in 2001 (Jolivet, 2002), and has also focused on combating age discrimination. The Europe 2020 Strategy set a goal of 75% labour market participation for women and men aged 20–64 by 2020 (Duchemin et al, 2012). The introduction of extended working life policies has been linked by some commentators with neoliberal ideologies and the retrenchment of welfare states (see Chapter Two; see also Foster, 2012a) because such policies are designed to enable welfare states to take less responsibility for pensions and to place the responsibility for pension provision increasingly on workers themselves. Critics of the 'Active Ageing' approach point out that it appears to be using a reductionist, economistic interpretation of active ageing overly focused on labour market activity (Mouleart and Biggs, 2012). It fails to consider adequately issues such as ill-health, the challenges of physically demanding work in later life and precarious employment (Vickerstaff, 2010). Linking pensions more closely to years of employment disadvantages women and men with periods of unemployment since women typically have interrupted periods of labour supply due to caring for dependent family members (Ginn et al, 2001; Dewilde, 2012).

Gender critique of generic work life policies

Extended working life policy approaches are narrowly focused on reducing state expenditure and do not adequately recognise the gendered impact of family/caring on pension outcomes (Ginn et al, 2001; Harrington Meyer, 2013). Feminist and, more recently, life-course scholars argue that the typical work–life biographies of women and men differ, with women in most countries expected to perform unpaid care for children and dependent family members (see Chapter Two; see also Ivosevic, 2009; Dewilde, 2012). Moreover, the history of retirement is closely tied to meanings of work in the male breadwinner model (Everingham et al, 2007: 152), calling into question the relevance of retirement to women, who have less clear distinctions between paid and unpaid work (Loretto and Vickerstaff, 2015). These very different patterns of engagement with 'work' have profound implications for all aspects of the extended working life agenda, with women in particular often ill-served by current foci and policies.

Women were also marginalised in the earlier (1990s/2000s) policy discourse of reversing early retirement. The institutionalisation of early retirement arose as one of the unintended results of maturing public pension systems, the creation of institutional pathways to early retirement and, in Europe, prolonged high unemployment (Cooke, 2006: 390). All of those processes affected men more than women, especially given structural issues leading to mass and involuntary early retirement in male-dominated industries (Beatty and Fothergill, 2007); as such, early retirement was often viewed as gender-neutral or even as a male 'issue'. However, early retirement was also prevalent among women (Ebbinghaus, 2006). Nevertheless, the focus of governments on tackling early retirement in order to address the potential economic and social effects of an ageing workforce was very clearly prompted by men's (dis)engagement with the labour market, not women's.

In recent decades, retirement patterns and behaviours have shifted. However, as retirement has shifted from being a singular, unidirectional 'event' to a much wider collection of possible transitions, gender is largely absent or, at best, loosely incorporated into notions of 'societal norms' of family roles and/or marital status. In particular, understanding of women's retirement processes has been limited because of 'a tendency to view women's retirement and retirement planning relative to normative understandings already established for men' (Wong and Hardy, 2009: 77).

Now that the focus is on extending working lives, it is implicitly assumed that women will take on 'male' models of retirement. This is an assumption that needs questioning. Back in 1998, Onyx (1998, cited in Everingham et al, 2007: 513) cautioned that historical changes in women's labour market engagement should not be interpreted as 'women simply desiring to take on male models of work'. Many women still structure their working lives around family care. Onyx argued for new models of retirement that would distinguish between the effects of different family and work situations on women's options in later life. She notes that this is in alignment with the dominant Western discourse of 'choice' (Onyx, 1998: cited in Everingham et al, 2007:521), but that women cannot easily realise this without opportunities for better work–life balance and education throughout the life course. European governments' welfare and employment policies are based on the assumption that women's employment outside the home will create more and new jobs to meet the requirement for caring and domestic work currently being carried out on an unpaid basis – that women's earnings will help keep families out of poverty and make a contribution to the rising costs of welfare (Esping-Andersen, 1999; Esping-Andersen et al, 2002). In fact, research using the concept of global care chains suggests that in many wealthy countries, much of the outsourced caring work is performed by migrants, leading to new inequalities between sexes, classes and ethnic groups (Yeates, 2009; Hochschild, 2012; Palenga-Möllenbeck, 2013). As yet, there had been limited feminist analysis of extended working life policies to interrogate largely untested underpinning assumptions (although for the body of work on pensions, see later). Nevertheless, we can extend critiques of welfare policies in general to analyse motivations behind encouraging female participation in the workforce.

Feminist challenges to welfare policies for women's paid and unpaid care

Lewis (2006) has been fiercely critical of Western European welfare states that have built their systems of social protection around the relationship between the male worker and the labour market. She argues that the gender–equality goal is subsumed or at best co-opted (in relation to work–life balance, see Stratigaki, 2004) in the process of achieving a good fit with the dominant policy preoccupation. For example, in the case of work–life balance, the business case is the dominant frame: 'Social policy, like equal opportunities policy, has historically been tied to the overarching goal of market-making' (Stratigaki, 2004: 432). Lewis sees this paradigm extending into the 21st century with employment of all able-bodied adults as a necessary prerequisite for economic growth and competition. Under this model, women are seen as an untapped labour reserve (Esping-Andersen and Sarasa, 2001). Similar assumptions appear to also underpin the focus on extended working life, with explicit reference to women as untapped potential contained in, for example, UK policy publications (Altmann, 2015), but with scant attention to women's needs as workers, paid and unpaid.

According to Lewis (2006: 426), the lack of attention to gender equality has been justified both by market considerations and 'continuing reluctance, especially on the part of the European Court of Justice, to consider unequal gender divisions in the family as well as in the labour market'. In relation to work–life balance policies, there has been little focus on promoting the equal sharing of unpaid care work or on changing the behaviour of men. Instead, gender equality is narrowly defined in a 'particular, partial and instrumental' way related to formal labour market participation but not care work (Lewis and Giullari, 2005: 78). Similarly, Crompton and Lyonette (2006) critique the motivations underpinning work–life balance policies in France, noting that support for mothers' employment has been pro-natalist rather than concerned with women's equality, while the motivation in the UK is alleviating child poverty. As policymakers have shifted emphasis from rights to responsibilities, from passive to active welfare, whereby recipients of welfare are encouraged to work and work is made to pay, 'It is now assumed that women as well as men will be "citizen workers"' (Lewis and Giullari, 2005: 79).

In practice, the individualised adult worker model has meant more work for women, who have tended to add paid work to existing care responsibilities, while men in many Western countries have decreased their amount of paid work, but only slightly increased care (Lewis and Giullari, 2005; Thevenon, 2011). The realities of the distribution of labour are ignored because:

> it is usually assumed by governments and policy experts that in the adult worker model of family, the work of care will increasingly move to the formal paid sector, which helps to account for the secondary place accorded to care on the policy agenda. (Lewis and Giullari, 2005: 77)

The assumption that care can be marketised and commodified is not proven. Choice is socially embedded and real choice would involve a complicated rebalancing of unpaid work between the market, the state, men and women. It would also take into account cultural factors, which Naldini et al (2016) have shown to significantly affect the likely outcomes of policies and state funding for elder care on older women carers' propensity to leave employment.

EU-level policy documents have placed considerable emphasis on the provision of formal childcare services; however, that does not necessarily positively affect rates of female labour market participation (Lewis and Giullari, 2005). For many women, the best jobs are those that enable them to reconcile work and family responsibilities, and while policies that promote that are helpful, they have tended to focus on women only, as if men have no responsibility to care. While there has been some attempt by some governments to introduce policies to encourage men to engage in unpaid care work, this is uneven at best (OECD, 2011a).

A further reason highlighting the inadequacy of the commodification of care in addressing gender inequality in employment and care arises from the conflation of labour and love in any caring role, identified by Lewis and Giullari (2005: 86) as 'a key process of female identity formation embedded in a gendered normative framework of obligations'. Such embeddedness may strengthen over the life course, which would suggest that assuming older women will 'choose' work over care is unfounded. The realities of the imperatives for older women to leave paid employment to take up caring roles are clear from OECD analyses. Their *Pensions at a glance, 2011* (OECD, 2011b) report showed different retirement pathways for women and men. For women, retirement accounts for the majority of labour market exit in only five out of 20 countries; most move out of work into the 'other inactive' category, most likely ceasing paid work to care for other family members. By contrast, more than half of exits for men in 11 countries are via retirement –where there was either a relatively low pension age or a range of early retirement options, or both. In another five countries, more than half of men leave employment because of unemployment or disability.

Gender and cumulative inequalities in later life

The failure of welfare systems, particularly pension schemes, to address the diversity that characterises women's lives and compensate for disadvantage in divisions between paid work and unpaid family care has continued to disadvantage women and has led to accumulated disadvantage – the key here is the balance between the distributive and non-distributive elements of a pensions system (Ivosevic, 2009; Vlachantoni, 2012). A life-course perspective on policies would acknowledge the accumulation of advantage or disadvantage over the life course, taking into account poor health, poverty and irregular employment in earlier life and their consequences for later-life transitions and circumstances (see Chapter Two; see also Cooke, 2006). As Cooke (2006: 388) notes, the extent to which the interrelated domains of work, education, family and health have been taken into account is unclear. He suggests that 'Welfare state policies can be considered life-course policies insofar as they affect the timing and experience of these various life-course transitions' (Cooke, 2006: 389).

Women face disadvantages when more contributions are required and pensions are tied closely to earnings, a point acknowledged by the OECD in response to gender critiques (Ginn, 2004; Corsi and D'ippoliti, 2009; OECD, 2015). However, their reports stop short of making clear recommendations to address issues of gendered life course disadvantages (OECD, 2013a). Instead, it is up to each country to find a means of balancing the sustainability of pensions while ensuring that women who provide unpaid care are not disadvantaged. The OECD (2015: 101) explicitly state that 'pension systems … are not typically intended to reduce inequalities between men and women…. That is probably as it should be', thus implying that such inequalities are acceptable. By contrast with its strong policy recommendations to address sustainability in the pension system, the OECD's approach to addressing gender inequalities in pension outcomes appears somewhat lukewarm and ambivalent.

A life-course perspective allied to a feminist political-economy perspective offers a useful means of analysing the way in which de-standardised retirement and pension reforms affect pension outcomes for women (Ginn et al, 2001; Dewilde, 2012; Foster, 2012a). A feminist political economy of ageing approach recognises the impacts that the social, normative, economic, cultural and political environment, including legislation, can have on women's capacity to provide for pensions. A life-course approach highlights the accumulation of inequalities across life courses. For example, if a person starts off with a social and/or economic disadvantage, this has a tendency to become exacerbated over the life course (Dannefer, 2003; Ferraro and Shippee, 2009). It also emphasises the importance of analysing life-course trajectories, such as women's tendency to take time out of the workforce for caring and acknowledging that many women are not aware of the need to save for pensions at the start of working life (Ní Léime et al, 2015). While a feminist political-economy perspective provides a lens through which to assess policies associated with extended working life, researchers also recognise the importance of local contexts for understanding individuals' lived experiences. From a policy perspective, that local context is shaped to a large extent by national-level policy frameworks and initiatives.

Overview of countries and policies

In all of the countries covered in this book, there have been policy debates and, in some instances, policy changes in the realm of pensions and policies intended to extend working lives. We discuss pension reforms in terms of how closely they adhere to the agenda of the OECD and the EU, as well as the extent to which the gender critique outlined earlier is supported. An overview of the broad scope of pension reforms is provided in Table 3.1. While individual country experiences are complex and the effects of one particular policy can sometimes minimise or neutralise the effects of another policy, the pension policies outlined here tend to have the following effects: requiring regular contributions for longer periods to qualify for a state pension scheme; averaging pensions over the entire or long portions of working life; and tying pensions closely to earnings. All these policies are inclined to increase gender inequality in pensions because of women's interrupted work–life trajectories and because of the gender pay gap (Ginn et al, 2001). When states (including Australia and Ireland) provide a minimum guaranteed pension and flat-rate provisions, this tends to reduce gender inequality in pension outcomes, depending on the level of the safety-net pension (Ginn et al, 2001; Ginn, 2004). Similar effects may be expected when countries do not base pensions on gendered actuarial life-expectancy estimates, which tend to disadvantage women since they live for longer. Systems with universal citizens' pensions mean that women who spend several years caring do not receive less than other pensioners. Systems that offer pension credits or disregards for years spent caring (including the UK and Ireland) can also help reduce pension inequality for women (Ginn, 2004; OECD, 2013a). Systems that allow part-time workers to make extra pension contributions can also reduce inequality, but only for women who can afford to make extra contributions. Gender differences in pension outcomes can also be reduced by redistributive features in the system, such as higher replacement rates for low income workers, as in the US.

Recent pension reforms typically encourage privatisation and individualisation. The privatisation of pensions is generally disadvantageous to women (Estes, 2004; Foster, 2011). Research based on six EU countries found that women's mean income relative to men's is considerably lower from private pensions than from public pensions in each country studied (Ginn, 2004); this is also true in the US (Street and Wilmoth, 2001). Other pension reforms that have been introduced include raising the state pension age, reducing incentives to take early retirement, linking pensions more closely to the duration of employment, encouraging citizens to increasingly finance their own individual private pensions and encouraging a change from defined benefit to defined contributions in occupational or private pension schemes. The likely impact of these reforms is mixed and needs to be considered in context. Raising the state pension age may be beneficial for some women who wish to continue working past the state pension age and who are in well-paid employment; however, it may be very difficult for women engaged in heavy labour such as cleaning or caring (Vickerstaff, 2010). Furthermore, there is unlikely to be suitable employment readily available for many older women and men, particularly during periods of economic recession (Foster, 2014).

Pension policies and reforms

Most pension systems were initially based on a male breadwinner model of family life. In many countries, women did not have pensions in their own right, but were constructed as dependants of their spouses/husbands (Ginn et al, 2001). Pension systems vary, with most countries having mixed systems of provision, with a first tier – residual, means-tested safety-net pension – funded by the state and a second tier of private and/or occupational pensions.

Typically, the OECD recommends 'diversifying' pension provision by encouraging individuals through tax incentives to provide their own private pensions. Several countries, including Ireland, the UK, the US and Sweden, have followed these recommendations and encouraged citizens to pay into private pensions by giving tax incentives. However, privatisation is recognised as being unfriendly to women, whose disadvantages in the labour market result in poorer pensions (Estes, 2004; Ginn and MacIntyre, 2013). For example, women's experience of privatisation has been largely negative in Ireland, with pensions losing up to 65% of their value during the recent economic crisis (Ní Léime et al, 2015). Very often, women cannot afford to contribute to private schemes, which have high administration costs and uncertain outcomes (Ginn and MacIntyre, 2013).

Another reform undertaken by some of the countries studied, such as the US, is switching from defined benefit pensions (where the level of pension is set out, usually at a proportion of final salary) to defined contributions (where the level of pension depends on stock market returns) in occupational pensions. This is also likely to affect women adversely since, unlike defined benefit pensions, which socialise risk and guarantee lifetime benefits based on a particular formula, defined contribution schemes do not provide a guaranteed outcome and seldom include a survivor benefit (Estes, 2004; Foster, 2011). When husbands die, this leaves women without a predictable income and, for those nearing retirement, without sufficient time to build up pensions of their own. The outcomes of defined contributions schemes are more risky than traditional defined benefit occupational pensions as outcomes depend on the performance of private markets (Russell, 2014).

One of the main policies advocated by the OECD is increasing the state pension age or normal retirement age. Most of the countries featured in this book increased the age of retirement and/or removed mandatory retirement. Some plan further increases. This varies from Portugal and Germany, both with moderate increases planned to reach 67 in 2029, to Ireland, where the state pension age is now 66, with plans to increase it to 68 by 2028, even though Ireland has a relatively low percentage of its population (12%) aged 65 or over. Australia, Germany, the US and the UK plan to increase the normal retirement age more gradually (see Table 3.2), although the timetable for increases has recently been shortened in the UK (Foster, 2014). The impact of these increases for women is likely to vary, depending on their occupation and preferences; women engaged in heavy labour for poor pay and in poor conditions may find it physically difficult to continue working until they are the right age to be fully eligible for state pensions, while others may welcome the opportunity to work for longer, for financial reasons and/or because they enjoy working (Ní Léime et al, 2015). In some countries (including the UK and Australia), women traditionally had a lower state pension age than men, but ages were recently equalised. The increase in women's state pension ages has already disrupted the expectations that they had of being eligible for a pension earlier, thus increasing their exposure to financial hardship (Foster, 2014). Mandatory retirement age was removed in the US in 1986, in Australia in 2001, in the UK in 2011 and in Ireland in 2016. The impact of this is positive for both men and women in that it removes a barrier to work, thus increasing their options after traditional retirement age.

In some countries, pension credits are awarded towards state pension entitlements for periods of time spent caring for children and/or older people, constituting a direct recognition of unpaid caring work as contributing to pensions. The number of years' credit given in 2014 for childcare varies: women get none in the US (although 35 years' total contributions requirement allows for some time out of the labour market) and Australia; women in Portugal get part-time work (for childcare purposes) credited as full-time work, but do not get credit for time taken out for childcare; credits for children up to 12 years old may be awarded in the UK; credits for children up to age 10 are awarded in Germany; time spent caring for children is disregarded in Ireland so long as at least 520 pension credits are made; and in Sweden, credits are available for parents of children up to five years for 480 days (OECD, 2015). The UK gives credits for those caring for older people in need of care since 2007 (Ginn and MacIntyre, 2013) and Ireland also gives credits for time spent caring for older people.

Policy measures giving people incentives to work around and past retirement age (flexible working) have been introduced to varying degrees (see Table 3.3). For example, Australia is to increase the age at which superannuation may be accessed from 55 to 60. A work bonus was introduced in 2009 allowing pensioners to work past retirement age and still receive a full pension. A similar measure was introduced in Ireland in 2006 and increased in 2007. Credit is given for deferment of the pension in the US up to age 70, and in Germany and Sweden after normal retirement age. These policies can have the mixed gendered impacts mentioned earlier, offering some women an opportunity to build up more pension entitlements, which is useful for women with gaps in employment. However, employment may be unavailable or not possible due to caring responsibilities or ill-health (Foster, 2014).

Table 3.2: Changes to state pension age/normal retirement age

Australia	Germany	Ireland	Portugal	Sweden	UK	USA
Women's standard pension age: increased to 65 in 2014 All: 67 by 2023(increase by 6 months every 2 years)	From 2012, increase in normal retirement age from 65 to 67 for those born after 1964 by 2029	Increase in standard pension age 66: 2014 67: 2021 68: 2028	Standard pension age = 66 in 2014 To increase in line with life expectancy	No retirement until age 61 Unlimited deferral possible Employers consent after 67 Collective agreements: contract Retirement age 65	State pension age in 2015: 65 for men; 62.5 for women Women's to increase to 65 in 2018 All to increase to 66 by 2020, 67 by 2028 To be reviewed regularly	Normal retirement age = 66 Will increase to 67 by 2022

Source: OECD (2015), various countries, and amended with subsequent legislative updates.

Table 3.3: Policies to encourage flexible working around retirement age

Australia	Germany	Ireland	Portugal	Sweden	UK	USA
Work Bonus – income-tested concession on employment income to encourage people of pension age to work	Pension benefits reduced by 3.6% each year below state retirement age 0.5% accrual to pension for each month after state retirement age	Exemption earnings of €200 per week in 2007 into means test for non-contributory pension Can work and claim contributory pension	Pension amount increased if retirement postponed beyond 65. Upper age limit of 70	Earned Income Tax Credit (EITC) enhanced EITC higher for those 65+ Employees' Social Security contributions lower for over 65s Can combine pension with work Reduced benefit for early retirement	No pension before state pension age Higher state pension if deferred	Early retirement: age 62 at reduced benefit Credit (8%) for deferment up to age 70 Can combine work and pension

Source: OECD (2013a, 2013b, 2013c, 2013d, 2013e, 2013f, 2013g, 2013h, 2015), various countries.

Policy reforms linking pensions more closely to earnings have been identified as likely to increase gender inequality in relation to pensions (Ginn et al, 2001) because of their gaps from employment for caring and because of gender wage gaps (Dewilde, 2012). Yet, despite the obvious disadvantage to many women, the OECD recommends tying pensions even more closely to time spent in paid employment. While some countries such as the UK reduced the amount of years necessary to earn a full pension, Ireland doubled the amount of contributions required to qualify for a minimum contributory pension and is committed to increasing the amount of years needed to qualify for maximum pensions to 30 by 2020 (OECD, 2013a). This clearly makes pension-building more difficult for women, who spend many years in unpaid caring work.

Another policy that may be helpful for extended working life is auto-enrolment in pension schemes, where people are automatically enrolled when they begin work and where opting out requires a deliberate choice. This is designed to overcome workers' (particularly women's) tendency to 'undersave' for their pensions. The UK has introduced auto-enrolment for occupational schemes and Ireland plans to introduce it. However, recent qualitative evidence indicates that for many women, low pay means that they cannot afford to contribute to pensions rather than 'choosing' to undersave (Ní Léime et al, 2015).

Flexible employment policies enabling people to work and earn a certain amount of money after retirement age and still receive a pension have been introduced in most of the countries featured in the book. The US, for example, has a long history of people working past state retirement age. American workers can continue working and postpone receiving Social Security until the age of 70. Several countries have also introduced incentives to encourage people to delay claiming pensions until after normal pension age and some (including Germany, Sweden and the US) have introduced actuarial reductions if people take out their pension before normal pension age. Again, the impacts of these reforms on women's patterns of extending working life will likely vary, depending on their occupation, level of pay and conditions, and work–life trajectories. For example, some women, if healthy and in a job with reasonable pay and conditions, may wish to continue, postponing receipt of their state pensions and receiving higher payments when they eventually claim them. However, for many others, these measures tend to remove choices by reducing pension income and this can have negative effects for women in poor health and/or those who are unable to find employment or engaged in unpaid caring (Ginn and MacIntyre, 2013; Foster, 2014).

Work–life balance employment policies: elder care and childcare

A holistic gender-informed analysis of extended working life policies must consider relevant current and previous employment policies in addition to pension policies, particularly policies related to caring and employment. Conservative countries and Mediterranean countries generally have low levels of state provision of leave for elder care and families are expected to provide care (Folbre, 2012). There is a legal obligation on families to provide care in Germany, while Scandinavian countries, including Sweden, provide high levels of state care and there is no legal obligation on families to provide care.

A range of flexible employment policies, including part-time or seasonal work, plus paid and unpaid leave, can enable some older workers to continue in paid employment while caring for a dependent adult relative (OECD, 2011a). Part-time work tends to be used more often to care for children than to care for an ill or dependent adult (OECD, 2011a). However, a relatively high proportion of workers use part-time work as a way to balance responsibilities for adult care in Sweden, Ireland, Germany and the UK, while a very small proportion do so in Portugal (OECD, 2011a). Some 60% of employed American carers had to make changes in their work schedule to accommodate caring (NAC and AARP Public Policy Institute, 2015).

Policies in the selected countries range from relatively long periods of care leave, either paid or unpaid or a combination of the two, or nothing at all. Only Australia and Sweden offer paid leave to workers to care for adult dependants (OECD, 2011a). None of the liberal or conservative welfare states offers paid leave. Germany, Ireland and some employers in the US provide unpaid leave to workers for caring, ranging from 12 weeks in the US to 104 weeks in Ireland (see Table 3.4).

Table 3.4: Policies for work and (adult) family care (2010)

	Australia	Germany	Ireland	Portugal	Sweden	UK	USA
Paid leave	10 days' care leave (since 2010)	No	No	No	100 days: for terminal care 80% of wage	No	No
Unpaid leave	2 days' emergency leave	Up to 6 months (emergency leave up to 10 days)	Up to 104 weeks (since 2001)	15 days' leave per year to care for ill or disabled spouse/ relative	No	Emergency leave 2 days	Large private companies: up to 12 weeks unpaid leave per year
Flexible work arrangements	May request if working for 12 months	Yes (part time), 6 months, renewable once	No		No	Carers can request flexible working (no time limit)	Up to 12 weeks' part-time work or leave Can revert to full time

Source: Adapted from OECD (2011a: 142–50, Table 4.A2.1); information for Portugal from Wall and Lietao (2015).

Policies to facilitate childcare and employment

Countries vary in relation to the kinds of supports that they offer to women to enable them to combine childcare with employment. As Table 3.5 shows, there is a wide range of approaches to maternity leave, ranging from the US, which offers no entitlement to paid maternity leave (although some employers and states provide it), to Portugal, Australia, Sweden and Germany, giving less than the OECD average of 17 weeks, while Ireland and the UK offer 26 and 39 weeks, respectively. However, Germany and Sweden offer very high levels of total paid leave for mothers (including both maternity and childcare leave), with relatively low amounts for the UK, Ireland, Portugal and Australia, and none for the US. All offer comparatively low levels of paid paternity leave, with only Portugal, Sweden and Germany providing above or near the OECD average, while Australia, the UK, Ireland and the US provide either none, minimal or low paid leave for fathers, thus

Table 3.5: Policies for work and childcare: paid maternity leave (weeks), April 2015

	Maternity leave	Total paid leave[a] for mothers	Paid leave for fathers
Australia	6.0	18.0	2.0 (paternity)
Germany	14.0	58.0	8.7 (parental)
Ireland	26.0	26.0	2.0 (paternity)
Portugal	6.2	30.2	21.3 (includes 4 weeks paternity)
Sweden	8.6	60.0	10.0 (includes 1.4 weeks paternity)
UK	39.0	39.0	2.0 (paternity
USA	0.0	0.0	0.0
OECD	17.7	54.1	8.2

Notes: The UK has recently introduced shared parental leave (for more details, see Chapter Nine). Ireland introduced paternity leave in 2016. [a] Includes maternity and childcare leave. Source: Adapted from the OECD Family Database (available: www.oecd.org/social/family/database.htm), Table PF2.1.A and Table PF2.1.B.

providing little incentive to share the work of childcare more equally (Ireland introduced two weeks' paid paternity leave in 2016).

In order to analyse how such policies affect older women's ability to stay in employment, the whole package of measures to support childcare and elder care needs to be considered in context, as the authors do in later country-specific chapters of this book.

In recent years, the policy regime in Germany has come to be described as ambivalent rather than conservative. On the one hand, women are now being encouraged to participate in the labour market, but care is still regarded as the responsibility of the family, and the burden of unpaid care falls mainly on women. For a Mediterranean country (typically regarded as familistic), Portugal appears to offer relatively generous maternity leave and offers 21.3 weeks of father-specific leave. Sweden, typical of social-democratic states, strongly supports gender equality in the workplace as a principle and offers generous (paid and unpaid) leave, specifying that 10 weeks must be father-specific. In countries where little maternity and or parental leave is provided, there is a high level of engagement of women in part-time work and casual work to enable women to reconcile work and caring responsibilities, for example, in the US, the UK and Australia. However, part-time work, which characterises many years of some women's working trajectories, typically results in lower pensions and can affect promotion prospects. There is also a varying degree of vertical and horizontal gendered occupational segregation (see Chapter One). For many women across all countries, there are gaps in employment, gaps in pay and, consequently, gaps in pensions. The employment patterns identified result in an unadjusted gender wage gap for full-time employees that ranges from the highest levels in Australia, the US and the UK, all between 17% and 18%, with Germany and Portugal next highest at 16–17%, Sweden at 15.1%, and Ireland being the lowest at 12.7%, while the OECD average is 15.5% (OECD, 2014b). This, in turn, translates into a gender pension gap that ranges from a high level of 44% and 43% for Germany and the UK, respectively, to Ireland and Portugal, with a gap of around a third, to Sweden, which has the lowest gap at 30% (Bettio et al, 2013). The employment and pension policies adopted by Sweden appear to act to reduce gender inequalities.

Conclusion

This preliminary overview suggests that most of the countries in the study have based their policies to extend working lives on the rationale promoted by the OECD and the EU of the generic, ungendered worker. Even though the work–life trajectories of men and women are typically different, most countries seem to have adopted pension policies designed with the homogeneous, individualised adult worker in mind. There is little evidence of recognition of gendered life courses in these policy reforms. The pension reforms that have been introduced, for the most part, encourage the individualisation and privatisation of pensions, the closer linkage of pension entitlements to earnings, and a lesser role for the state in pension provision. There appears to be very little recognition by policymakers of the likely adverse impact of these reforms for women, although scholars have been highlighting these concerns recently (Ginn, 2003, 2004; Foster, 2011, 2012b, 2014; Ginn and MacIntyre, 2013; Foster and Walker, 2015).

We have argued in this chapter that a more detailed contextualised analysis using a gender and life-course perspective is needed at the country level to assess the likely impacts of policy reforms. For these reasons, in our analysis of pension systems and recent reforms from a gender perspective at the country level, we will extend the methodology devised by Ginn, Street and Arber in 2001, where it is recognised that paying attention to both access to and the amount of pensions is analytically important (Ginn et al, 2001).

Following the framework set out earlier, the individual country chapters will discuss the main features of each country's pension system, the recent and/or future reforms of pensions, and policies intended to extend working life, and assess from a gendered life-course perspective to what extent they are likely to produce adequate employment and pensions for women or to increase gendered inequality (Ginn et al, 2001: 8). The authors will discuss the current employment and pensions policy situation for each country in detail, as well as providing a brief socio-economic contextual discussion describing how the current situation evolved. They will develop a holistic analysis incorporating a life-course perspective, based on the policy framework set out in Table 3.1. This will include consideration of interconnected policies, such as: family care leave; maternity, parental and paternity leave; whether there is education/training on pensions; and the normative environment and sometimes gender-biased policies that existed when current older workers joined the workforce. This will help us to understand the intersection of gender and age inequalities as they are implicated by extending working lives.

References

Altmann, R (2015) *A new vision for older workers: Retain, retrain and recruit*, London: Department of Work and Pensions.

Beatty, C. and Fothergill, S. (2007) Moving older people into jobs: Incapacity Benefit, Labour's reforms and the job shortfall in the UK regions, in W. Loretto, S. Vickerstaff and P. White (eds) *The future for older workers*, Bristol: Policy Press, pp 65–88.

Bettio, F., Tinios, P. and Betti, G. (2013) *The gender gap in pensions in the EU*, Luxembourg: European Commission.

Cooke, M. (2006) Policy changes and the labour force participation of older workers: evidence from six countries, *Canadian Journal on Aging*, 25(4), 387–400.

Corsi, M. and D'Ippoliti, C. (2009) Poor old grandmas? On gender and pension reforms in Italy, *Brussels Economic Review, Cahiers Economiques de Bruxelles*, (52)1, 35–56.

Crompton, R. and Lyonette, C. (2006) Work–life 'balance' in Europe, *Acta Sociologica*, 49(4), 379–93.

Dannefer, D. (2003) Cumulative advantage/disadvantage and the life course: cross-fertilizing age and social science theory, *The Journals of Gerontology. Series B, Psychological Sciences and Social Sciences*, 58(6), S327–37.

Dewilde, C. (2012) Life course determinants and incomes in retirement: Belgium and the United Kingdom compared, *Ageing and Society*, 32, 587–615.

Duchemin, C., Finlay, L., Manoudi, A. and Scott, D. (2012) *European Employment Observatory Review: Employment policies to promote active ageing 2012*, Luxembourg: Publications Office.

Ebbinghaus, B. (2006) *Reforming early retirement in Europe, Japan and the USA*, Oxford: Oxford University Press.

Esping-Andersen, G. (1999) *Social Foundations of Postindustrial Economies*, Oxford: Oxford University Press.

Esping-Andersen, G. (2002) *Why we need a new welfare state*. New York: Oxford University Press.

Esping-Andersen, G. and Sarasa, S. (2001) The generational conflict reconsidered, *Journal of European Social Policy*, 12, 5–21.

Estes, C.L. (2004) Social Security privatization and older women: A feminist political economy perspective, *Journal of Aging Studies*, 18(1), 9-26.

European Commission (2009) *Dealing with the impact of an ageing population in the EU (2009 ageing report)*, Brussels: European Commission.

European Commission (2012) *White Paper: An Agenda for Adequate, Safe and Sustainable Pensions*, Brussels: European Commission

Everingham, C., Warner-Smith, P. and Byles, J. (2007) Transforming retirement: re-thinking models of retirement to accommodate experiences of women, *Women's Studies International Forum*, 30, 512–22.

Ferraro, K.F. and Shippee, T.P. (2009) Aging and cumulative inequality: how does inequality get under the skin?, *Gerontologist*, 49(3), 333–43.

Folbre, N. (2012) *For love and money: Care provision in the United States*, New York, NY: Russell Sage Foundation.

Foster, L. (2011) Privatisation and pensions: what does this mean for women?, *The Journal of Poverty and Social Justice*, 19(2), 103–15.

Foster, L. (2012a) Active ageing and pensions in the European Union, *Journal of Comparative Social Welfare*, 28(3), 223–34. Available at: http://doi.org/10.1080/17486831.2012.753022

Foster, L. (2012b) Using a political economy and life course approach to understand gendered pension provision in the UK, *Sociology Compass*, 6(1), 883–96.

Foster, L. (2014) Women's pensions in the European Union and the current economic crisis, *Policy & Politics*, 42(4), 565–80.

Foster, L. and Walker, A. (2015) Active and successful aging: a European policy perspective, *The Gerontologist*, 55(1), 83–90. Available at: http://doi.org/10.1093/geront/gnu028

Ginn, J. (2003) *Gender, pensions and the life course: How pensions need to adapt to changing family forms*, Bristol: The Policy Press.

Ginn, J. (2004) European pension privatization: taking account of gender, *Social Policy and Society*, 3(2), 123–34.

Ginn, J. and MacIntyre, K. (2013) UK pension reforms: is gender still an issue?, *Social Policy and Society*, 13(1), 91–103.

Ginn, J., Daly, M. and Street, D. (2001) Engendering pensions: A comparative framework, in J. Ginn, D. Street and S. Arber (eds) *Women, work and pensions: International issues and prospects*, Buckingham: Open University Press, 1–10.

Harrington Meyer, M. (2013) Changing social security in the US: rising insecurity?, *Social Policy and Society*, 12(1), 135–46. DOI: 10.1017/S1474746412000486

Hochschild, A.R. (2012) Global care chains and emotional surplus value, in A. Giddens and W. Hutton (eds) *On the edge: Living with global capitalism*, London: Jonathan Cape, pp 130–46.

Ivosevic, V. (2009) *Pension reforms in Europe and their impact on women*, Brussels: Education International.

Jolivet, A. (2002) *Active strategies for older workers in France. Active strategies for older workers*, Brussels: ETUI, 245–74.

Lewis, J. (2006) Work/family reconciliation, equal opportunities and social policies: the interpretation of policy trajectories at the EU level and the meaning of gender equality, *Journal of European Public Policy*, 13(3), 420–37.

Lewis, J. and Giullari, S. (2005) The adult worker model family, gender quality and care: the search for new policy principles and the possibilities and problems of a capabilities approach, *Economy and Society*, 34(1), 76–104.

Loretto, W. and Vickerstaff, S. (2015) Gender and flexible working in later life, *Work Employment and Society*, 29 (2), 233–49.

Mouleart, T. and Biggs, S. (2012) International and European policy on work and retirement: reinventing critical perspectives on active ageing and mature subjectivity, *Human Relations*, 66(1), 22–43.

NAC (National Alliance of Caregiving) and AARP Public Policy Institute (2015) Caregiving in the United States: 2015 report, Washington, DC, USA.

Naldini, M., Pavolini, E. and Solera, C. (2016) Female employment and elderly care: the role of care policies and culture in 21 European countries, *Work, Employment and Society*, 30(4), 607–30.

Ní Léime, Á., Duvvury, N. and Callan, A. (2015) Delayed retirement: gender, ageing and work in austerity, in K. Walsh, G. Carney and Á. Ní Léime (eds) *Ageing through austerity: Critical perspectives from Ireland.* Bristol: Policy Press, 63–78.

OECD (Organisation for Economic Co-operation and Development) (2006) *Live longer, work longer*, Paris: OECD.

OECD (2011a) Policies to support family carers, in OECD (ed) *Help wanted? Providing and paying for long-term care*, Paris: OECD. Available at: http://dx.doi.org/10.1787/9789264097759-9-en

OECD (2011b) Trends in retirement and working at older ages, in OECD (ed) *Pensions at a glance 2011: Retirement-income systems in OECD and G20 countries*, Paris: OECD Publishing. Available at: http://www.oecd-ilibrary.org/finance-and-investment/pensions-at-a-glance-2011_pension_glance-2011-en;jsessionid=51ckpmkm1s9qk.x-oecd-live-02

OECD (2013a) *Pensions at a glance, 2013, OECD and G20 indicators*, Paris: OECD.

OECD (2013b) *Thematic follow-up review of policies to improve labour market prospects for older workers, Australia (situation mid-2012)*, Paris: OECD.

OECD (2013c) *Thematic follow-up review of policies to improve labour market prospects for older workers, Germany (situation mid-2012)*, Paris: OECD.

OECD (2013d) *Thematic follow-up review of policies to improve labour market prospects for older workers, Ireland (situation mid-2012)*, Paris: OECD.

OECD (2013e) *Thematic follow-up review of policies to improve labour market prospects for older workers, Portugal (situation mid-2012)*, Paris: OECD.

OECD (2013f) *Thematic follow-up review of policies to improve labour market prospects for older workers, Sweden (situation mid-2012)*, Paris: OECD.

OECD (2013g) *Thematic follow-up review of policies to improve labour market prospects for older workers, UK (situation mid-2012)*, Paris: OECD.

OECD (2013h) *Thematic follow-up review of policies to improve labour market prospects for older workers, USA (situation mid-2012)*, Paris: OECD.

OECD (2014) Employment database. Available at: https://www.oecd.org/gender/data/genderwagegap.htm

OECD (2015) *Pensions at a glance 2015: OECD and G20 indicators*, Paris: OECD. Available at: http://dx.doi.org/10.1787/pension_glance-2015-en

Onyx, J. (1998) Issues affecting women's retirement planning, *Australian Journal of Social Issues*, 33(4), 379–93.

Palenga-Möllenbeck, E. (2013) New maids – new butlers? Polish domestic workers in Germany and commodification of social reproductive work, *Equality, Diversity and Inclusion: An International Journal*, 32(6), 557–74.

Russell, J. (2014) *Social insecurity. 401(k)s and the retirement crisis*, Boston, MA: Beacon Press.

Stratigaki, M. (2004) The cooptation of gender concepts in EU policies: the case of reconciliation of work and family, *Social Politics*, 11(1), 30–56.

Street, D. and Wilmoth, J. (2001) Social insecurity? Women and pensions in the US, in J. Ginn, D. Street and S. Arber (eds) *Women, work and pensions: International issues and prospects*, Buckingham; Philadelphia, PA: Open University Press, 120–41.

Thevenon, O. (2011) Family policies in OECD countries: a comparative analysis, *Population and Development Review*, 37(1), 57–87.

Vickerstaff, S. (2010) Older workers: the unavoidable obligation of extending our working lives, *Sociology Compass*, 4(10), 869–79.

Vlachantoni, A. (2012) Financial inequality and gender in older people, *Maturitas*, 72(2), 104–7.

Wall, K. and Lietao, M. (2015) Portugal, leave notes. Available at: http://www.leavenetwork.org/lp_and_r_reports/country_reports/

Wong, J. and Hardy, M. (2009) Women's retirement expectations: how stable are they?', *Journal of Gerontology: Social Sciences*, 64B(1), 77–86.

Yeates, N. (2009) *Globalizing care economics and migrant workers: Explorations in global care chains*, Houndmills, Basingstoke: Palgrave Macmillan.

Part Two:
Extended working life in
seven OECD countries

FOUR

The Australian empirical landscape of extended working lives: a gender perspective

Elizabeth Brooke

Introduction

Australian government policies to extend working lives have been promulgated in four intergenerational reports (2002–15), similar to policy directions proposed in other advanced economies. These reports advocate extending workforce participation, with targets for workers aged 55–64, regardless of gender, to mitigate the projected economic and fiscal consequences of an ageing population. This chapter analyses the distinctive Australian policy context and empirical landscape of extended working lives and considers the implications of this 'ungendered' exhortation for older women's working and post-working lives.

The neoliberal political context that influences the extension of working lives interconnects the liberalisation of global trade boundaries powering global competition, downward pressure on national labour forces and contractionary state welfare expenditure, through 'minimal regulation of the labour market and a lean, adaptable welfare state that urges its citizens to work' (Beck, 2006: 79). The neoliberal objective privileges 'productive' relations while subordinating multiplicities of social identities, including gender, age and ethnicity, to global economic power arrangements. A feminist political-economy critique exposes the inequality consequences for women of extending their working lives within the neoliberal institutional context.

Government policy discourses promoting extended working lives

The Australian government's *2015 intergenerational report* commits the government to restoring 'intergenerational equity' as 'future generations will not only have to fund their own government services, they will be funding the services used by Australians today' (Commonwealth of Australia, 2015, xix). The *2015 intergenerational report* proposes raising the pension age to 70 by 2035 as a means to re-establish future 'intergenerational equity', while, at the same time, labour force participation rates are projected to fall. The discourse of 'active ageing' is promoted as a form of productive ageing, which purports to present 'great opportunities for older Australians to keep participating in the workforce and community for longer, and to look forward to more active and engaged retirement years' (Commonwealth of Australia, 2015: viii). Without the government's budget 'repair strategy' to bring the budget back to a 'sustainable surplus', the policy scenario projects that gross debt will reach 125% of gross domestic product (GDP) by 2054/55 (Commonwealth of Australia, 2015: viii–ix). Neoliberal constructions of budget 'repair' and 'surplus' form the gold standard of recovery from the global recession, in contrast with the rhetorical frame of 'austerity' used in the Eurozone.

The *2015 intergenerational report* policy discourse suggests that women constitute the labour segment with the greatest potential to increase labour force participation. This report states that in 1975, only 46% of women aged 15 to 64 had a job, rising to 66% in 2015, and by 2054/55, female employment is projected to increase to around 70%. 'Nonetheless, Australia's current female participation rates remain lower than some other advanced economies such as Canada and New Zealand, and more can be done to encourage women to enter and stay in the workforce' (Commonwealth of Australia, 2015: ix).

Australian women's labour force participation in later working lives has increased in the current century. In the first decade of the 21st century, the labour force participation rate of women aged 60–64 doubled, from 21.7% to 43.2%, compared with a one-third increase for men, from 46.5% to 61.7% (McDonald, 2011: 26). Compared with previous generations, contemporary older women have higher qualifications and increased duration in the workforce, which will help extend their working careers until traditional retirement age (Wilkins and Wooden, 2014: 418). Yet, notwithstanding recent substantial increases in women's labour force participation, their career trajectories are still truncated compared with men's. In 2013, the average age at retirement for recent retirees (those who have retired in the last five years) was 59.6 years for women and 63.3 years for men, with only 9% of women who retired in 2013 retiring at over 65 years, compared to 25% of men (ABS, 2013a).

Disconnected dualities in government policy responses

Recent public policy reports promoting extended working lives have examined age discrimination in employment (Australian Human Rights Commission and Urbis, 2013; Australian Human Rights Commission, 2015, 2016). These reports, however, have not considered age and gendered life courses in conjunction, but rather bifurcated discrimination based on age and discrimination based on gender. The most recent report, *Willing to work* (Australian Human Rights Commission, 2016), subsumes women under the foreground focus on age, rather than interconnecting age and gender discrimination. The *National prevalence survey of age discrimination in the workplace* (Australian Human Rights Commission, 2015) conducted in late 2014, based on around 2000 randomly selected population-based telephone interviews, aimed to document the prevalence, nature and impact of workplace age discrimination against Australians aged 50 years and older. Gender was similarly subsumed under the focus on age within the analysis of workforce engagement (Australian Human Rights Commission, 2015). A previous report on the prevalence and depth of broadcast, advertising and print media stereotypes of and negative attitudes towards older Australians focused on ageism and elided discussion of relational age and gender stereotypes (Australian Human Rights Commission and Urbis, 2013). These reports underscore the hiatus in 'joined-up' age and gender policies supporting extended career trajectories, which have generally fallen between the cracks, given separate government portfolio responsibilities for ageing and for women.

Despite abolition of mandatory retirement in Australia in the mid-1990s, the male pension age of 65 remains as a proxy for workforce exit. Age-related reasons of 'reached retirement age/eligible for superannuation/pension' formed the primary reason for retirement for recent retirees who worked in the last 20 years (44% of men and 30% of women). Yet, reaching the anachronistic 'retirement age' of pension eligibility masks the distinction between choice and discriminatory, involuntary exit to retirement.

Theorisations of retirement have distinguished gendered meanings and relational considerations in retirement transitions at the border of the paid 'productive' workplace and 'retirement' (Onyx and Benton, 1996; Moen et al, 2005; Loretto and Vickerstaff, 2013). Calasanti (2005) comments that ageism includes categorisation, stereotyping and prejudice, but the most important aspect is exclusionary behaviour. Exclusionary organisational processes that marginalise women in workplaces, including individualisation, informalisation, 'controlled' flexibilisation and managing 'out' to retirement, also limit women's extended working lives (Brooke, 2014).

Neoliberal policies of employment and 'welfare' rationalisation across the life course

The cascading trinity of public policy pillars

Australia has a trinity of retirement income pillars: the first pillar, the Aged Pension, is a means-tested public pension; the second pillar, the Superannuation Guarantee, is a compulsory employer contribution to an employee's superannuation account; and the third pillar comprises private income consisting of earned income and investment returns. McDowell's (2014) review of gender and work theorisations concluded that most key theorists of work and employment in the new millennium had a 'productionist' focus related to employment in the paid workforce, ignoring the reproduction of the labour force. This trinity of interconnected, cascading macro-level public retirement policies privileges the 'productionist' imperative over the gendered life course.

The first pillar, the Aged Pension, instituted in 1909, is based on a means-tested income support system. Most Australians (70%) receive a part pension after eligibility at 65 years of age. The Aged Pension replaces around one quarter of average male ordinary time earnings and is paid to individuals (Department of Human Services, 2016). Lower wages predispose women to dependency on the pillar of public pensions, which are subject to contractionary budget policies (Butler, 2015). Reductions in pensions have disproportionate effects on women, who comprise 57.4% of aged pensioners and 68.8% of those on carers' payments. Women are more likely to receive the maximum rate of pension than men: 60.48% compared to 57% (Workplace Gender Equality Agency, 2015). Around 55.7% of women on aged and carers' payments are single, compared with 40.3% of men, while 71.8% of single age pensioners are women and around one in three women on the single rate remain in poverty (Harmer, 2009). Being a single-person pensioner household has cascading effects on a range of indicators of inequality, including housing stress, expenditure pressures and food insecurity (Harmer, 2009).

The Australian government's policy discourse on future 'intergenerational inequity' rationalises extending the pension age to 70 (by 2035) from the current setting of 67 years (by 2023). Further changes in pension systems are intended to yield government savings through changed benefit computation and ceilings on eligibility

(Parliament of Australia, 2015). These include benchmarking pensions to the Consumer Price Index, replacing the current higher level of Male Total Average Weekly Earnings and a freeze on means-test limits for all benefits and pensions. These measures will affect the payment rates and eligibility conditions for pension payments to the aged, veterans, carers, people with disabilities, single parents and unemployed people. The government estimates that AUD$1.5 billion will be saved over four years (2015–19) through a freeze on the income and asset-test threshold for all Australian government payments (Parliament of Australia, 2015).

The measures proposed in the 2014/15 federal budget to counter the projected government deficit attributed to ageing demography and 'intergenerational equity' will disproportionately affect older women, the majority of pensioners, who have lower wages and educational attainment, interrupted careers, and a lower duration of work than men in comparable age cohorts (McDonald, 2011; Wilkins and Wooden, 2014; Australian Government Productivity Commission, 2015): 'Compared with men, women earn relatively low wages, accumulate lower retirement savings and are dependent on both private and public transfers as sources of retirement income' (Jefferson, 2005).

The neoliberal rationalisation of government income support provisions in response to Australia's deteriorating debt-to-GDP ratio increases women's vulnerability, due to their greater reliance on such benefits. Australia's contractionary pensions policy also exacerbates international inequalities given Australia's current average pension expenditure of 3.5% of GDP compared to the Organisation for Economic Co-operation and Development (OECD) average of 7.9%. The Australian pension poverty rate measured by the level of population with less than 50% of the median household income (adjusted for population size) is 36%, the second highest of OECD countries and nearly three times the OECD average of 13% (OECD, 2015).

Women are the predominant *carers* for children and adults over the life course, with the consequence of fractional working time arrangements and episodic labour force withdrawal. As Connell (2005) maintains, 'work–life balance' is a conservative expression of a radical impulse, expressed as a demand for 'balance' because of the impossibility of realising equality within an institutional system that subordinates home to economy. The survey of disability, ageing and carers (ABS, 2012a) indicates that there are more female carers (56%) than male carers (44%) and that one in five carers were aged between 55 and 64 years. There were nearly twice as many female as male primary carers caring for someone with a disability or long-term health condition aged between 55 and 64. These carers included those who were employed and those who were not in paid work. According to 'Caring in the community Australia' (ABS, 2012b), female carers' full-time participation in the labour force declines sharply with age. Based on Australian Bureau of Statistics (ABS) data, the number of female carers aged 45–64 years in full-time work decreased 14-fold (from 42,700 to 3300) for female carers aged 65 and over (Brooke, 2015). Notably, this reduction in workforce participation takes place against the backdrop of a declining workforce participation rate for women (45–64 years), falling from 43.2% to 6.7% (65 years and over) (McDonald, 2011).

The relationship between caring and health has been analysed using data from the longitudinal Household, Income and Labour Dynamics in Australia (HILDA) survey (Wave 6) (Harmer, 2009). Two to four times the proportion of women primary carers report their health as being only fair or poor compared with other women of a similar age. The inverse relationship between female caring, workforce participation and health exposes the need for policies supporting the health and well-being of carers, potentially by the coordination of public and private elder-care policies.

Further regulatory tightening of carers' provisions is forecast in new government policies. The government-funded parental leave of 18 weeks (at AUD$657 per week) is to be rationalised to avoid 'duplication' of employer parental leave schemes. The costs to women of government transferring public parental leave provision support to employers has been estimated at between AUD$4000 and AUD$11,400, depending on the employers' provisions (Baird and Constantin, 2015). Compulsory part-time employment for single mothers on Supporting Parents Benefit and a shift to unemployment benefits is required from the time the youngest child turns eight. Tightening eligibility for benefits will induce greater workforce participation among those able to find employment. However, the problem with this approach is a lack of active labour market policies required to meet increasing activity requirements and to support and extend women's careers across the life course.

The third intergenerational report of 2010 states that targeted pension reductions, particularly in Disability Support Pensions (DSPs), will compensate for projected increases in Aged Pensions in 2049/50 (Commonwealth of Australia, 2010: 62). Routes to disability pensions are being rationalised as exit from the workforce through health/disability, and are the second-most common reason for retirement, for 25% of men and 21% of women (ABS, 2013a). DSPs will require increased work activity or retraining for at least 15 hours per week, with eligibility contingent on assessed impairment level (Department of Human Services, 2016). This public expenditure contraction targets the beneficiary group that relies most on household income derived from transfer payments. An analysis of HILDA (Wave 6) reveals that poverty levels were highest among DSP recipients, who were more than 90% dependent on transfers (Harmer, 2009: 40).

In summary, government policies advocating extended working lives are based on 'ungendered' working lives that privilege a 'productionist' over 'reproductionist' perspective (McDowell, 2014). Neoliberal policy directions raising productivity through increased workforce participation constitute a 'push' towards the labour market unsupported by active labour market policies. Concurrently, 'pulls' out of the labour market are rationalised by public sector constraints on income support and eligibility requirements for carers' beneficiaries and those with disabilities.

The second pillar of Australian retirement incomes, the Superannuation Guarantee, is a compulsory employer contribution to an employee's superannuation account, currently 9.5% and scheduled to increase to 12% by 2026. The Productivity Commission review of the superannuation system recommended raising the age of preservation, the age at which people can access their superannuation, from 55 to 60 years in 2025, to offset the gap between the pension age of 67 in 2025 and 70 by 2035, in order to achieve AUD$7 billion in savings (Australian Government Productivity Commission, 2015). Hence, current policies of working longer are re-inscribed within the employment-based superannuation system, which is extending preservation ages. At the time of retirement (60 to 64 years of age) in 2013/14, men had more than twice the amount in superannuation than women. Average superannuation balances at the time of retirement were AUD$292,500 for men and AUD$138,150 for women (Clare, 2015). Median account balances, indicative of the concentration of low balances for most women, were AUD$100,000 for males aged 60–64 but only AUD$28,000 for females. Superannuation concessions currently privilege male high-income earners through full-time earnings and taxation concessions (Keegan et al, 2012: 17). Around 55% of women between 65 and 69 years of age reported having no superannuation, and women with low balances are more likely to be married to men with low superannuation balances. Hence, many recent female retirees would need to substantially rely on the Age Pension in their retirement (Clare, 2015).

Successive pillars interconnecting work and retirement systems preserve the gender gap in retirement incomes. Women's high levels of part-time work and interrupted careers due to reproductive and caring responsibilities interact with private employment-based superannuation to magnify inequalities. Data released by the Workforce Gender Equality Agency in 2016 show a gender gap in superannuation of 19.3%, even for full-time workers. Wealthier individuals with higher superannuation savings are more likely to extend working lives; by contrast, individuals with low superannuation are likely to exit work earlier and rely on the pension. Thus, most of the fiscal gains by individuals associated with increased preservation ages come to wealthier households (Australian Government Productivity Commission, 2015: 14).

Women who work longer accumulate disadvantages due to gendered transitions and economic 'step downs' across the working life course. Analysis of superannuation balances based on a 2009 ABS survey of income and housing costs for 2009/10 shows almost no change in the median superannuation balances of women over the two decades from their early 30s to their late 40s, while the median superannuation balance for men doubles (Keegan et al, 2012: 9). By ages 50 to 54, the typical man has about three times as much superannuation as the typical woman. In 2009/10, most women aged 45–54 had less than half of the superannuation needed for a modest retirement (Keegan et al, 2012), a gender gap that is exacerbated by women's longer life expectancy.

Women who care for children, people with moderate disabilities and people with poor educational attainment are all projected to have less than half the superannuation of someone who has been in full-time employment for 40 years or more (Australian Government Productivity Commission, 2015: 49). Superannuation can be withdrawn as a lump sum. Withdrawal of the entirety of superannuation as a lump sum is associated with being single, having low net wealth and expenditure on 'the essentials', such as rent, personal care items and power' (Australian Government Productivity Commission, 2015). Bray (2013) analysed wealth and debt trends for those approaching retirement between 2002, 2006 and 2010 based on the HILDA survey, finding that individuals exhausting superannuation before Aged Pension age of 65 had very small balances (relative to those not exhausting their superannuation), were twice as likely relative to the general population to be on income support payments and were more likely to be female (61%), renters (22%) or single (38%). Fifty-one percent had a disability or long-term health condition (Bray, 2013: 105). Within this gendered superannuation distribution, Indigenous Australian women had two thirds of the average superannuation balance of women in the non-Indigenous Australian population (Clare, 2012).

Superannuation provides incentives to extend working lives for those in high-end occupations, making disproportionate gains. By contrast, incentives to remain working to accrue superannuation decline with low income, which is used for daily living expenses. The policy of working longer disadvantages women due to the gendered nature of superannuation. Women's workforce exits for caring, fractional working time and earlier retirement shorten the period for accumulation of superannuation. As Ginn et al (2001: 2) have noted: 'Constraints on women's employment due to their performing the bulk of unpaid domestic and caring work, together with gender discrimination in the labour market, leave women less able to accumulate earnings-related pensions'. There is a lack of policy compensation for 'reproductive' relations at life-course transitions within this trajectory.

The institutional conveyor belt connects inequalities in superannuation to pensions, creating a trajectory of 'de-accumulation' that has been conceptualised by life-course theorists (see O'Rand, 1996; Dannefer, 2003). O'Rand (1996) has delineated how structural arrangements operate to stratify cohorts by allocating differential opportunities for the accumulation of value and reward over the life course. The institutional arrangements of pensions consolidate lower incomes from waged work as the first pillar of accumulated disadvantage. Women's disproportionate representation as pensioners constitutes a successive, connected 'de-accumulation' work and post-retirement trajectory over the gendered life course.

The third pillar on which retirement incomes rest, wages and employability, is subject to neoliberal trade liberalisation and global competition policies. Beck posits that the continued existence of radical social inequalities between regions and cultures, as well as within nation-states, is an essential prerequisite for global business substitution strategies. In accordance with this logic, 'the governments of various countries are pursuing a *political strategy of downwards mobility* in order to attract foreign capital and hold on to it in the longer term' (Beck, 2006: 151, emphasis in original). In Australia, trade displacement, liberalisation and the deindustrialisation of markets in the manufacturing sector have decimated that segment of the labour force, shifting 'away from lower skilled jobs towards a higher skilled, service based economy' (Australian Government Department of Employment, 2014).

An analysis of older women's (55+) participation by industry sector based on ABS data for 1995–2015 (ABS, 2015), shown in Figure 4.1, demonstrates that industry workforce participation and growth was highest in the more localised service sector industries of health care and social assistance, which increased by 84.8% over the period, followed by education and training (+83.3%) and retail (+65.1%). Participation in emerging global competitive industries increased similarly despite starting from far lower bases: professional scientific and technical services (+82.3%) and the financial and insurance industry (+83.7%).

Figure 4.1: Female employment over age 55, by industry (1995–2015)

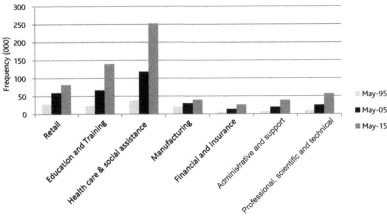

Source: ABS (2015).

Employment growth is highest in the health care and social assistance industry, currently employing 12.1% of the total workforce, projected to increase to 16.3% from 2013 to 2018 (Australian Government Department of Employment, 2014). In 2012, 89% of direct care workers in residential facilities were women, while direct care workers over 55 comprised around 27% of the workforce (King et al, 2012). Older women positioned in local services are increasingly exposed to globalised service sector competition as care work becomes a more competitive labour segment through globalisation. Australian women face increased competition from migrant care workers, comprising 21% of direct care workers (King et al, 2012). There is an increasing need for unionisation and collective agreements regulating remuneration to protect localised care workers from the downward wage pressures exerted by global labour competition. As Sassen (2008) notes, there are contradictory strategies that promote migration from the periphery and tacitly tolerate or even encourage the employment of immigrants, minority ethnic groups and women in the highly segmented labour markets at the centre.

Protracted working lives privilege high-end male-dominant managerial, professional and skilled occupations. For men over 65, managers and professionals make up an increasing proportion of those employed, while technical and trades workers, as well as clerical and administrative workers, comprise a decreasing proportion. For women, with the exception of managers, there have been no occupational increases in employment (McDonald, 2011: 37). Information technology occupations are comprised of low proportions of workers over 55 and women, forming around one fifth of the workforce (Brooke, 2009).

Political strategies of downward mobility are reflected in global industrial relations policies that institute pervasive inequalities between countries regarding standards of dignified work, occupational health, environmental protection and socio-cultural inequalities (Beck, 2006). Growth in earnings inequality in Australia is derived from neoliberal deregulation in the 1990s, privatisation and the privileging of the market over the state. The profit-maximising strategies in high-value globalised occupations and the most globally competitive high-value industries are associated with the highest gender wage gaps: male-dominated financial services, assets and professional, technical and scientific occupations. In November 2014, the average gender pay gap for all Australian industries was 24%. It was highest in the globally competitive finance industry for full-time employees (35.0%) followed by rental, hiring and real-estate services (28.4%), and professional and scientific services (27.3%). The lowest gender pay gaps were in localised industries of education and training (9.3%) and public administration and safety (8.7%) (Workplace Gender Equality Agency, 2016).

Individualisation and the deregulation of employment relations

Trade liberalisation through new free trade agreements such as the Trans-Pacific Partnership systematically institute industrial deregulation, including 'reductions in contractual and trade union approved standardizations and forms of organizing human labour' (Beck, 2006: 151). Flexibilisation of working time has de-standardised working time linked to tasks and individualised employment relations. The fragmented labour force creates precarity at the individual level, reflecting that a 'prevailing trend in most advanced sectors of most advanced societies is the general diversification of working time', which 'ends up in fact, being measured in terms of each worker's and each job's differential capacity to manage time' (Castells, 2009: 473). The 'precariat' is subject to employment insecurity through practices of unregulated hiring and inadequate protection against arbitrary dismissal (Standish, 2011). The level of casual employment, while fluctuating over two decades (1993–2013), increased slightly for men (from 15% to 21.2%), while decreasing for women (from 31% to 26.7%) (see Wilkins and Wooden, 2014: 426). More broadly, forms of precarity embrace contractualisation, labour hire, outsourcing and the flexibilisation of working hours, undermining labour's capacity to respond to employers' requirements for flexible labour forces. Working-time patterns are strongly gender-segmented, with 14% of men working part time in 2013, compared with 43.4% of women (ABS, 2013b). As Castells (2009: 255) comments: 'The new model of global production and management is tantamount to the simultaneous integration of work process and disintegration of the workforce'.

Low valuation is embedded in gendered pay hierarchies and the structure, design and implementation of payment systems (Grimshaw and Rubery, 2007). Women's lower remuneration across the life course relative to men's is built on gendered wage inequalities, which are reproduced in individual agreements. The Australian Workplace Gender Equality Agency reports that among full-time employees whose pay was set by individual agreement, average weekly total cash earnings were substantially higher for men than women, yielding a gender pay gap of 21.7%. For workers whose pay was set by award only, the difference in full-time earnings was reduced and men earned only slightly more than women (Workplace Gender Equality Agency, 2016).

'Gendered' unemployability and workforce detachment

Older women are more likely to become discouraged workers compared to older men, who are more likely to actively seek jobs by using the public employment services and electronic and social media used by national agencies to measure unemployment (ABS, 2013c). On average, women on pensions have had less engagement with the labour market than men, and labour market re-engagement presents particular problems for women (Harmer, 2009). While 55- to 64-year-old women's unemployment rate (3.2%) was actually lower than men's (4.1%) (ABS, 2013b), the extended underemployment rate of women (including unemployment, discouraged jobseekers and people not actively looking for work due to perceived lack of employment opportunities) is comparatively higher than men's. For example, at age 45–54, women's extended underemployment rate was 13%, compared with 7.7% for men (ABS, 2013b). Australian government policy in the 2014/15 Budget targeted the long-term (six months and over) older unemployed group through the employer 'Restart' subsidy, which has been funded for AUD$524.8 million over four years. Preliminary findings indicate that the take-up has been by younger men aged 45–55, with lower participation by older women, who are generally more likely than men to be discouraged from active job-seeking (ABS, 2013b). Re-engagement in work requires gendered unemployment interventions that counter tendencies towards workforce detachment. The policy of targeting individual employers is a short-term, individualised and passive instrument of 'sheltered' employment, as opposed to active labour market measures aligning with mainstream training, which builds women's workforce capabilities.

Cascading trajectories of 'de-accumulation'

The feminist political economy of extended working lives builds on the neoliberal 'political strategy of downwards mobility' (Beck, 2006: 151) of globally flexible labour forces. Neoliberal Australian retirement income pillars are built on gender gaps in wages (24%), superannuation (19.3%) and Age Pension reliance by 56.4% of women and 71.8% of single women, which cascade to a low-road 'de-accumulation' life-course trajectory. Gendered inequalities are rendered 'invisible' this way, constituting a covert instrument of global economic crisis management. Low-road employment trajectories act as disincentives to extend working lives and promote early exit to 'retirement'. There is an emerging bifurcation between those included in and excluded from working lives, with further downstream fault lines in inequalities, including health, housing and food insecurity.

In four intergenerational reports responding to claims of economic and fiscal crises invoked by demographic ageing, government discourse has avoided the term 'austerity', substituting 'intergenerational equity' instead. Despite Australia's lesser exposure to the fallout of the global crisis compared with North America and Europe, recent declines in commodities based on trade with China have lowered national GDP and global competitiveness. Neoliberal policy directions have prioritised productivity through workforce participation, accompanied by contractionary policies of reducing eligibility requirements and entitlements for income beneficiaries across the life course through 'minimal regulation of the labour market and a lean, adaptable welfare state that urges its citizens to work' (Beck, 2006: 79).

Age and gender discrimination interrelate to undermine opportunities for extending working lives. Bodily signs of old age have been linked with the political and cultural promotion of activity and promotion of productive engagement and 'active' ageing (see Katz, 2000; Estes et al, 2003; Walker, 2010). The normative productive ageing perspective intermeshes with gendered performative expectations of the youthful male and female body (Calasanti, 2005). Age and gender relations are interwoven within complex relational trajectories across working lives. Identifying and naming gendered and ageing stereotypes embedded in these trajectories should inform the analysis of discriminatory barriers limiting extended working lives.

As discussed, rendering gendered inequalities invisible by ignoring them constitutes an instrument of crisis management at the macro level enacted successively by institutional wages and superannuation gender gaps and rationalised pension incomes. Absorbing and rendering invisible women's 'reproductive relations' within the system of 'productionist' relations (McDowell, 2014) and global labour competition re-institutes class and gender inequalities over the working and post-working life course. The interaction between the neoliberal state 'push' to extend working lives and 'pull' to rationalise welfare expenditure institutionalises systems of inequality that 'interact as they engage in processes of production, reproduction and distribution, which in turn shapes, reinforces, and sometimes engages existing ideologies of masculinity and femininity, and gender-based systems of advantage and disadvantage' (McMullin and Berger, 2006: 214).

Conclusion: countervailing responses and public policy directions

At each gendered working life-course stage, countervailing and compensatory instruments are required to support 'reproductive' and 'productive' relations. Extending working lives requires multi-level strategies at macro-, industry and organisational levels to counter existing gendered and ageist policies. Countervailing policies across women's working and non-working lives are required to neutralise the cascading deterioration of retirement income through low-road wages, superannuation and pension policies. These institutional policies require fundamental restructuring to increase pension and superannuation levels, and to provide compensation for age and gendered careers. Historically, organisations representing labour forces and advocacy organisations from the ageing and welfare sectors have operated in relative isolation; however, stakeholder organisations are currently connecting policies across working and post-working lives (eg Council for the Ageing, National Seniors Australia). Cross-sectoral coalitions that represent industry, superannuation, unions, government and advocacy organisations are essential to develop adequate responses to extend working lives within the neoliberal context of globalisation. Obtaining a seat at the budget table to support a restructured 'accumulation' trajectory for women will inevitably require the renegotiation of government neoliberal policies.

At the macro-level, Australia is redirecting its industry policy towards globally competitive new economy technologies. Hence, prolonging women's working lives requires skills aligned with competitive labour segments within the globally transformative knowledge economy, concomitant with opportunities to be equally remunerated. Government employment policies can provide transferable mainstream training and transcend the individualised, short-term, protectionist policies of employer subsidies in order to build women's longer-term workforce capacity. As the superannuation system is built on the normative tacit assumption of a full-time male worker, compensatory policies that accommodate interrupted career episodes, such as parental leave, could improve outcomes for women. At the government level, industrial relations support to standardise and/or regulate flexible employment is required to compensate for disadvantages in negotiating power due to individualised employment relations. Industrial relations protections that resist downwards pressures on global labour forces are imperative.

At the industry level, industry restructuring demands investment in training that takes into account gendered career trajectories. Transitions to new economy employment likely require flexible work, training and certainly equal remuneration for both men and women. Such transitions also include those from education to work, from reproductive and caring responsibilities to paid work, and from work to retirement, which should accommodate multidirectional pathways. This would require that men also take carers' leave. The Australian Human Rights Commission (2014) found that 27% of fathers taking two weeks' parental leave experienced discrimination, mostly through negative attitudes, discrimination in pay and conditions.

This chapter has focused on national patterns configuring older Australian women's working lives rather than the micro-level complexity of identities embedded within women's lived experiences. Such relational perspectives would take into account 'multiplicities of cultural, social and political intersections in which the concrete array of "women" are constructed' (Butler, 2007: 19). Exposing and naming the composition of attitudinal discrimination embedded within relational intersectionalities is invaluable. Future research should map the processes articulating intersectionalities in social identities that also limit the extension of working lives.

Extending working lives requires cross-sectoral strategies and coordination at government, industry and organisational levels responsive to intersectionalities. Government-coordinated cross-sectoral programmes, such as those experienced by workers in Finland, require systematic initiatives to create outcomes that are not disadvantageous for most women. Without institutional strategies supporting accumulation across the working and post-working life course, polarisation between those included and those excluded from working lives will remain predictably gendered and extend across many fault lines of inequalities, including health, housing and opportunities for social participation.

References

ABS (Australian Bureau of Statistics) (2012a) Disability, ageing and carers, Australia: Summary of findings, Cat 4430.

ABS (2012b) Caring in the community Australia, Cat 4436.0.

ABS (2013a) Retirement and retirement intentions, Australia, July 2012 to June 2013, Cat 6238.0.

ABS (2013b) Australian labour market statistics, July, Cat 6105.0.

ABS (2013c) Job search experience, July, Cat 6322.0.

ABS (2015) *Labour force, Australia, detailed, quarterly*, February, Cat 6291.0.55.003.

Australian Government Department of Employment (2014) *Employment outlook to November 2018, based on the Department of Employment's 2014 employment projections*, Canberra: Australian Government Department of Employment.

Australian Government Productivity Commission (2015) *Superannuation policy for post-retirement, Productivity Commission research paper, chapter 1*, Canberra: Commonwealth of Australia.

Australian Human Rights Commission (2014) *Supporting working parents: Pregnancy and return to work national review – report*, Sydney: Australian Human Rights Commission.

Australian Human Rights Commission (2015) *National prevalence survey of age discrimination in the workplace. The prevalence, nature and impact of workplace age discrimination amongst the Australian population aged 50 years and older*, Sydney: Australian Human Rights Commission.

Australian Human Rights Commission (2016) *Willing to work, national inquiry into employment discrimination against older Australians and Australians with disability*, Sydney: Australian Human Rights Commission.

Australian Human Rights Commission and Urbis (2013) *Fact or fiction? Stereotypes, research report*, Sydney: Australian Human Rights Commission.

Baird, M. and Constantin, A. (2015) *Analysis of the impact of the government's MYEFO cuts to paid parental leave*, Women and Work Research Group, December, Canberra: Australian Business School.

Beck, U. (2006) *Power in the global age: A new global political economy*, Cambridge: Polity Press.

Bray, J.R. (2013) *In the red and going grey? Wealth and debt as Australians approach age pension eligibility age and retirement*, Social Policy, Evaluation, Analysis & Research Centre, Research School of Economics, SPI Working Paper 04/2013, October, Canberra: The Australian National University.

Brooke, E. (2014) Older women's work–life transitions: competing regimes, XV111 ISA World Congress of Sociology RC 11, Seoul, Korea, 13–19 July.

Brooke, E. (2015) *Appreciating value: Measuring the economic and social contributions of mature age Australians*, Canberra: National Seniors Productive Ageing Centre.

Brooke, L. (2009) Prolonging the careers of information technology workers: continuity, exit, or retirement transitions?, *Ageing and Society*, 29, 237–56.

Butler, J. (2007) *Gender trouble: Feminism and the subversion of identity*, New York, NY, and London: Routledge.

Butler, M. (2015) *Advancing Australia: The politics of ageing*, Melbourne: Melbourne University Press.

Calasanti, T.M. (2005) Ageism, gravity, and gender: experiences of aging bodies, *Generations*, 29(3), 19–24.

Castells, M. (2009) *The rise of the betwork society: The information age: Economy, society and culture 1* (2nd edn), Oxford: Wiley Blackwell.

Clare, R. (2012) *Equity and superannuation – the real issues*, Canberra: Association of Superannuation Funds of Australia Limited.

Clare, R. (2015) *Superannuation account balances by age and gender*, Canberra: Association of Superannuation Funds of Australia Limited.

Commonwealth of Australia (2010) *Australia to 2050: Future challenges*, circulated by The Honourable Wayne Swan MP, Treasurer of the Commonwealth of Australia, Canberra: Commonwealth of Australia.

Commonwealth of Australia (2015) *2015 intergenerational report. Australia in 2055*, The Honourable J.B. Hockey MP, Treasurer of the Commonwealth of Australia, Canberra: Commonwealth of Australia.

Connell, R.W. (2005) A really good husband, work/life balance, gender equity and social change 2003, *Australian Journal of Social Issues*, 40(3), 369–83.

Dannefer, D. (2003) Cumulative advantage/disadvantage and the life course: cross-fertilizing age and social science theory, *Journal of Gerontology: SOCIAL SCIENCES*, 58B(6), S327–S337.

Department of Human Services (2016) Payments for older Australians. Available at: http://www.humanservices.gov.au/customer/services/centrelink/age-pension

Estes, C., Biggs, S. and Phillipson, C. (2003) *Social theory, social policy and ageing, a critical introduction*, Maidenhead, Berkshire: Open University Press and McGraw Hill Education.

Ginn, J., Daly, M. and Street, D. (2001) Engendering pensions: a comparative framework, in J. Ginn, D. Street and S. Arber (eds) *Gender and later life*, Thousand Oaks, CA: Sage Publications.

Grimshaw, D. and Rubery, J. (2007) *Undervaluing women's work*, Manchester: European Work and Employment Research Centre, University of Manchester.

Harmer, J. (2009) *Pension review report*, Canberra: Commonwealth of Australia.

Jefferson, T. (2005) Women and retirement incomes in Australia: a review, *Economic Record*, 81(254), 273–91.

Katz, S. (2000) Busy bodies: activity, aging and the management of every day life, *Journal of Aging Studies*, 14(2), 135–52.

Keegan, M., Harding, A. and Kelly, S. (2012) A growing divide? Retirement incomes by gender in Australia, paper prepared for the 32nd General Conference of The International Association for Research in Income and Wealth, Boston, USA, 5–11 August.

King, D., Mavromaras, K., Wei, Z., HeJoshua, B., Healy, K., Macaitis, M. and Smith, I. (2012) *National aged care workforce census and survey report*, Canberra: Department of Health and Ageing.

Loretto, W. and Vickerstaff, S. (2013) The domestic and gendered context for retirement, *Human Relations*, 66(1), 65–86.

McDonald, P. (2011) Employment at older ages in Australia: determinants and trends, in T. Griffin and F. Beddie (eds) *Older workers: Research readings*, Canberra: NCVER, Department of Education, Employment and Workplace Relations, pp 25–41.

McDowell, L. (2014) Gender, work, employment and society: feminist reflections on continuity and change, *Work, Employment and Society*, 28, 825–37.

McMullin, J.A. and Berger, E.D. (2006) Gendered ageism and sexism, the case of unemployed older workers, in T. Calasanti and K. Slevin (eds) *Age matters: Realigning feminist thinking*, New York, NY: Routledge, pp 201–23.

Moen, P., Sweet, S. and Swisher, R. (2005) Embedded career clocks: the case of retirement planning, in R. MacMillan (ed) *The structure of the life course: Standardised? Individualized? Differentiated?* Advances in Life Course Research 9, University of Minnesota, Minneapolis, MN: Elsevier, pp 237–65.

OECD (Organisation for Economic Co-operation and Development) (2015) Pensions at a glance 2015. Available at: http://www.oecd.org/els/public-pensions/

Onyx, J. and Benton, P. (1996) Retirement: a problematic concept for older women, *Journal of Women and Aging*, 9(2), 19–34.

O'Rand, A. (1996) The precious and the precocious: understanding cumulative disadvantage and cumulative advantage over the life course, *The Gerontologist*, 36, 230–8.

Parliament of Australia (2015) Changed indexation and eligibility for benefits. Available at: http://www.aph.gov.au/about_parliament/parliamentary_departments/parliamentary_library/pubs/rp/budgetreview201415/indexation

Sassen, S. (2008) *Territory, authority, rights. From medieval to global assemblages*, New Jersey, NJ: Princeton University Press.

Standish, G. (2011) *The precariat: The new dangerous class*, London: Bloomsbury.

Walker, A. (2010) The emergence and application of active ageing in Europe, in G. Naegele (ed) *Soziale Lebenslaufpolitik. Sozialpolitik und Sozialstaat. VS Verlag*, Wiesbaden: Sozialwissenschaften.VS verlag fur Sozialwissenschaften, pp. 585–602.

Wilkins, R. and Wooden, M. (2014) Two decades of change: the Australian labour market 1993–2013, *The Australian Economic Review*, 47(4), 417–31.

Workplace Gender Equality Agency (2015) Women's economic security in retirement, perspective paper.

Workplace Gender Equality Agency (2016) WGEA data explorer. Available at: https://www.wgea.gov.au

Extended working lives in Germany from a gender and life-course perspective: a country in policy transition

Anna Hokema

Introduction

Extending working lives, especially by closing the well-established routes to early retirement, has been an important German policy goal in recent decades. Although the country has been perceived as successful in these efforts (see, eg, Eichhorst et al, 2009), the effective retirement age was 62.7 in 2014 (OECD, 2015), which is still considerably lower than the state pension age. Furthermore, these policy changes come at a heavy cost for some subgroups of future pensioners. Notably, when a feminist political economy of ageing and life-course perspective is applied (see Chapter Two), a more differentiated picture arises, one that does not show a success story for all.

Many policy areas of the German welfare state that are important for understanding the gendered implications of extended working lives have been reformed over the years – not only employment and pensions, but also child- and long-term care. I argue that policy reforms in these areas have often been based on different agendas or contradictory goals, which makes a clear-cut conclusion difficult in respect to their outcomes in the long run. For example, Germany has initiated several important reforms to increase childcare provision and parental leave schemes in order to improve the situation for families and to encourage women to return to paid work sooner. However, at the same time, the labour market was liberalised to increase atypical employment rather than standard employment, and state pension replacement rates were reduced. The latter developments are harmful for future pension incomes because they reduce the chances of building an adequate income for old age. Interestingly, the pension reform of

2014 reintroduced one early-retirement option for a transitional period and gave stronger acknowledgement of childcare. The latter policy might especially help female pensioners.

Hence, this chapter seeks to answer the questions as to what welfare policy reforms were enacted to extend working lives and whether they succeeded in their goal. First, the German welfare state is briefly sketched; then, the most important reforms for the issue of extending working lives are described. Finally, the impact of those reforms is tentatively assessed from a gender-sensitive perspective.

The institutional context of extending working lives

The German welfare state has typically been classified as belonging to the corporatist-conservative regime type (Esping-Andersen, 1990), with its emphasis on public insurance, earning-related payments, the goal of status maintenance and a strong focus on care provision by the family. Furthermore, inherent in the welfare state is the promotion of a dominant family model, including ideas about gender roles and the division of paid and unpaid labour between men and women in the family context. For Germany, at the cultural and institutional level, the male breadwinner and female housewife model was dominant from the beginning of the 20th century; however, it did not become lived practice until after the Second World War in the Federal Republic of Germany (Pfau-Effinger, 2004). Welfare state policies in the areas of employment, pensions, childcare and taxation supported the household division of labour, for example, through the protection of wives through the rights derived from their spouses (Kuller, 2010). In contrast, family and gender policy in the German Democratic Republic (GDR) followed the adult worker model because the state supported the full-time employment of women and provided extensive external childcare. This can be explained by two factors: first, female labour supply was needed in the economy; and, second, gender equality was a propagated policy goal (see, eg, Ostner, 2010). However, the lived reality looked different. While female labour market participation was high, the remaining unpaid caring and household work was mainly left to women as well (Boeckh et al, 2011). From the 1960s onwards, the dominant family model in Federal Republic of Germany evolved into a male breadwinner and female part-time worker model, which still left the bulk of unpaid family care to women (Kuller, 2010). Again, this family model was strongly supported by the West German welfare state. Examples include half-day-only childcare provision and the inclusion of part-time work in health and unemployment insurance.

An adult worker model, which would entail the equal distribution of unpaid and paid work between men and women in the family context, was never fully implemented and is not the lived reality of contemporary Germans. Unpaid household and caring activities are still not equally shared between men and women, and the German tax system still favours married couples where one partner is the main breadwinner and the other earns nothing or very little. Furthermore, childcare provision and all-day schools are only slowly becoming the norm and unpaid long-term care carried out by family members is still encouraged. In sum, German welfare policies still leave the majority of caring obligations to the family, which makes the full-time employment of both men and women difficult. Yet, family policy since the turn of the 21st century has been described as moving away from the male breadwinner/female home-based care for children model (Ostner, 2010). New policies encourage childbearing and support parents, especially mothers, to stay in or return to work. A generous paid parental leave scheme that only pays out the maximum amount when both parents take time off was introduced. However, the effects of this on pension saving will only be observable in future years and underlines the need for a gendered life-course perspective for this topic.

The German labour market and its framing welfare institutions, such as the education and unemployment protection systems, have traditionally supported and are based on long and stable working lives. Employment protection was high and standard employment arrangements were the norm. Intra- and inter-labour market mobility was low, especially when compared to other countries. In case of unemployment, generous benefits were paid out for long periods. The aim of the system was to maintain the former living standard and status of the unemployed person, and to facilitate the return to a job that fitted the individual's qualification level. However, after unification and a period of high unemployment rates, the so-called *Hartz* reforms (2003–05) transformed the unemployment protection system and increased flexibilisation by proliferating atypical employment (for more detail, see Jacobi and Kluve, 2007). Over recent decades, one of the most important changes to the German labour market was the increasing participation of women. The female employment rate of the working-age population (15-64) rose from 46.5% in 1970 to 73.1% in 2015 (OECD, 2016a) and is nowadays among the highest of the countries featured in this book. However, Germany also has the highest rate of female part-time employment, with 48.1% of women in part-time jobs (OECD, 2016b). Mothers, especially, work part time and interrupt paid work when having their children.

The German pensions system complements the labour market institutions. Pension levels in retirement are related to work incomes and the length of the working career is paramount. The public pension insurance scheme is a pay-as-you-go system, with current pensions financed by current contributions (Schulze and Jochem, 2006). Moreover, the system is characterised by a generous first-pillar state pension – aimed at maintaining pre-retirement living standards. Occupational and private pensions were of lesser importance historically, although they are gaining in significance. Meyer and Pfau-Effinger (2006) argue that the German pension system is based on a moderate male breadwinner model because women, and especially wives, can accrue their own pension rights through paid employment but are also insured and protected through rights derived from their spouses. In case of widowhood, the remaining partner can claim a survivor's pension, which makes up 55% of the deceased spouse's pension amount. Furthermore, in the event of divorce, pension entitlements are shared for the period of the marriage. Until the first decade of this century, Germany featured a strong early-retirement culture. Early labour market exit was the norm for many employees and was strongly subsidised by the German welfare state (Jacobs et al, 1991). Many recent social policy reforms suggest that Germany has moved away from its former welfare system and goals. However, this applies only partly to current generations of older workers and pensioners.

Welfare state reforms relevant to extending the working lives of men and women

Political and social debate about the unsustainability of the public pension insurance system started in the 1980s, triggered by slowing economic performance, high unemployment rates and demographic changes. The unification of East and West Germany pressurised the necessity to make several increases in state subsidisation of the pension insurance scheme, and contribution rates were increased several times to keep the public pension system functional. Hence, from the 1990s onwards, German governments embarked on a series of 'incremental reforms' (Anderson, 2015: 184) to reduce pension spending by extending working lives and also by lowering replacement rates.

The pension ages of different groups were raised and harmonised. Early retirement without deductions at 60 for the unemployed or those participating in early-retirement schemes had been the main paths to early retirement in Germany. The pension age for these groups was first raised and eventually phased out. Second, women's state pension age was increased gradually to 65 as from 2004 and this was fully realised in 2012. Third, the German pension system gave persons with long (35 years) and especially long (45 years) employment careers the possibility to retire before the state pension age. Both these early-retirement options were phased out, although the latter was reintroduced in 2014, as will be described later (Steffen, 2015). Fourth, the German pension system offers disability pensions and invalidity and partial invalidity pensions to people who are (chronically) ill and cannot work. The pension age for the disability pension has been raised to 63 and the eligibility criteria for the invalidity pensions have been tightened. Lastly, in the reforms of 2009, the state pension age of both men and women was gradually raised to 67 by 2029, starting in 2012. Early retirement in Germany from 63+ is still possible, but is permanently penalised by pension deductions of 0.3% for each month of retirement before the state pension age, which can add up to a maximum of 18.5%.

All of these reforms have been extremely unpopular with the German electorate. Anderson argues that the pension reform of 1997 partly explains why Kohl's Christian Democratic–Liberal government lost the 1998 election (Anderson, 2015: 184). Similarly, the Social Democrats appear to be still paying the price for the *Hartz* reforms and the pension age increase to 67; it also damaged the party's relationship with the trade unions (see, eg, Behrens, 2013: 214). In contrast, the pension reform of 2014 has been criticised as an election gift from the grand coalition of the Christian Democratic Union and Social Democratic Party to the electorate since the pension for especially long employment careers was partially reintroduced, allowing individuals with 45 years of contributions and credited periods to retire at 63 without pension deductions (Bundesministerium für Arbeit und soziale Sicherung, 2014). Some have described this as a U-turn from the policy of extending working lives (for an overview of different viewpoints, see Rasner, 2014a). Additionally, it has been argued that it has missed its intended aim of easing the burden on low-skilled or physically hard working persons that have problems staying in employment until 67 (Bauknecht and Naegele, 2016: 154). Furthermore, the 2014 pension reform increased childcare credits for children born before 1992 and improved disability pensions (Bundesministerium für Arbeit und soziale Sicherung, 2014).

One long-standing goal of the German pension system was eroded, namely, the maintenance of living standards in old age through the public pension. In two pension reforms in 2001, the importance of the first-pillar public pension was reduced and the uptake of private and occupational pensions was encouraged. The first reform introduced measures to the pension calculation formula that would slowly reduce the public pension replacement rate (Schulze and Jochem, 2006). In 1990, it was as high as 55% of the average income; by 2015, it was already reduced to 47.5% and will eventually go down to 43% in 2030 (Institut für Arbeit und Qualifikation, 2015a). The aim of the second reform was to encourage people to cover that pension gap by introducing tax subsidies for the uptake of private pensions and, more generally, giving more responsibility to the individual with respect to pension saving (Schulze and Jochem, 2006).

Reforms of the German unemployment protection system were also crucial to extending working lives and discouraging early retirement. One of the most important regulations that facilitated early labour market departure was the so-called '58-years-rule', which expired in 2007. It had allowed unemployed individuals aged 58 and over to indicate that they would draw a pension from the earliest point possible and would then receive unemployment benefits for two years. Such individuals were taken out of unemployment statistics and did not have to search for a new job. Once this possibility expired, unemployed people had to keep searching for a job until the age of 63, which constitutes the earliest possibility to draw a pension with deductions. The only exception is that older unemployed individuals are allowed to draw Unemployment Benefit for longer than younger ones. The fewer early-retirement schemes that still exist are agreed upon in labour agreements or organised in workplaces. They are less common, less generous and no longer subsidised by the state (Buchholz et al, 2013). The *Hartz* reform introduced and proliferated marginal employment – so-called mini-jobs or midi-jobs – which also affect older workers, as will be seen later. The mini-job is the more common work arrangement. It is marginal employment that pays an income of €450 a month or less; employees do not have to pay social insurance contributions and employers only have to pay a reduced fixed amount (Jacobi and Kluve, 2007). Employees can opt to pay into the pension system; since 2013, the rule has been changed to opt out.

The reforms of the last decades not only aimed at extending working lives, but also recognised that more people experienced discontinuous employment careers (Bonoli, 2003), which is harmful for their old-age incomes, especially in social insurance countries where lifetime earnings and pension benefits are closely linked. Women are particularly affected because German mothers interrupt their work when having children and often return to part-time work. This employment behaviour disadvantages them in respect to pension incomes. The reforms of recent decades have tried to remedy this to a certain degree through a lower pension age for women (until 2012) and, from 1986, with contribution credits for each child. Several reforms increased the value of the credits. Also, when the main carer works part time in the first 10 years after a child is born, the income is treated as an average full-time income in the calculation of the pension (Eichenhofer et al, 2012: 162). Furthermore, periods spent caring for a person needing long-term care, on maternity leave, unemployed, ill or in vocational training are also counted towards the qualifying period for pension eligibility. However, measures to compensate for longer spells of unemployment or other forms of atypical employment were not implemented.

Furthermore, recent reforms tried to reconcile not only the care of children and employment, but also caring for people in need of long-term care and employment. The public long-term care insurance has measures to support carers, but they are not as generous as those for looking after children. People who care for a relative for more than 15 hours and work less than 30 hours a week have their pension insurance contributions paid by the long-term care insurance. Second, people caring for close relatives in need of long-term care can take up to 10 days of paid leave a year when a sudden care crisis arises. The long-term care insurance then pays 90% of the net income and also pays contributions to health, pension and unemployment insurance for carers. Third, policies implemented in 2008 and reformed in 2012 and 2014 aimed to better combine long-term care at home and employment. Workers in companies with more than 25 employees can take unpaid leave (*Pflegezeit*) for up to six months to provide long-term care and also have the right to an interest-free loan. Relatives also have the right to reduce their employment for 24 months to a minimum of 15 hours a week when looking after a person in need of long-term care at home (*Familienpflegezeit*). Both leave options can be taken in succession but are not allowed to exceed 24 months (Bundesministerium für Familie Senioren Frauen und Jugend, 2015). Despite these reforms, policies concerning carers of people in need of long-term care have been criticised for failing to meet the goal of adequately supporting carers because of the lack of financial support (see eg, Leitner and Vukoman, 2015: 102). Realistically, these leave options can only be taken up when the financial support comes from somewhere else, such as a main breadwinner (for more detail, see Frericks et al, 2014: 70).

This constitutes the bulk of reforms that were enacted over the past decades to prolong the working lives of men and women in Germany. The question remains as to how far these numerous reforms have extended working lives in a country with a long-standing 'early-retirement culture' (Buchholz et al, 2006).

Extended working lives?

In 2015, 69.4% of 55 to 64 year olds were employed (OECD, 2016a), a large increase that surpasses the goal of 50% agreed by the European Union. However, several researchers observe that the increase is partly explained by demographic developments, namely, the increasing share of older people in the overall population (see, eg, Dietz and Walwei, 2011). A more informative approach uses employment ratios compared to the population in the respective age group. Using that lens, the employment–population ratio of the age group of 55 to 64 year olds has also markedly increased, from 35.5 in 1985 to 66.2 in 2015 (OECD, 2016a).

However, unpacking the labour force participation rate paints a more differentiated picture. As Table 5.1 shows, the employment rate of 55 to 64 year olds is still very diverse. The rate of 55 to 59 year olds is very high (81.1%), influenced by demographic effects, an increasing female employment rate and the overall positive labour market situation. In contrast, the labour force participation rate of 60 to 64 year olds is 56.2%. Still, this reflects a very large increase from 19.4% to 56.2% in 20 years. A second obvious point is the gender difference in employment. In 2015, only 50.2% of women aged 60 to 64 were employed, just above the 'Lisbon goal' of 50%. In the 1980s, however, it was as low

Table 5.1: Labour force participation rates of age group 55–69 in Germany (%) (1985–2015)

Age	Sex	1985	1990	1995	2000	2005	2010	2015
55 to 59	Men	77.1	75.8	72.3	76.1	82.2	84.8	86.1
	Women	36.3	39.1	47	55.7	64.5	70.3	76.2
	All persons	55.8	57.5	59.7	65.9	73.3	77.5	81.1
60 to 64	Men	33.3	33.6	28.4	30.2	40.7	53.7	62.7
	Women	10.1	10.4	10.2	13.3	22.9	35.5	50.2
	All persons	19.4	21.3	19.1	21.6	31.7	44.4	56.2
65 to 69	Men	–	–	–	7.4	8.5	10.9	18.5
	Women	–	–	–	3.1	4.8	6.6	11.2
	All persons	–	–	–	5.1	6.6	8.6	14.7

Source: Own compilation from OECD (2016a).

as 10.1% because of the lower female state pension age, which was increased from 2004 onwards.

There are also strong regional differences in the work arrangements of older workers. In 2007, only 50% of working West German women worked in full-time jobs, the other half worked part-time or in marginal employment, while 60% of East German women worked full time. In contrast, 88.2% of West German men and 84.6% of East German men were in full-time employment (Brussig, 2010: 4). People in this age group in lower-qualified jobs also work more often in part-time and marginal work arrangements (Brussig, 2010: 6). While the employment rate of older workers has increased, some groups work more than others and more older workers are in atypical work arrangements, which is detrimental to the accumulation of pension rights in the German pension system.

Table 5.1 also shows the rising employment rate for the age group 65 to 69, despite German employers and employees strongly perceiving state pension age as an age boundary. Scherger (2015: 18) has argued that this increase can partly be explained by the increasing employment rates of older workers before the pension age, which creates 'a kind of spillover effect'. This means that staying on in the same job is more likely, or that the probability of taking up work again is higher, if the end of the career job was not so long ago. Possible reasons for increased employment beyond pension age are the wish to pursue a meaningful activity, to be socially integrated and, to a lesser extent, to increase income in old age (Hokema and Scherger, 2015).

The employment rate of the 55 to 64 age group indicates that not all people are employed, but nor are they necessarily in retirement yet, especially since many routes to early retirement have been closed. More older workers therefore need to register as unemployed. The employment rate of older workers has fluctuated over the last decade, linked to overall economic performance. Germany currently features a record low overall unemployment rate and came through the financial crisis relatively unharmed. The latter point holds especially true for older workers. During the crisis, agency workers were dismissed most often and fixed-term contracts were not prolonged. The share of older workers in this kind of employment is relatively low (Dietz and Walwei, 2011: 367). In 2015, 5.2% of people aged 60 to 64 were registered as unemployed (OECD, 2016a). Dietz and Walwei (2011) argue that the unemployment rate of older German workers is a problematic labour market indicator because there are other welfare state benefits that they can receive and hence it does not measure inactivity accurately. For example, older Germans may be on invalidity or disability benefits or are not registered as unemployed, as is often the case for older women (Dietz and Walwei, 2011: 365).

Another complexity is that people participating in early-retirement schemes – now organised by the employer – appear in national statistics as (full-time) employed, even if they have already left the labour market. Fröhler (2015) quotes a study which shows that 75% of private firms with more than 20 employees (approximately 44% of all employees) still offer a company-based and company-organised early-retirement option, which usually takes the form of partial retirement (Fröhler, 2015: 14). Other Germans opt to retire at some point between 63 and 65 with pension deductions, as described earlier. In 2014, 23.9% of all people entering the pension system did so with pension deductions (Institut für Arbeit und Qualifikation, 2015b).

Additionally, since 2014, another early-retirement option was reintroduced, namely, the pension at 63 without pension deductions. First calculations by the Federal Employment Agency show that the rate of increase of people working in the age group 60 to 64 has slowed down, and unemployment rates have also dropped after implementation (Hartmann and Reimer, 2015: 4). However, it is especially men working in technical jobs based on vocational training who qualify for this early-retirement option because they fulfil the requirement of 45 years of contributions and credited periods (Hartmann and Reimer, 2015: 3). Accordingly, the fairness of this policy reform can be questioned because it again favours men with long work biographies (Rasner, 2014a). The age component for this option will be raised to 65 from 2016 onwards (two-month increases per year). Accordingly, only current generations benefit from this reform measure.

Clearly, the German pension system still features several options to leave the labour market before reaching the state pension age. Another pathway is invalidity pensions. Hagen and Himmelreicher (2014) show that gender and marital status are decisive with respect to the illnesses that lead to the need for an invalidity pension. Women and single people are more affected by psychological illnesses while men and people living in a partnership are more affected by somatic illnesses (Hagen and Himmelreicher, 2014: 8). The numbers of invalidity pensions granted have fluctuated strongly over the past 20 years. They decreased from the 1990s onwards and started to increase again from 2008. Since that time, about 20% of those entering the pension system each year receive an invalidity pension (Hagen and Himmelreicher, 2014: 7). Receiving an invalidity pension is often the end of a long history of illness, including interrupted employment careers; hence, pensions are low. In 2014 in West Germany, the average invalidity pension for men was €737 and for women was €702, compared to €1020 for men and €566 for women for an average old-age pension (Deutsche Rentenversicherung Bund, 2015: 34–35).

The average effective age of labour market exit was 62.7 in 2014 (OECD, 2015) and, accordingly, people accept or need to accept permanent pension deductions and lower pensions. This is not surprising, but it is the opposite to what might be expected under effective policies to extend working lives for older workers generically. However, it is consistent with a strategy for reducing state pension costs. As mentioned earlier, leaving the labour market does not necessarily mean entering the pension system. According to Brussig (2012: 1), in 2010, only a third of 65 year olds entered the pension system from employment. Older workers have problems staying in work until state pension age because they are either unfit or unwilling, and/or employers are still unwilling to keep them. Romeu Gordo and Simonson (2016: 81) show that 71% of people entering the pension system between 2009 and 2011 transitioned directly from employment. These two results cannot be directly compared because the two studies used different age parameters and data sets. However, both show that people who do not enter retirement directly from employment, but who are unemployed, sick or inactive in other ways, spend an increasingly longer time between employment and being retired, which affects their pension amounts negatively (Romeu Gordo and Simonson, 2016: 81).

One reason for inactivity before state pension age is providing unpaid care for relatives, which is done more often by women than men. When caring for relatives, people often reduce or leave paid work, although a sizable number were not employed before caring (Bestmann et al, 2014: 14–15). Bestmann et al estimate that 39% of people between 50 and 65 are carers; Unger and Rothgang (2013) report considerably higher numbers when looking only at women of working age. Unger and Rothgang also show that women who take over caring responsibilities in midlife acquire lower pension rights than non-caring women. This involves both a selection and causal effect, meaning that women who take over caring responsibilities already have lower pension rights than non-caring ones before the caring period begins and that the pension rights acquired through the pension insurance while caring do not compensate adequately (Unger and Rothgang, 2013: 34–6), and it is not known whether informal carers make use of the unpaid leave schemes mentioned earlier. The responsible ministry answered a parliamentary inquiry by stating that the numbers of individuals using the scheme was unknown and that individuals taking time out have no obligation by law to report this information. What is known is that 115 German individuals applied for an interest-free loan in 2015 to cover a period of full-time care, of which 73 were women and 43 were men (Deutscher Bundestag, 2016). The explanatory value of this information is, of course, small but suggests that such measures are not used much.

All women, not just those providing long-term care for others, receive lower public pensions than men. In 2011, German woman received, on average, €603 a month, compared to a man, who receives, on average, €1,103 from the public pension insurance (TNS Infratest Sozialforschung, 2013: 23). This represents a gender pension gap. Married women, in particular, receive the lowest individual pension payments, also compared to divorced and single women (see, eg, Fasang et al, 2013). Married women are covered by their husband's pension payments but Fasang quotes Orloff (1993: 319), who writes: 'women are often a husband away from poverty'. Pension incomes of East German women (who lived and worked in the GDR) are currently higher than their West German counterparts, mainly because East German women combined family responsibilities with a speedier return to full-time employment and interrupted their employment for shorter periods (see, eg, Rasner, 2014b). However, current generations of women of working age in the eastern part of Germany show higher part-time employment rates than earlier and that may lead to lower pensions in the future.

One way of increasing the individual pension claims of mothers has been the introduction and increase of pension credits for children. However, Möhring's (2014) study shows that care entitlements in the pension system do not fully close the pension gap of mothers because caring-related career interruptions and part-time employment after having children cannot be adequately compensated by those measures when compared to childless women with more continuous work biographies. This is especially the case in pension systems like Germany's, which do not feature a basic citizens' pension. Additionally, the motherhood credits do little to help to reduce old-age poverty because they are included in the means test for income support. Women, in general, are more affected by old-age poverty than men, especially divorced women. However, old-age poverty and women's disproportionate risk is not such a burning issue compared to poverty rates in other age groups. Martens showed that 2.3% of over 65 year olds receive means-tested income support and 1.9% receive housing support, concluding that 4.2% of people over the pension age are poor (Martens, 2014). He predicts an increase of old-age poverty to 7%

in the next 10 years as a result of lowered pension replacement rates and retirements by individuals with less orderly work careers than the current generation of pensioners.

Conclusion

Many different measures were implemented in Germany to extend the working lives of both men and women over the past two decades. The employment rate strongly increased for the age group. Working until pension age is mostly realised by men and highly qualified workers. Women and lower-qualified workers tend to leave the labour market earlier. If they do work, it is more often in part-time or marginal work arrangements that are increasingly part of German employment. However, atypical working arrangements are penalised by the German pension system.

The German pension system still offers several early-retirement options; however, they mostly involve permanent pension deductions. Other early-retirement routes have been closed or eligibility criteria tightened. Hence, many pensioners enter the pension system from other states, such as sickness or unemployment. This leads to even deeper status differences in respect to pension payments in retirement, which are already inherent in the German pension system.

Women's labour market participation has increased over the last decades, translating into higher individual pension incomes, especially for East German women. West German women traditionally interrupted their employment careers when they became mothers and returned to employment in part-time jobs, which has impacted their pension incomes negatively. Measures to compensate for this have been only moderately successful. It remains to be seen how the family policy efforts to encourage women to return to the labour market sooner will play out in future generations of older workers.

Data for this chapter are from disparate sources, which were often not directly comparable. However, the sources support the conclusion that future public pension incomes will be lower and more polarised. It remains to be seen whether people will be able to compensate for the reduced replacement rates of the public pension with payments from occupational and private pensions or extended work. Some research predicts an increase in old-age poverty rates. Women's disadvantage seems likely to persist. Many commentators call for more flexible ways of combining work and retirement in later stages of the work biography to make the extension of working lives possible for more people. The current pension system already allows this to a certain extent by offering partial pensions, but this option is hardly used.

References

Anderson, K.M. (2015) Pension reforms in Europe: context, drivers, impact, in S. Scherger (ed) *Paid work beyond pension age. Comparative perspectives*, Basingstoke: Palgrave Macmillan, pp 177–97.

Bauknecht, J. and Naegele, G. (2016) Successful yet insufficient: German policies for higher employment rates among older age groups, *Australian Journal of Social Issues*, 51(2), 147–65.

Behrens, M. (2013) Germany, in J.K.C. Frege (ed) *Comparative employment relations in the global economy*, London: Routledge, pp 206–26.

Bestmann, B., Wüstholz, E. and Verheyen, F. (2014) Pflegen: Belastung und sozialer Zusammenhalt. Eine Befragung zur Situation von pflegenden Angehörigen [Caring: stress and social cohesion. A survey of the situation of caring relatives]. Available at: http://www.tk.de/centaurus/servlet/contentblob/699766/Datei/140125/Bestmann-Pflegen-Belastung-und-sozialer-Zusammenhalt-2014.pdf

Boeckh, J., Huster, E.-V. and Benz, B. (2011) *Sozialpolitik in Deutschland* [Social policy in Germany], Wiesbaden: VS Verlag.

Bonoli, G. (2003) Two worlds of pension reform in Western Europe, *Comparative Politics*, 35(4), 399–416.

Brussig, M. (2010) Anhaltende Ungleichheiten in der Erwerbsbeteiligung Älterer; Zunahme an Teilzeitbeschäftigung [Continuing inequality in employment of older people; increase of part-time employment], *Altersübergangreport*, 2010/03. Available at: http://www.iaq.uni-due.de/auem-report/2010/2010-03/auem2010-03.pdf

Brussig, M. (2012) Weiter steigendes Renteneintrittsalter, mehr Renteneintritte aus stabiler Beschäftigung, aber zunehmend geringere Altersrenten bei Langzeitarbeitslosen. Aktuelle Entwicklungen beim Rentenzugang [Further increase in age on entering pensionable retirement, more pensionable retirements after stable employment, but increasingly lower old age pensions for long-term unemployed], *Altersübergangs-Report*, 2012-02. Available at: http://www.iaq.uni-due.de/auem-report/2012/2012-02/auem2012-02.pdf

Buchholz, S., Hofäcker, D. and Blossfeld, H.-P. (2006) Globalization, accelerating economic change and late careers. A theoretical framework, in H.-P. Blossfeld, S. Buchholz and D. Hofäcker (eds) *Globalization, uncertainty and late careers in society*, London: Routledge, pp 1–24.

Buchholz, S., Rinklake, A. and Blossfeld, H.-P. (2013) Reversing early retirement in Germany. A longitudinal analysis of the effects of recent pension reforms on the timing of the transition to retirement and on pension incomes, *Comparative Population Studies – Zeitschrift für Bevölkerungswissenschaft*, 38(4), 881–906.

Bundesministerium für Familie Senioren Frauen und Jugend (2015) Die neue Familienpflegezeit [The new family care scheme]. Available at: http://www.bmfsfj.de/BMFSFJ/aeltere-menschen,did=212400. html

Bundsministerium für Arbeit und soziale Sicherung (2014) Das Rentenpaket [The pension package]. Available at: http://www. rentenpaket.de/rp/DE/Startseite/start.html

Deutscher Bundestag (2016) Antwort der Bundesregierung auf die Kleine Anfrage der Abgeordneten Elisabeth Scharfenberg, Kordula Schulz-Asche, Maria Klein-Schmeink, weiterer Abgeordneter und der Fraktion BÜNDNIS 90/DIE GRÜNEN – Drucksache 18/7160 [Response to the minor interpellation from the Members of Parliament Elisabeth Scharfenberg, Kordula Schulz-Asche, Maria Klein-Schmeink, and further members and the parliamentary group BÜNDNIS 90/DIE GRÜNEN – Parliamentary printing matter 18/7160].

Deutsche Rentenversicherung Bund (2015) *Rentenversicherung in Zahlen 2015 [Pension insurance in numbers 2015]*, Berlin: Deutsche Rentenversicherung Bund.

Dietz, M. and Walwei, U. (2011) Germany – no country for old workers?, *Journal for Labour Market Research*, 44(4), 363–76.

Eichenhofer, E., Rische, H. and Schmähl, M. (eds) (2012) *Handbuch der gesetzlichen Rentenversicherung SGB VI [Handbook of the statutory pension insurance – social insurance code VI]*, Köln: Luchterhand.

Eichhorst, W., Marx, P. and Thode, E. (2009) Arbeitsmarkt und Beschäftigung in Deutschland 2000–2009 [Labour market and employment in Germany 2000–2009]. IZA Research Report, No. 22.

Esping-Andersen, G. (1990) *The three worlds of welfare capitalism*, Cambridge: Polity Press.

Fasang, A.E., Aisenbrey, S. and Schömann, K. (2013) Women's retirement income in Germany and Britain, *European Sociological Review*, 29(5), 968–80.

Frericks, P., Jensen, P.H. and Pfau-Effinger, B. (2014) Social rights and employment rights related to family care: family care regimes in Europe, *Journal of Aging Studies*, 29, 66–77.

Fröhler, N. (2015) Vom Staat zum Betrieb. Der Übergang in den Ruhestand im sozialpolitischen Wandel [From the state to the workplace. The social political change of the transition into retirement], *Informationsdienst Altersfragen*, 42(2), 13–19.

Hagen, C. and Himmelreicher, R.K. (2014) Starke Zunahme von Erwerbsminderungsrenten wegen psychischer Erkrankungen bei westdeutschen Frauen. Analysen zu individuellen, sozialen und regionalen Unterschieden beim Zugang in Erwerbsminderungsrente in Deutschland [Strong increase in disability pensions for psychological illnesses of West German women. Analyses of individual, social and regional differences of the receipt of disability pensions in Germany], *Informationsdienst Soziale Indikatoren*, 51, 6–11.

Hartmann, M. and Reimer, K. (2015) Hintergrundinformation: Auswirkungen der Rente ab 63 Jahren nach langjährigen Beitragszeiten auf den Arbeitsmarkt [Background information: effects of the pension at 63 after long years of contribution on the labour market]. Available at: http://statistik.arbeitsagentur.de

Hokema, A. and Scherger, S. (2015) Working pensioners in Germany and the UK: quantitative and qualitative evidence on gender, marital status, and the reasons for working, *Journal of Population Ageing*, 9 (1/2), 91–111.

Institut für Arbeit und Qualifikation (2015a) Entwicklung des Netto-Rentenniveaus vor Steuern 1990 - 2029 und 2030: Netto-Standardrente vor Steuern (45 Versicherungsjahre) in % des durchschnittlichen Jahresentgelts [Development of the net replacement rate before tax 1990–2029 and 2030: net standard pension before tax (45 years of contribution) in % of the average annual income], *Sozialpolitik-aktuell.de – Infografiken mit Kurzanalysen*. Available at: http://www.sozialpolitik-aktuell.de/tl_files/sozialpolitik-aktuell/_Politikfelder/Alter-Rente/Datensammlung/PDF-Dateien/abbVIII37.pdf

Institut für Arbeit und Qualifikation (2015b) Abschläge im Rentenzugang, Altersrenten 2014 [Deductions when entering the pension system, old age pensions 2014], *Sozialpolitik-aktuell.de – Infografiken mit Kurzanalysen*. Available at: http://www.sozialpolitik-aktuell.de/tl_files/sozialpolitik-aktuell/_Politikfelder/Alter-Rente/Datensammlung/PDF-Dateien/tabVIII13.pdf

Jacobi, L. and Kluve, J. (2007) Before and after the Hartz reforms: the performance of active labour market policy in Germany, *Journal for Labour Market Research*, 40(1), 45–64.

Jacobs, K., Kohli, M. and Rein, M. (1991) Germany: the diversity of pathways, in M. Kohli, M. Rein, A.-M. Guillemard and Gunsteren, H (eds) *Time for retirement: Comparative studies of early exit from the labor force*, Cambridge: Cambridge University Press, pp 181–221.

Kuller, C. (2010) Ungleichheit der Geschlechter [Gender inequality], in HG Hockerts and W. Süß (eds) *Soziale Ungleichheit im Sozialstaat: Die Bundesrepublik Deutschland und Großbritannien im Vergleich [Social inequality in the welfare state: Germany and the UK in comparison]*, München: R. Oldenbourg Verlag, pp 65–89.

Leitner, S. and Vukoman, M. (2015) Zeit, Geld, Infrastruktur? Vereinbarkeitspolitik für pflegende Angehörige [Time, money, infrastructure? Compatibility policies for caring relatives], *Gender – Zeitschrift für Geschlecht, Kultur und Gesellschaft*, 7(1), 97–112.

Martens, R. (2014) Vorausberechnung regionaler Altersarmut: Zunahme in Ballungsräumen und in Ostdeutschland [Projections of regional old age poverty: increase in congested urban areas and East Germany], *Vierteljahrshefte zur Wirtschaftsforschung*, 83(2), 95–113.

Meyer, T. and Pfau-Effinger, B. (2006) Gender arrangements and pension systems in Britain and Germany: tracing change over five decades, *International Journal of Ageing and Later Life*, 1(2), 67–100.

Möhring, K. (2014) Der Einfluss von Kindererziehungszeiten und Mütterrenten auf das Alterseinkommen von Müttern in Europa [The influence of child-rearing periods and mothers' pensions on the old age incomes of mothers in Germany], *Vierteljahrshefte zur Wirtschaftsforschung*, 83(2), 139–55.

OECD (Organisation for Economic Co-operation and Development) (2015) *Pensions at a glance 2015: OECD and G20 indicators*, Paris: OECD Publishing. Available at: http://dx.doi.org/10.1787/pension_glance-2015-en

OECD (2016a) Labour market statistics: labour force statistics by sex and age: indicators, OECD Employment and Labour Market Statistics (database). Available at: http://dx.doi.org/10.1787/data-00310-en

OECD (2016b) Labour market statistics: full-time part-time employment – national definitions: incidence, OECD Employment and Labour Market Statistics (database). Available at: http://dx.doi.org/10.1787/data-00301-en

Orloff, A.S. (1993) Gender and the social right of citizenship: the comparative analysis of gender relations and welfare states, *American Sociological Review*, 58, 303–28.

Ostner, I. (2010) Farewell to the family as we know it: family policy change in Germany, *German Policy Studies*, 6(1), 211–44.

Pfau-Effinger, B. (2004) Socio-historical paths of the male breadwinner model – an explanation of cross-national differences, *British Journal of Sociology*, 55(3), 377–99.

Rasner, A. (2014a) Early retirement at 63: fair compensation or pension giveaway?, *DIW Roundup*, 9.

Rasner, A. (2014b) Geschlechtsspezifische Rentenlücke in Ost und West [Gender pension gap in Eastern and Western Germany since reunification], *DIW Wochenbericht*, 40, 976–85.

Romeu Gordo, L. and Simonson, J. (2016) Veränderungen von Rentenübergangsformen und Erwerbsdauern: Auswirkungen auf das individuelle Renteneinkommen [Changes in transitions into retirement and length of employment: impacts on individual pension incomes], *Sozialer Fortschritt*, 65(4), 77–83.

Scherger, S. (2015) Introduction: paid work beyond pension age – causes, contexts, consequences, in S. Scherger (ed) *Paid work beyond pension age: Comparative perspectives*, Basingstoke: Palgrave Macmillan, pp 1–30.

Schulze, I. and Jochem, S. (2006) Germany: beyond policy gridlock, in E.M. Immergut, K.M. Anderson and I. Schulze (eds) *The handbook of West European pension politics*, Oxford: Oxford University Press, pp 660–712.

Steffen, J. (2015) Sozialpolitische Chronik [Social political chronicles]. Available at: http://www.portal-sozialpolitik.de/sozialpolitische-chronik

TNS Infratest Sozialforschung (2013) *Alterssicherung in Deutschland 2011 (ASID 2011): Lebens- und Einkommenssituation im Alter von Personen mit und ohne Migrationshintergrund* [Old age provision in Germany 2011 (ASID 2011): Life and income situation in old age of persons with or without migration background], Berlin: Bundesministerium für Arbeit und Soziales.

Unger, R. and Rothgang, H. (2013) Auswirkungen einer informellen Pflegetätigkeit auf das Alterssicherungsniveau von Frauen [Effects of informal caring activities on the level of the old age income of women], *FNA-Journal*, 4/2013.

SIX

Extended working life, gender and precarious work in Ireland

Áine Ní Léime, Nata Duvvury and Caroline Finn

Introduction

Policies designed to extend working life have been introduced relatively recently in Ireland, but the pension age has been increased more quickly and steeply compared to other countries such as Germany, the UK, France or Poland (OECD, 2015a). This chapter considers the likely gender impacts of these policies. As is true for several other countries, the extended working life agenda has been ushered in and accompanied by alarmist headlines in the media warning against the prospect of unsustainable pension systems, which are argued to be the inevitable result of demographic ageing.

However, there has been little explicit discussion by policymakers of the gender implications of extended working life policies (OECD, 2015a). There is a limited number of reports and articles in the academic literature raising the issue of gender equity and pensions, and/or extended working life, but, for the most part, there has been little debate about whether these policies are the only or best possible solution to demographic ageing and whether they should be applied indiscriminately to all workers (Murphy and McCashin, 2008; Duvvury et al, 2012; Ní Léime et al, 2015). Organisations such as the National Women's Council of Ireland (NWCI) have raised the issue of women's unequal access to pensions in various pre-Budget submissions and in the consultation on the Green Paper on pensions (Cousins and Associates, 2008). However, concerns raised by the NWCI and others in relation to women affected by previous discriminatory legislation (discussed later) appear not to have been addressed in introducing extended working life policies. Public debate from 2008 onwards has been dominated by the public debt crisis and only recently have opposition politicians raised the issue of the possible adverse effects for women of pension reforms in the Dail – the Irish Parliament (Dail Debates, 2014). In a neoliberal environment, trades unions, as happened in other countries, have been forced to choose between protecting rights for their existing members and accepting deteriorating working conditions and pensions for future members (Russell, 2014). When recent pension reforms were introduced in 2012, the recession was at its most severe and there was little overt protest (although the Irish Congress of Trade Unions held a conference on the issue entitled 'Wake up to state pension reform' in 2012). It is likely that, for pension recipients, the impact of reforms is only now beginning to be experienced fully.

The political and socio-economic context within Ireland shaped the environment in which extended working life policies were introduced. International policy bodies typically promote these policies as being necessary to achieve cost containment in order to sustain pensions (OECD, 2006). Extending working life is also advocated as part of the Active Ageing agenda promoted by the European Union (EU) (OECD, 2006; Foster, 2012). In Ireland, this Active Ageing agenda was outlined in a number of policy documents, the most recent being the National Positive Ageing Strategy (Department of Social and Family Affairs, 2007, 2010; Department of Health, 2013). The narrow focus on cost containment could well lead to crude policies that construct work–life trajectories as homogeneous and do not sufficiently address the diversity among older workers. Feminist critics highlight the fact that debates about the changing nature of retirement tend to assume that all workers have long uninterrupted careers. They do not account for the greater involvement of women in performing society's unpaid care work (Lewis, 2006, 2007). A feminist political economy of ageing approach highlights the impact of legislation, social norms, structures such as gender segregation in the labour market and the impact of economic conditions on work–life trajectories. This approach acknowledges the need for policy analysis that pays attention not only to pensions and employment policy in isolation, but also to family-friendly policies and gendered divisions of labour in the home (Lewis, 2007). Since work–life trajectories are deeply gendered, there is a need for a life-course approach that considers the impact of previous policies that affected women at earlier stages in their lives (Dannefer, 2003; Dewilde, 2012).

In this chapter, we present a contextualised discussion of the current nature of women's participation in the labour market, including the diversity of occupation and employment status and family-friendly policies, and discuss how this shapes pension provision. We outline the structure of the pension system, describing women's current outcomes in terms of the type and level of pensions. We then turn to a discussion of reforms that have been introduced to pensions and employment policy and consider the likely gender implications of these reforms, drawing on experiences in other countries and the Organisation for Economic Co-operation and Development's (OECD's) projections. Finally, undertaking new analysis of the most recent data available, we assess the impact of the recession, particularly on precarious employment among older workers, and consider the impact of health disparities on employment and pension prospects. We discuss possible alternative policy approaches and/or modifications that would ensure that gender equality as well as cost containment are pursued.

Women's labour market participation

Ireland was historically known as a strong male breadwinner state with low levels of support for women to participate in the labour market (Mahon, 1998). Gender-equality legislation was not introduced until the mid-1970s after Ireland joined the European Community. There was a 'marriage bar' in place until 1973, where women working in public sector employment were legally obliged to leave their jobs on marriage. Equal pay legislation was introduced only in 1977. Taxation and social welfare policies constructed women as dependants, favouring a male breadwinner model of employment and discouraging married women from working (O'Connor, 1998). Therefore, there were very low employment rates for women, particularly older women, in Ireland. The economic boom in the early 2000s, along with the individualisation of taxes in 2000, created a strong demand for labour and better after-tax income for second earners. Many older women (who had been forced to leave due to the marriage bar) returned to the labour market at this time; there was a sharp increase in the employment rates of older women (aged 55–64) from 38.4% in 2005 to 48.1% in 2014 (OECD, 2016d). Some of this increase is attributable to the introduction of anti-age discrimination legislation in 1998 and its expansion in 2000 and 2004 to cover people aged 65 and over, removing upper recruitment ages and thus facilitating the entry of older women into the workforce.

There is evidence in Ireland of interruptions in women's labour market participation for caring for children and older people. Women with children aged under five are less likely than men to be in paid employment – for example, 81.9% of men as opposed to only 59.5% of women in a household with children aged 1–3 years were in paid employment in 2013 (Central Statistics Office, 2013a). They are more likely than men to be in part-time employment – women's share of part-time employment was 68.1% (68.5% for women aged 55–64 years) in 2014 compared to 35.9% for men (OECD, 2016a). Additionally, women are concentrated in low-paid sectors. This leads to relatively low levels of pension provision for Irish women (discussed later in the chapter).

Family-friendly policies help alleviate some of the economic disadvantage that women experience across the life course. After Ireland joined the European Community in 1973, the government had to introduce gender-equality legislation. Maternity leave of 14 paid weeks and four unpaid weeks was introduced in 1981. Today, Ireland has an increased level of paid and unpaid maternity leave of 42 weeks (26 weeks paid and 16 weeks unpaid). Two weeks of statutory paid paternity leave was introduced in 2016 (Campbell, 2015). Unpaid parental leave was increased from 14 to 18 weeks in 2013. Parents are entitled to protection of their Social Insurance contributions for the period of parental leave. Both parents have an equal separate entitlement to parental leave (OECD, 2016c). Childcare costs in Ireland are among the highest in the EU (45% of the average wage compared to 16% for the EU) and this is a barrier to women's employment (Daly, 2010). There is a free pre-school childcare year that helps with childcare costs, but they still form a considerable barrier.

Ireland also has policies to assist with eldercare. A Carer's Benefit scheme, introduced in 2000, enables workers to take time out from the labour market and be paid at a replacement rate of 34.5% for up to 104 weeks to care for dependent older people and to then return to work. There is also a Carer's Allowance, introduced in 1990, which means that citizens can claim an allowance from the state for caring for a vulnerable family member. Most (77.5% in 2014) recipients are women (Department of Social Protection, 2014).

Women's labour force participation in Ireland increased steadily from the 1990s to about 54.7% in 2007 (just before the economic crisis). However, women face several structural constraints in the labour market. First, there is horizontal segregation of women into low-paid areas of the workforce (Ní Léime et al, 2015; OECD, 2016a). Women are more likely to be in poorly paid jobs in the services sector, such as caring, cleaning or retail work (Central Statistics Office, 2013a, Russell and McGinnity, 2014). There is a substantial gender wage gap; in 2013, the gender wage gap in Ireland was 14.4%, which is a little lower than the OECD average of 16.4% (Eurostat, 2015). This is probably partly due to the prevalence of women in public sector jobs such as teaching and nursing, which tend to be well-paid (Arulampalam et al, 2007; Kelly et al, 2009). Equally, there is vertical segregation in the labour market, with women being predominantly located in the middle/

lower part of organisations (Central Statistics Office, 2013a). Given existing gender norms, many women have interruptions in their labour market trajectories to care for children and dependent family members (Bettio et al, 2013). For similar reasons, part-time employment was higher for women than men – 35.4% of employed women were in part-time employment compared to 12.5% for men in 2014 (OECD, 2016b). These various factors directly and indirectly affect women's earnings and pension building. Evidence suggests that women with greater interruptions often return to lower-paid jobs and may miss out on promotion prospects since crucial career building often coincides with childbearing years (Russell, 2002). These structural features of the labour market, together with gendered caring norms, shape women's labour force participation and pension building.

Rates of paid employment grew particularly steeply for older women in recent decades. The labour force participation rate of women aged 60–64 increased from 17% in 1998 to 34.5% in 2013 (Central Statistics Office, 2013a). The gender wage gap increases with age. Data from the National Employment Survey in 2009 indicated that the gap in annual earnings for women and men aged 20–29 was about 10% whereas the gap for those in the age group 50–59 was 37% (Central Statistics Office, 2011). While Ireland's employment rates for older women have increased recently, discriminatory legislation in the past adversely affects the pension building of today's older workers and retirees. We now provide an overview of the pension system and assess the current outcomes for women and pensions.

Ireland: pension system and reforms

The state pension system has two tiers: state pensions and voluntary private pensions. There are two state pensions available to citizens aged 66 and over. One is a flat-rate means-tested, pension, called the state non-contributory pension. This is a low level pension worth €219 per week in 2015 that provides a replacement of 34.7% of the average industrial wage, which is low by international standards (OECD, 2015b). In 2014, 28% of the population received the state non-contributory pension, and the majority (62.4%) of those receiving this are women (Department of Social Protection, 2014: 61).

There is also a somewhat higher state contributory pension. The level of this pension is based on the number of years spent in the paid labour market. The maximum amount is €230.30 per week (OECD, 2014). This maximum rate replaces 43% of median earnings, which is considerably below the OECD average of 57.9% (OECD, 2014).

Women typically have a lower level of pension because of labour market interruptions and only 35.6% of those receiving the state contributory pension are women (Department of Social Protection, 2014: 61). There is also a gender disparity in the coverage of the state contributory pension, with 64% of men and 58% of women aged under 70 receiving a contributory pension (OECD, 2014).

There is a second tier of voluntary occupational and private pensions. In 2015, 46% of women as compared to 47% of men had occupational pensions; however, the level of these pensions is lower for women given the nature of their engagement in paid employment (Central Statistics Office, 2016b). The government has been strongly encouraging citizens to pay into personal pensions by giving tax relief on pension contributions (Department of Social and Family Affairs, 2007; Hughes, 2014). Personal Retirement Savings Accounts (PRSAs) were introduced in 2003 with the intention of increasing private pension coverage. There is currently a low level of private pension coverage, with women having less than half the coverage rates (11%) of men (25%) (Central Statistics Office, 2016b). Overall, then, current coverage and amounts of pensions are lower for women, with older women being more dependent on social transfers (Central Statistics Office, 2013a). Among older women, those who are single, divorced or widowed are likely to be less financially well off in retirement (Central Statistics Office, 2013b).

Certain elements of the Irish pension system are women-friendly. The non-contributory pension provides a safety net, though low by international standards, for women who have no other means of support. There are pension credits for years spent out of paid employment caring for children up to the age of 12 and for older people, reflecting an understanding of the life-course perspective (see Chapter Two). Parents can claim a maximum of 20 years' pension credits. These were introduced in a Home-maker's Scheme introduced in 1994. However, these were not backdated, so several cohorts of women who were affected by the marriage bar and were out of the labour market prior to 1994 do not receive these credits and so are disadvantaged in pension building.

A wide range of pension reforms introduced in 2012 and 2014 encouraged the extension of working life and privatisation of pensions. One such reform was raising the state pension age. Ireland's population is relatively young, with only 12.72% aged 65 and over in 2014 (OECD, no date). Yet, the state pension age is being raised rapidly from 65 pre-2012 to 66 in 2012, 67 in 2021 and 68 in 2028. This change affects women (and men) negatively if they are in poor health, engaged in physically demanding work and/or unable to find employment. It removes the option of retirement with a contributory state pension for those who had expected to retire at 65 and have little time to adjust and build pension contributions. They may be unemployed since there is evidence of age discrimination in the labour market in Ireland, despite legislative measures to protect against it (Russell et al, 2008).

The mandatory retirement age is being abolished in Ireland in 2017 in line with OECD recommendations. However, employers will have the right to impose fixed-term contracts if they can justify it on objective grounds. In Ireland, the average effective age of retirement for the period 2009–14 was 65.4 years for men and 62.6 years for women, higher than the OECD average of 64 years for men and slightly lower than the average of 63.1 years for women (OECD, 2015a). The recession arguably led to contradictory reactive policies by the government, who undermined their previous Active Ageing policies by introducing incentives for certain public sector employees to retire early in order to reduce the public sector pay bill in the short term. Certain categories of public sector employees were encouraged to leave public sector jobs early before a specific date after which their pensions would be reduced.

A number of measures were introduced in 2012 that tied the amount of pension benefits more closely to participation in the formal, paid labour market. The amount of contributions required to qualify for a minimum level of state contributory pension was doubled from 260 to 520 (10 years of contributions). There was an increase in the number of rate bands from September 2012, which effectively meant lower rates of pension benefits for those with lower contributions (mainly women). The underlying rationale for these changes was that of the 'need to generate savings', as conveyed by ministerial staff in notes prepared for the minister of social protection. The introduction was strongly opposed by trade union leaders as being unduly harsh on women with interrupted work histories. Interestingly, the minister rebutted that 'core rates have been protected' and, moreover, that 'those with lower earnings and those with shorter contribution histories, mostly women, have and will continue to obtain the best value for money from the fund due to the distributive nature of the fund' (Ryan, 2014).

It is planned to change in 2020 from the current yearly averaging system to a total contributions system to be averaged over the person's entire working life. A total of 30 years of contributions – 1/30th for each year – will be required for a maximum pension and the minimum pension is set at just a third of the maximum. These reforms link pensions more closely to labour market participation and are disadvantageous to many women but particularly to older women with greater gaps in their work trajectories (Ní Léime et al, 2015). In its review of the Irish pension system, the OECD report cites an actuarial projection which predicts that the changes will mean fewer people having 80–100% pensions by 2020. It acknowledges that these measures will have a larger impact on women's pensions in 2020 compared to men's (OECD, 2014). It is also planned to reduce the number of years for which credit for care work will be given from 20 to 10 in 2020 (Department of Social and Family Affairs, 2010). It appears that this intensification of women's disadvantage is anticipated and does not appear to be a concern to either the OECD or the Irish government. If as a result of these reforms, women have less access to state pensions, the OECD and the government presumably expect them to increasingly provide for their own private pensions. However, substantial evidence indicates that many women are unable to afford private provision and are even more disadvantaged when pensions are privatised (Ginn, 2004; Ginn and MacIntyre, 2013).

Ireland's employment rates for older women have increased recently, but a legacy of discriminatory legislation adversely affects the pension building of today's older workers and retirees. There are at least some family-friendly policies in Ireland. We now give an overview of employment reforms and assess the current outcomes for women and pensions.

Ireland: employment reforms for older workers

One of the first Active Ageing employment policy recommendations promoted by the EU was the target set at the Stockholm Summit in 2001 of 50% employment for men and women in the 55–64 age groups to be achieved by 2010. The Irish government introduced various measures designed to pursue this objective, including strengthening anti-age discrimination legislation (originally introduced in 1998) in 2000 and 2004 to cover people aged 65 and over. An increase in the proportion of older women in the labour market was facilitated by the removal of upper age limits for recruitment due to anti-age discrimination legislation. Many older women were recruited or returned to the public service at this time. Employment rates for men aged 55–64 were 64.9% in 2001 and 58.7% in 2013 – this decrease was caused by the sharp increase in unemployment during the recession. The EU Commission subsequently set a target participation rate of 75% to be achieved by 2020 for all workers aged 20–64. In pursuit of this, Ireland set a short-term target of 69–71% by 2014, and this was to include older workers (FORFÁS, 2011). Employment rates for older workers aged 55–64 are 61.4% for men and 44.7% for women in 2014 – considerably lower than the 75% target, as well as by Northern European standards (Eurostat, 2015).

Measures to facilitate flexible working around retirement age have been introduced. An exemption from employment earnings of €100 per week was introduced into the means test for the non-contributory pension in 2006 and increased to €200 in 2007. While this is beneficial for those who are healthy, it is of little benefit to those who are unable to find work or whose health is compromised (Vickerstaff, 2010). Job-search requirements for older workers have been introduced; jobseekers have to actively seek employment or engage with employment and training services. This is likely to be challenging for older workers given the high levels of unemployment since the recession.

State agencies such as the Citizens Information Service and the Equality Authority have produced information materials to inform employers and employees of employment rights, equality and family leave legislation. The Equality Authority also supports equality mainstreaming in training programmes and among employers. Older workers (over 55) have access to training schemes. Research in Ireland suggests that ageism exists in the Irish labour market and often acts as a barrier to recruitment and retention for older workers (Russell et al, 2008; Ní Léime, 2010).

Implications of reforms in the context of recession: precarious employment and gender

In Ireland, the global recession had serious implications for employment generally and for older workers in particular. The crisis was precipitated by an overheated property bubble, leading to high levels of public debt when the government bailed out the banks. This led to very high levels of unemployment, peaking at 15.3% in 2012; while unemployment rates were higher among younger workers, they also increased for older workers. By 2014, unemployment rates for men aged 55–59 were 11% for men and 7.8% for women (Central Statistics Office, 2016a). The recession also meant that many private pension funds lost their value, causing hardship to women (and men) who had responded to government urgings to invest in these pensions. There is evidence that some women have discontinued these pensions because they are no longer able to afford them and have lost trust in them due to steep declines in their value (Ní Léime et al, 2015). Some women had hoped that equity in their homes would help supplement their pensions.

Property values collapsed dramatically in the recession, resulting in the loss of property equity as a strategy to bolster low pensions (Duvvury et al, 2012). Impacts on pension provision were only one dimension of the crisis; an equally disturbing trend is the changing nature of employment relations. Drawing on new analysis of the latest data available, we explore the gendered dimensions of the expansion in precarious employment, particularly for older workers.

It appears that, following global trends, precarious work is becoming more prevalent in the Irish labour market, particularly since the recession. Precarious work (although the definition is contested, see Chapter One) includes part-time work, particularly involuntary part-time work, seasonal, zero-hour and temporary contracts (Vosko, 2008; Standing, 2014). The trends outlined in Table 6.1 present new data analysis pointing to the increasing precarity of employment. Part-time and vulnerable work, traditionally the preserve of women, have become somewhat 'masculinised' in Ireland since the recession. Men's part-time employment rose systematically across the recession – almost doubling from 2007 to 2012 – while women's part-time employment increased marginally across the period. Overall, the recession has exacerbated the precarity of Ireland's labour market, though women continue to dominate both part-time and temporary employment. EU-SILC (European Union Statistics on Income and Living Conditions) data

Table 6.1: Contract type and hours of work in Ireland, by year and sex

Percentage of total population in employment in Ireland by type of contract and year								
		2007	2008	2009	2010	2011	2012	% change, 07–12
Male	Permanent	93.2	93.1	92.7	91.2	90.3	90.4	−3.0
	Temporary	6.8	6.9	7.3	8.8	9.7	9.6	41.1
Female	Permanent	90.3	90.4	90.6	89.9	89.7	89.9	−0.5
	Temporary	9.7	9.6	9.4	10.1	10.3	10.1	4.2
Percentage of total population in employment in Ireland by hours of work and year								
		2007	2008	2009	2010	2011	2012	% change, 07–12
Male	Full time	92.5	91.8	88.9	87.8	86.8	85.7	−7.4
	Part time	7.5	8.2	11.1	12.2	12.2	14.3	91.1
Female	Full time	65.4	65.2	64.9	64.4	63.9	63.9	−2.4
	Part time	34.6	34.8	35.1	35.6	36.1	36.1	4.4

Source: Authors' own calculations derived from EU-SILC microdata.

suggest that much of this part-time employment is involuntary, with 45% of men and 29% of women reporting in 2013 that they would like to work more hours but cannot do so (source: authors' calculation from EU-SILC data).

Two key trends emerge from our analysis of older workers in the Irish labour market. First, there has been an increase in precarious employment overall for most workers, especially men. Male workers turned to part-time employment in a scarce job environment. Precarious employment has become more prevalent in sectors and among socio-economic groups that in the past were insulated from this type of employment (Lewchuk et al, 2013).

Second, older women's involvement in employment actually increased over the course of the recession. However, this increase in the employment of older women occurred in the context of deteriorating working conditions overall. Overall, weekly wages declined by about 2.65% between 2010 and 2014, with sharp declines in wages in education, health and arts and recreation (Central Statistics Office, 2014). Table 6.2 demonstrates that the gender gap in earnings increased for particular groups of women. For older workers, aged 55–64 years, the gender gap in earnings, having reduced in 2010, began to widen from 2011, with a sharp increase in older men's average income.

For older workers in precarious employment, it may not be possible to find or retain employment, particularly if they experience ill health. Previous research has demonstrated that job insecurity is associated with an increased risk of poor health – both physical and mental. Persistent job insecurity has the strongest negative association with health (Ferrie et al, 1995; Burgard et al, 2007; László et al, 2010). This is important given the context of the recent economic crisis and the increasingly complex nature of employment in the labour market. While job insecurity is certainly not a new phenomenon, increased 'flexibility' in labour markets along with the recent recession have left the positions of workers increasingly insecure. Findings regarding the differential impact of insecure employment on the health of men

Table 6.2: Gender gap (%) in mean annual employee cash income (€), by age group

		2007	2008	2009	2010	2011	2012
Gender gap in income (%)	15 years +	38.50	37.95	36.66	31.18	31.32	27.67
	55–65 years	49.75	47.97	41.85	35.43	35.85	39.00

Source: Authors' analysis of EU SILC microdata.

and women are contested. Some researchers argue that new forms of precarious employment interact with patriarchy, damaging women's health more than men's (Ferrie et al, 1995; Menéndez et al, 2007). Others argue that it is more detrimental for men's health as norms around the division of labour cause men to feel more threatened by being in precarious employment (Cheng et al, 2005). Others report that there were gender differences in the health impacts of precarious employment (László et al, 2010). Data from the Irish Longitudinal Study of Ageing (TILDA) study indicate that older workers are more likely to experience a variety of health challenges, to report that health problems have limited their activities in the past six months and to report that health problems have limited the type of work that they can do (see Table 6.3).

Table 6.3: Health conditions of older employed workers, by age and sex

Male	Depression	Back pain	Arthritis	High blood pressure	Limiting activities	Limits on type of work
50–54	3.7	14.1	1.2	20.3	9.27	6.95
55–59	3.8	12.3	1.5	29.8	10.67	6.48
60–64	3.2	11.9	1.4	33.2	8.94	8.14
65+	2	10.9	2.2	44.3	15.21	12.61
Female						
50–54	6.6	13	2	18.5	9.71	6.96
55–59	7.5	13	2.5	25.1	14.1	7.14
60–64	6.4	14.3	1.1	35.8	12.7	5.66
65+	5.1	12	6.54	28	6.54	3.67

Source: Authors' own calculations from TILDA microdata.

One assumption of extended working life policy is that older workers aged 65 and over are healthy enough to continue working, which Table 6.3 in fact counters. Additionally, workers in physically demanding occupations such as construction work or cleaning are more likely to develop work-related health challenges. In fact, examination of TILDA data for those taking early retirement for health reasons shows high rates for men in manual occupations; 13% of unskilled men reported retiring early due to ill health compared to 5.9% for the professional and managerial/technical categories (source: TILDA microdata).

Conclusion

From the analysis presented here, it appears that extended working life policies were introduced in Ireland without adequately considering the gender implications. The unidimensional nature of employment and pension policy reform does not allow for variations in employment status and pension outcomes across diverse groups of workers by gender, occupation, employment status, precarity and health.

Extended working life policies are based on the assumption that workers are homogeneous and free to participate in the labour market, as assumed by the adult worker model. Yet, it is clear that many workers (typically women) are not always free to participate in the labour market due to the prevailing social norm that they are primarily responsible for providing unpaid care for dependent family members (Lewis, 2007; Russell and McGinnity, 2014). In fact, in Ireland, a substantial proportion of women are not in the labour market and the breadwinner/homemaker model is still common, although there are an increasing number of dual-earner households (Murphy, 2012). Scholars from a feminist political economy of ageing approach have pointed out that adult worker model assumptions may not hold for many women whose health may be compromised from physically and emotionally demanding caring roles and who may be concentrated in low-paid employment (Ginn et al, 2001; Foster, 2012).

Given the strong influence of caring norms on labour market participation and pension building for women in particular, there is a need for a coordinated policy approach. We must consider not only pension and employment policies in isolation, but also the impact of family-friendly policies, if we are to understand gender-differentiated outcomes. We need to analyse policies that support the reconciliation of paid work in the formal labour market with unpaid caring, including maternity and parental leave (Lewis, 2006; Chau et al, 2016).

Certain groups of workers are disadvantaged under the current pension system and this is likely to be exacerbated by the proposed pension and employment reforms and the growing informality of labour markets. This includes men and women in precarious and/or low-paid employment and those in occupations that demand heavy physical and/or emotional labour. Our new analysis of recent data highlights the growing precarity in the Irish labour market and the health challenges faced by certain groups of older workers engaged in onerous and/or precarious work. It cannot be assumed that these workers can easily find or retain employment after the state pension age. A universal citizen's income payment (see Chapter Three) may provide the best policy option for these groups.

Pension reforms need to be reconsidered. Privatising pensions and raising the state pension age across the board are problematic, especially for women, who tend to be more reliant on state non-contributory pensions. Presenting extended working life as the inevitable solution to demographic ageing obscures the fact that this reflects a particular political choice. It would be possible, for example, to support increased pension costs by increasing general taxation, removing or reducing tax breaks for private pensions, and using this money to increase the level of the state non-contributory pension.

If the current pension system is to be maintained, measures to protect those adversely affected need to be introduced. For example, raising the state pension age should not be imposed in a uniform manner across all occupations. Linking pension building more closely to labour market participation means that women (and men) in low-paid employment will find it more difficult to manage on the now lower state contributory pension. A life-course perspective shows that certain cohorts of women such as those affected by the marriage bar have been doubly discriminated against by not being given pension credits/ disregards for the time they spent caring. They should be included in the Home-maker's Scheme.

Employment policies could help address the current imbalance whereby women undertake the majority of caring for young, old and vulnerable family members (Murphy, 2014). Increased paternity leave should be available to men to facilitate them to engage in caring and be given to men on an equal basis by employers and by the government.

Finally, a number of lines of enquiry in research need to be pursued if the issue of gender and extended working life is to be comprehensively analysed and addressed in Ireland. There needs to be qualitative research into the processes by which women and men in different occupations and different forms of employment, secure and precarious, arrive at disparate pension outcomes. An intersectional approach to analysis would help uncover more precisely how gender and other dimensions intersect across the life course. This could be complemented by quantitative research that draws upon longitudinal data sets such as TILDA and Study of Health and Retirement in Europe (SHARE) data. This would enable an informed comprehensive analysis of extended working life policy in the Irish context.

References

Arulampalam, W., Booth, A.L. and Bryan, M.L. (2007) Is there a glass ceiling over Europe? Exploring the gender pay gap across the wage distribution, *Industrial & Labor Relations Review*, 60(2), 163–86.

Bettio, F., Tinios, P. and Betti, G. (2013) *The gender gap in pensions in the EU*, Luxembourg: Publications Office.

Burgard, S.A., Brand, J.E. and House, J.S. (2007) Toward a better estimation of the effect of job loss on health, *Journal of Health and Social Behavior*, 48, 369–84.

Campbell, K. (2015) Fathers have their day as paternity leave on the way, *The Irish Times*, 6 November. Available at: http://www. irishtimes.com/business/work/fathers-have-their-day-as-paternity-leave-on-the-way-next-year-1.2418335

Central Statistics Office (2011) Quarterly national household survey: Pension provision quarter 4 2009, Cork/Dublin: Central Statistics Office.

Central Statistics Office (2013a) Women and men in Ireland 2013. Available at: http://www.cso.ie/en/releasesandpublications/ep/p-wamii/womenandmeninireland2013

Central Statistics Office (2013b) Survey on Income and Living Conditions (SILC): Thematic report on the elderly, Dublin: Central Statistics Office.

Central Statistics Office (2014) Earnings and labour costs, quarterly report, Cork/Dublin: Central Statistics Office.

Central Statistics Office (2016a) Quarterly National Household Survey: Quarter 1 2016. Available at: www.cso.ie/en/releasesandpublications/er/qnhs/quarterlynationalhouseholdsurveyquarter12016/

Central Statistics Office (2016b) Quarterly National Household Survey: Pension provision quarter 4 2015 summary, Cork/Dublin: Central Statistics Office.

Chau, R.C., Foster, L. and Yu, S.W.K. (2016) Defamilisation and familisation measures: can they reduce the adverse effects of pro-market pension reforms on women in Hong Kong and the UK?, *Critical Social Policy*, DOI: 10.1177/0261018315621989.

Cheng, Y., Chen, C.W., Chen, C.J. and Chiang, T.L. (2005) Job insecurity and its association with health among employees in the Taiwanese general population, *Social Science & Medicine*, 61, 41–52.

Cousins, M. and Associates (2008) *Report on the consultation process for the Green Paper on pensions*, Dublin: Stationery Office.

Dail Debates (2014) April. Available at: http://oireachtasdebates. oireachtas.ie/debates%20authoring/debateswebpack.nsf/takes/dail2014041600009

Daly, M. (2010) Ireland. In-work poverty and labour market segmentation. A study of national policies, peer review in social protection and social inclusion and assessment, *Social Inclusion*, European Commission, DG Employment, Social Affairs, and Equal Opportunities.

Dannefer, D. (2003) Cumulative advantage and the life course: cross-fertilizing age and social science knowledge, *Journal of Gerontology*, 58b: S327–37.

Department of Health (2013) *Positive ageing starts now: The national positive ageing strategy*, Dublin: Stationary Office.

Department of Social and Family Affairs (2007) *Green Paper on pensions*, Dublin: Stationery Office.

Department of Social and Family Affairs (2010) *National pensions framework*, Dublin: Stationery Office.

Department of Social Protection (2014) Statistical information on social welfare services, 2014. Available at: https://www.welfare.ie/en/Pages/Annual-SWS-Statistical-Information-Report-2014.aspx

Dewilde, C. (2012) Lifecourse determinants and incomes in retirement: Belgium and the United Kingdom compared, *Ageing and Society*, 32(4), 587–615.

Duvvury, N., Ní Léime, Á., Callan, A., Price, L. and Simpson, M. (2012) *Older women workers' access to pensions: Vulnerabilities, perspectives and strategies*, Galway: NUI Galway.

Eurostat (2015) News release: employment rate of people aged 20 to 64 in the EU up to 69.2% in 2014. Available at: http://ec.europa.eu/eurostat/documents/2995521/6823708/3-07052015-AP-EN.pdf/7e507ea0-43c7-452f-8e6a-b479c89d2bd6

Ferrie, J.E., Shipley, M.J., Marmot, M.G., Stansfeld, S. and Smith, G.D. (1995) Health effects of anticipation of job change and non-employment: longitudinal data from the Whitehall II study, *British Medical Journal*, 311(7015), 1264–9.

FORFÁS (2011) *Annual report 2011*, Dublin: FORFÁS.

Foster, L. (2012) Active ageing and pensions in the European Union, *Journal of Comparative Social Welfare*, 28(3), 223–34.

Ginn, J. (2004) European pension privatisation: taking account of gender, *Social Policy and Society*, 3(2), 123–34.

Ginn, J. and MacIntyre, K. (2013) UK pension reforms: is gender still an issue?, *Social Policy and Society*, 12(1), 91–103

Ginn, J., Street, D. and Arber, S. (eds) (2001) *Women, work, and pensions: International issues and prospects*, Buckingham and Philadelphia, PA: Open University Press.

Hughes, G. (2014) Have personal retirement accounts met their objectives in Ireland?, in M. Szczepanski and J.A. Turner (eds) *Social security and pension reform: International perspectives*, Kalamazoo, MI: Upjohn Institute for Employment Research, pp 39–62.

Kelly, E., McGuinness, S. and O'Connell, P. (2009) *The public–private sector pay gap in Ireland: What lies beneath?*, ESRI Working paper no. 321, Dublin: Economic and Social Research Institute.

László, K.D., Pikhart, H., Kopp, M.S., Bobak, M., Pajak, A., Malyutina, S., Salavecz, G. and Marmot, M. (2010) Job insecurity and health: a study of 16 European countries, *Social Science & Medicine*, 70(6), 867–74.

Lewchuk, W., Lafleche, M., Dyson, D., Goldring, L., Meisner, A., Procyk, S., Rosen, D., Shields, S., Viducis, P. and Vrankulj, S. (2013) *It's more than poverty: Employment precarity and household well-being*, Toronto: Poverty and Employment Precarity in Southern Ontario (PEPSO).

Lewis, J. (2006) Work/family reconciliation, equal opportunities and social policies: the interpretation of policy trajectories at the EU level and the meaning of gender equality, *Journal of European Public Policy*, 13(3), 420–37.

Lewis, J. (2007) Gender, ageing and the new social settlement: the importance of delivering a holistic approach to care policies, *Current Sociology*, 55, 271–86.

Mahon, E. (1998) Class, mothers and equal opportunities to work, in E.R. Drew and E. Mahon (eds) *Women, work and the family in Europe*, London: Routledge, pp 170–81.

Menéndez, M., Benach, J., Muntaner, C., Amable, M. and O'Campo, P. (2007) Is precarious employment more damaging to women's health than men's?, *Social Science & Medicine*, 64(4), 776–81.

Murphy, M. (2012) *Careless to careful activation: Making activation work for women*, Dublin: National Women's Council of Ireland.

Murphy, M. (2014) Interests, institutions and ideas: explaining Irish social security policy, *Policy & Politics*, 40(3), 347–65. Available at: http://dx.doi.org/10.1332/030557312X626640

Murphy, M. and McCashin, A. (2008) *Pensions: What women want. A model of pensions that guarantees independence*, Dublin: National Women's Council of Ireland.

Ní Léime, Á. (2010) Decision-making among older workers in the Irish Civil Service, PhD dissertation, Trinity College Dublin, Ireland.

Ní Léime, Á., Duvvury, N. and Callan, A. (2015) Pension provision, gender, ageing and work in Ireland, in K. Walsh, G. Carney and Á. Ní Léime (eds) *Ageing through austerity: Critical perspectives from Ireland*, Bristol: The Policy Press, pp 63–78.

O'Connor, P. (1998) *Emerging voices: Women in contemporary Irish society*, Dublin: Institute of Public Administration.

OECD (Organisation for Economic Co-operation and Development) (no date) Elderly population. Available at: https://data.oecd.org/pop/elderly-population.htm

OECD (2006) *Live longer, work longer: Ageing and employment policies*, Paris: OECD.

OECD (2014) *OECD review of Irish pension system*, Paris: OECD.

OECD (2015a) Recent pension reforms, in OECD (ed) *Pensions at a glance, 2015,* Paris: OECD Publishing, pp 15–43.

OECD (2015b) Gross pension replacement rates, in OECD (ed) *Pensions at a glance 2015: OECD and G20 indicators*, Paris: OECD Publishing. Available at: http://dx.doi.org/10.1787/pension_glance-2015-14-en

OECD (2016a) Gender wage gap (indicator). Available at: http://www.oecd.org/gender/data/genderwagegap.htm

OECD (2016b) Part-time employment rate (indicator). Available at: https://data.oecd.org/emp/part-time-employment-rate.htm#indicator-chart

OECD (2016c) OECD Family Database. Available at: http://www.oecd.org/els/family/database.htm

OECD (2016d) *OECD labour force statistics, 2015,* Paris: OECD. Available at: http://www.keepeek.com/Digital-Asset-Management/oecd/employment/oecd-labour-force-statistics-2015/participation-rates-and-unemployment-rates-by-age-and-sex-ireland_oecd_lfs-2015-table124-en#.V5uMivkrLb0

Russell, H. (2002) *Getting out of the house: Women returning to employment, education and training*, Dublin: Liffey Press in association with the Economic and Social Research Institute.

Russell, H. and McGinnity, F. (2014) Under pressure: the impact of recession on employees in Ireland, *British Journal of Industrial Relations*, 52(2), 286–307.

Russell, H., Quinn, E., King O'Riain, R. and McGinnity, F. (2008) *The experience of discrimination in Ireland: Analysis of the QNHS equality module*, Dublin: The Equality Authority and the Economic and Social Research Institute.

Russell, J. (2014) *Social insecurity 401(k)s and the retirement crisis*, Boston, MA: Beacon Press.

Ryan, C. (2014) No country for old women as females bear burnt of pension cuts, *Irish Examiner*, 17 March. Available at: http:// www.irishexaminer.com/viewpoints/analysis/no-country-for-old-women-as-females-bear-brunt-of-pension-cuts-262241.html

Standing, G. (2014) *The precariat: The new dangerous class*, New York, NY: Bloomsbury.

Vickerstaff, S. (2010) Older workers: the unavoidable obligation of extending our working lives, *Sociology Compass*, 4(10), 869–79.

Vosko, L.F. (2008) Temporary work in transnational labour regulation: SER-centrism and the risk of exacerbating gendered precariousness, *Social Indicators Research*, 88(1), 131–45.

SEVEN

Ageing and older workers in Portugal: a gender-sensitive approach

Sara Falcão Casaca and Heloísa Perista

Introduction

Extending working life and increasing the employment rates among older workers has been a major policy focus in Portugal over the last two decades in a general context of demographic decline and population ageing, as well as concerns about the financial sustainability of social security. The declining trend in the birth rate and low fertility rates is particularly worrying in countries similar to Portugal, where the Synthetic General Fertility Index (ISF) fell from 3.20 in 1960 to 1.23 in 2014 (Pordata, no date). Low fertility rates, along with the decrease in the proportion of individuals registered as economically active, the rise in average life expectancy and increasing numbers of older people, have all been seen as factors placing increasing strain on the Portuguese social security, pension and health systems.

A comprehensive national strategy regarding extended working life has never been fully developed in Portugal as policies have developed in a fragmented, ad hoc basis. Moreover, policies and incentives to extend working life have tended to be gender-blind and have ignored the respective gendered implications of people being retained in the labour market (Bould and Casaca, 2012). Simultaneously, the urgent need for formal care provision has been largely disregarded by policy debates and reforms. The lack of attention to the issue of formal care provision is especially critical in countries such as Portugal, where the availability of such provision has always been rather low (Casaca and Bould, 2012). Austerity reforms have imposed further cuts and restrictions on welfare provision in a context where people, and women in particular, live longer but are often in need of care. In fact, *healthy* life expectancy has not increased very quickly. Data show that in 2013, life expectancy at birth is higher for women than it is for men

137

(84 and 77.6 years, respectively); yet, when healthy life expectancy is considered, figures are lower for women (62.2 years) than for men (63.9 years). With regard to life expectancy after 65, women can expect to live healthily 9.3 years longer, whereas men can expect to live healthily for another 9.6 years at the same age (Eurostat, no date).

Studies indicate that people aged 50+ regularly care for a partner or parent with health problems or disabilities (Eurofound, 2014). In Southern European countries, where gender regimes continue to be based on 'familialism' and traditional gender ideologies are deeply ingrained in society, the onus of an extended working life is felt, above all, by women. The significant amount of time that they devote to care and unpaid work may also limit women's availability to remain in the labour market (Addis, 2006; Kauppinen, 2010; Bould and Casaca, 2012).

The first section of this chapter discusses the gendered impacts of Portuguese policy reforms in the pensions and welfare systems, leading to extended working lives. Anti-discrimination legislation and the intervention of the national machinery and of other social actors in issues relating to age, gender and disability are the focus of the second section. A third section highlights distinctive patterns and the progress that has been made associated with critical issues still existing in relation to gender and age as they may influence extended working life. The analysis centres upon material deprivation and poverty, social protection, education and training, employment and work, and the work–family life balance. Finally, the chapter concludes with some general considerations relating to the current Portuguese debate about extended working life and gender.

Extending working lives and policy reforms in Portugal

Active ageing and the extension of working life are topics that have been widely discussed and are clearly visible in both European Union (EU) and national policy agendas, with Portugal adopting the National Strategy for Active Ageing, a working document that set out a comprehensive approach and was integrated into the National Employment Plan for 2005–08. This strategy was not, however, further developed after 2009. The government adopted the National Action Programme of the European Year on Active Ageing and Solidarity between Generations, but a comprehensive policy programme was never designed (Naumann, 2013). Over the last decade, policy reforms in Portugal have been marked by the encouragement of a delay in retirement and the penalisation of early retirement, as well as by cuts in social protection, namely, in pensions.

In 2007, the Portuguese pension system was significantly reformed, following the approval of the new Basic Social Security Law. The Law established a new formula for calculating pensions, which is no longer based on the best 10 years of remuneration in the last 15 years of work, but on the whole working-life trajectory. This reform has tended to impact more negatively on women than on men because their working-life remuneration is usually lower than men's, thereby creating a greater risk of poverty for older women (see also Bould and Casaca, 2012; Perista and Perista, 2012a).

The main measures introduced by this reform included: incorporating a sustainability factor into the calculations, linking the value of pensions to the evolution of life-expectancy estimations at the age of 65; new indexation rules designed to moderate periodic adjustments of pensions; encouraging the postponement of retirement by increasing the financial penalty for early retirement and granting bonuses for those who delay their retirement; and revision of the criteria for means testing for non-contributory benefits, along with a new non-contributory allowance for the elderly (the Solidarity Supplement for the Elderly) (see Baptista et al, 2015). These measures were designed from a gender-blind perspective, not anticipating the respective gender-differentiated implications.

The Portuguese reforms have occurred in a very specific context, not only in the aftermath of the global recession (2008–09), but with the signing of the bailout agreement in 2011. The so-called Memorandum of Understanding between the Portuguese government and the European Commission, in liaison with the European Central Bank and the International Monetary Fund, brought important changes to the Portuguese pension system. At the tax level, the main changes included both permanent measures (eg higher withholding tax rates and a decrease in the specific tax deductions applicable to income from pensions) and temporary measures (eg the Extraordinary Solidarity Surcharge and the Extraordinary Surcharge on Personal Income) (see Baptista et al, 2015). Furthermore, pensions above €1500 were significantly reduced.

As far as social security is concerned, some permanent changes were also introduced: an increase in the legal retirement age with full benefits, which in 2014, was 66 years old for both men and women and will subsequently evolve in line with life expectancy at 65; a decrease in the reference value of the Solidarity Supplement for the Elderly, which led to a significant reduction in the number of recipients of this non-contributory welfare allowance, with women representing the majority of such recipients; a change in the design of the sustainability factor, altering the reference year from 2006 to 2000; and reductions in survivors' pensions, penalising widows in particular. Two major social security-related temporary measures were also introduced during this period: the suspension of the regime allowing for early retirement, with the exception of long-term involuntary unemployment; and the freezing of pension benefits, with the exception of the lowest pensions (see Baptista et al, 2015). The new government that came into force at the end of November 2015 is planning to revise some of these measures, aimed at raising the income of pensioners.

As mentioned earlier in the chapter, in recent years, extended working lives have been encouraged. Working after retirement age while receiving a pension is also possible and encouraged: pensioners who remain in work, either as independent workers or employees, will now see their pensions supplemented. Furthermore, extended working life is encouraged by other incentives that are in place, such as employers being exempt from paying the employers' share of social security contributions when hiring older workers in order to promote the reintegration into the labour market of unemployed persons aged 55 or over.

There has been widespread discussion in policymaking and public discourse in Portugal concerning doubts relating to the sustainability of the public social security system, which, in turn, has encouraged a trend towards privatisation. However, in 2011, even the tax incentives encouraging contributions to private pension schemes were revoked, but many individuals who can afford to do so still invest in retirement saving plans. Capping – the introduction of thresholds on earnings from work that are liable to social contributions – has also been part of the policy agenda.

In Portugal, the economic crisis and the subsequent austerity policies have impacted greatly on pensions and welfare policies, with a disproportionately negative effect on older women (as detailed later in the chapter in the section on material deprivation and poverty) (see also Bastos et al, 2009).

Anti-discrimination legislation and intersectional issues: age, gender, disability

As already mentioned, active ageing has become a popular concept over the last decade in a trend that is instrumentally driven, largely motivated by economic and financial concerns (Bould and Casaca,

2012). Under the scope of the European Year 2012 for Active Ageing, the National Action Programme comprised various actions aimed at increasing older workers' participation in employment, such as: giving priority for unemployed persons aged 55 or over registered in public employment services; a Senior ReMobilisation Programme to encourage reintegration into the labour market; retraining measures; and support for self-employment (Governo de Portugal, 2012). This policy document states that gender equality is a cross-cutting criterion to be taken into account; nevertheless, any discussion of the gendered impacts of the planned measures is completely absent.

For the first time, under the scope of the European Year for Active Ageing and Solidarity between Generations (2012), the national official machinery in charge of promoting gender equality, citizenship and non-discrimination – the Commission for Citizenship and Gender Equality (CIG) – launched a study aimed at analysing the main issues regarding gender and ageing and at formulating policy recommendations for a more inclusive society (Perista and Perista, 2012a, 2012b). No other specific policies or measures were implemented from an intersectional perspective, bringing together gender and ageing issues.

CIG is the official mechanism responsible for implementing public policies to promote gender equality. As far as gender equality is concerned, the main policy instruments are the National Action Plans, including the National Plan for Equality, Gender, Citizenship and Non-Discrimination. Some plans have envisaged specific measures to support particularly vulnerable groups of women – older women and lone mothers with scarce economic resources, and women with disabilities. This is the case with measures of affirmative action designed to be implemented in favour of these groups in areas such as employment, vocational training, access to social housing and social facilities (Measure 3.2.3 – National Action Plan for Equality 2003–06). In recent action plans, measures are too vague and difficult to monitor – such as the measure 'to improve the quality of life of older women' (National Action Plan for Equality, Citizenship and Gender – 2007–10, Section 2.4) – or are even absent from the reference policy framework (National Action Plan for Equality, Gender Citizenship and Non-Discrimination – 2011–13). As to the 5th National Plan for Gender Equality, Citizenship and Non-Discrimination 2014–17, currently in force, older women are again identified as particularly vulnerable. A gender perspective, or a specific focus on older women, is adopted in several measures in specific domains such as social protection, access to information and knowledge, and health.

The 5th National Plan to Prevent and Combat Domestic and Gender-Based Violence 2014–17 includes, in three of its measures, a specific focus on violence against older people. Other National Action Plans do not include a specific focus on age and/or gender. This is the case with the National Health Plan 2012–16. A Strategy for the Protection of the Elderly was approved by the government in 2015. The law approving this strategy focused on the protection of older people's fundamental rights, mainly regarding the definition of a new incapacity regime and the criminalisation of any actions violating these rights. No specific mention of gender-specific rights is made in this law.

In spite of some ad hoc initiatives, where gender is considered in one place and age in another, there has been no comprehensive and integrated intersectional approach to extended working life, at least in terms of the legal framework or of the actions of the national machinery or other relevant social actors in Portugal. It is worth mentioning that no non-governmental organisation exists in Portugal with a specific focus on gender and age-based discrimination. Furthermore, extended working life, namely, in terms of the adoption of a gender-sensitive approach, is not a topic that has been on the agenda of civil society organisations. As to the social partners, their contribution, and that of the trade union confederations in particular, to the ongoing discussion on pension reforms has mainly focused on the negative impacts of the reforms on pensioners' incomes and their vulnerability to poverty, but without a particular focus on women's distinctive vulnerabilities.

What do we know about gender and age in Portugal: distinctive patterns, processes and critical issues

Only a few studies have been conducted in Portugal into intersecting gender and age issues. The next sections systematise their main contributions. Moreover, current data have also been collected and analysed in order to highlight the main processes and critical issues currently faced by the country on these issues.

Material deprivation and poverty

There has been a significant increase in the poverty rate in Portugal in the last few years, as evidenced by recently released European Union Statistics on Income and Living Conditions (EU-SILC) data (INE, no date), rising from 17.9% in 2011 to 19.5% in 2014 for Portuguese of all ages. Women are particularly vulnerable to poverty, with the female poverty rate standing at 20.5% and the male rate at 18.8% in 2014.

Using a poverty line anchored to 2009, the evolution of the poverty rate between that year and 2014 shows an increase from 17.9% to 24.2%. A similar evolution has been recorded in the relative at-risk-of-poverty gap by poverty threshold, which rose significantly from 24.1% in 2011 to 30.3% in 2013, decreasing to 29% in 2014. This relative at-risk-of-poverty gap is higher among older women compared to older men (19.3% and 17.0%, respectively, in 2014).

Older people have been among the most severely affected by the increasing poverty rates according to EU-SILC because for those in poverty in old age, employment or economic rebounds are unlikely to provide opportunities for non-working older people to change their financial situation and escape poverty. The latest poverty statistics highlight the rise in the poverty rate among the older population aged 65 and over (from 14.6% in 2013 to 17.1% in 2014). The older women's poverty rate is considerably higher than that of men: 19.1% and 14.4%, respectively, in 2014. Furthermore, considering their labour market status, pensioners are the ones who have witnessed the greatest increase in their poverty rate, rising from 13.2% in 2012 to 14.5% in 2014. Women pensioners, again, were particularly prone to poverty, at a rate of 15.3%, compared with 13.6% for male pensioners, in 2014. Using a poverty line anchored to 2009, the evolution of the poverty rate between that year and 2014 shows an increase from 21% to 24% among people aged 65 and over.

Gender-sensitive studies have shown that poverty is not a gender-neutral condition as the number of poor women exceeds that of men, and women and men experience poverty in different ways (see also Perista et al, 1993). Moreover, poverty is seen as a multidimensional concept as it is not only related to insufficient income, but also involves deprivation in terms of well-being in the various areas of people's lives. Furthermore, a micro-level analysis, based on qualitative information, would be particularly relevant in order to:

> disclose the complexity inside the *black box* and to understand gender relations as power relations within the family, to look at patterns of both cooperation and conflict, as well as at the division of labour, and the processes of bargaining and decision-making surrounding the allocation, sharing and control of household and individual resources. (Bastos et al, 2009: 777)

It is possible to conclude that the literature is still rather scarce in Portugal. More empirical evidence is needed to better understand the intricacies surrounding the issue of material deprivation, poverty and extended working lives from the perspective of a gendered life course, as argued in Chapter Two.

Social protection

Recent political developments have triggered some initiatives leading to the introduction of social protection reforms in early 2016. The so-called 'Income Package' aims at initiating the return to earlier income levels for families, namely, by increasing the level of pensions (general and social regimes), restoring the reference value of the social solidarity income and the minimum income benefit, restoring the previous equivalence scales, and increasing the three lowest levels of the child and family allowance.

As mentioned, the poverty rate has been rising among the older population, which may be a worrying sign of the erosion of the buffering effect of pensions and other social transfers, such as the social solidarity income. The reforms of the conditions for entitlement to non-contributory social benefits, implemented in 2010 and reinforced in subsequent years, had perverse effects. Those reforms were 'an alteration that was needed, implemented at the worst possible moment due to the economic and financial crisis, and driven mainly by the need to cut costs' (Rodrigues, 2011: 2).

Women are overrepresented among pensioners, comprising 59.6% of all pension recipients, 47.8% of recipients of an invalidity pension, 53% of recipients of an old-age pension and 81.6% of recipients of a survival pension in 2014 (Estatísticas da Segurança Social, no date). This overrepresentation makes women particularly prone to the freezing of (or even cuts to) pensions and the consequent reduction of their buffering effect in terms of financial security. Moreover, the gender gap in pensions in Portugal remained at 31% in 2012. Women's average monthly pensions were only €606, compared to men's average monthly pensions of €880 (EIGE, 2015). Portugal is also among the member states showing a deterioration in the gender gap in pensions, as well as increased gender pension gap asymmetries in the younger age cohorts. The situation for older Portuguese women worsens significantly for those aged 65 to 69 years (33% gap, on average) in light of recent austerity measures, as compared to those aged 75 years or over (22% gap in pensions) (EIGE, 2015).

Another issue related to social protection that is highly relevant for interpreting the gender pension gap in Portugal is the fact that time spent caring for children is not considered in terms of earning pension credits. According to recent estimates (OECD, 2015), a woman on an average wage who interrupts her career for five years to care for two young children would lose about 10% in pension income on average. If we consider a 10-year interruption, the loss in her pension income would rise to 21%. This represents the greatest disadvantage recorded among the 34 Organisation for Economic Co-operation and Development (OECD) countries. Pension credits only exist in Portugal for women who work part-time in order to care for their children. In the case of part-time workers, women's social security contributions are counted as if they had a full-time job (OECD, 2015).

In recent years, the buffering effect of social protection has been decreasing in Portugal. According to the EU-SILC, in 2014, the poverty rate before social transfers amounted to 47.8%, an increase of 2.4% compared to 2011, although remaining at the same level as in 2013. By including pensions, the poverty rate would be 26.4% (25.5% and 26.7% in the two previous years), while the inclusion of other social transfers decreases the rate to the aforementioned 19.5%. Thus, the influence of transfers other than pensions contributes to a reduction in the poverty rate of 6.9% (6.8% in 2013), which illustrates the continued erosion of the buffering effect of social transfers other than pensions in recent years.

Education and vocational training

Despite the important progress that has been made in the last few decades, Portuguese society is still characterised by relatively low levels of education. Data from the 2011 Census show that the illiteracy rate was 5.2% in 2011; the proportion of women who are illiterate (6.8%) is considerably higher than in the case of men (3.5%) (Pordata, no date). From a gendered life-course perspective, it is worth stressing that illiteracy and low levels of education are particularly evident among older people, and older women in particular, further exacerbating their vulnerability in the labour market, particularly in terms of their incompatibility with highly skilled and better-paid jobs. Considering the population aged 15+ in 2014, 11.9% of women and 5.5% of men lack formal education credentials of any kind.

Nearly 52% of women and 62% of men aged 15+ completed only basic education (INE, no date). However, women are also overrepresented among the highly educated: the percentage of women aged 15+ with higher education is lower than for men in the same age group, 19% and 13.6%, respectively. Furthermore, women are currently 59% of students in higher education in 2013–14 (Pordata, no date). Adequate monitoring and assessment of the interactions between increased access of younger women to education and their integration into the labour market would be crucial to estimate the concrete impacts of these changing patterns in a gendered life-course perspective.

As regards access to training over the life course, women are less likely to have undergone training over their working lives paid for or provided by their employer in Portugal (24% of women and 32% of men); overall in the EU, 33% of women and 34% of men in employment or self-employment received such training (EIGE, 2015). Moreover, Eurostat data show that the percentage of the Portuguese population aged 50–74 that is involved in education and training activities is very low, barely above 1% and less than one third of the corresponding average for the EU27 countries (Perista and Perista, 2012a). Such low participation in formal educational and vocational training schemes places serious constraints on the potential quality of employment at any time during the life course and may compromise continuity in the labour market in later life.

Employment and work

Portugal has often been clustered together with the Mediterranean and Southern European countries in terms of welfare state provisions, gender ideologies and family characteristics (Casaca and Damião, 2011). This categorisation is seen as controversial by some Portuguese researchers, who tend to point out the particular features of the Portuguese context and the country's state of development (for further discussion, see Wall and Amâncio, 2007; Arcanjo, 2011). Moreover, as far as women's employment is concerned, the country is also marked by relevant singularities. Portuguese women have had a long tradition of participation in employment (Ferreira, 1999; Torres et al, 2004; Wall and Amâncio, 2007; Casaca, 2012). This holds particularly true for women aged 25–54 – an age cohort in which the employment rate is relatively high (see Table 7.1), well above that of the countries usually included in the Mediterranean cluster of welfare states (Casaca, 2012). Furthermore, the vast majority of Portuguese women are employed on a full-time basis (see Table 7.1). The figures for full-time employment are lower in older age cohorts, but still relatively high when compared to four of the other seven countries under analysis, and marked by a relatively small gender gap. The main reason reported by women for working on a part-time basis is the difficulty in finding a full-time job, thereby suggesting that this is mostly involuntary part-time work

(Casaca and Bould, 2012). In Portugal, non-voluntary part-time work is particularly high for women, while it is also prevalent among young male workers. The highest gap for involuntary part-time work is found in older cohorts, where the percentage of women involved in involuntary part-time work is nearly double the percentage of men.

Table 7.1: Distinctive patterns of employment in Portugal (2014)

	Women	Men
Employment rates **(25–54 years old)**	74.3%	80.6%
% of full-time employment in total employment **(15–64 years old)**	87.4%	92.4%
% of full-time employment in total employment **(55–64 years old)**	78.3%	85.1%
Involuntary part-time employment as percentage of the total part-time employment (15–64 years old)	53.7%	42.3%
Involuntary part-time employment as percentage of the total part-time employment (55–64 years old)	39.8%	21%

Source: Eurostat: Labour Force Survey.

A relatively high full-time employment rate for women is also found among those who have children, as well as a low gender gap in full-time employment at younger ages. This feature also places Portugal close to the 'Nordic universal breadwinner model' (Karamessini and Rubery, 2014), with most women and men working on a full-time basis throughout adulthood and without any interruption throughout their life course (Torres et al, 2004; Wall and Amâncio, 2007; Casaca, 2012).

Despite such continuity in employment, women tend to be concentrated in the lowest-paid and most precarious jobs in the economy (Casaca, 2012). Moreover, the gender pay gap remains high, with Portuguese women still earning 17.9% and 20.8% less than men in terms of basic wages and total earnings, respectively, in 2013 (CITE 2015).[1] This explains, in part, the gender gap in pensions, mentioned earlier in the chapter. In line with the European Directives and trends elsewhere, early retirement has been discouraged and even financially penalised.

As regards vulnerability in the labour market, the unemployment rate is slightly higher for men in older age cohorts (55–64 years old), and slightly lower among those aged 15–64 (see Table 7.2). For the older age group, the rates are well above the average within the

EU28. Occupational segregation on the grounds of gender seems to account for these patterns as the first industries to be harshly hit by the financial and economic crisis were male–dominated (construction, manufacturing, automotive repair and maintenance) (Casaca, 2012). As for temporary work, there are relatively high levels in Portugal compared to the average of the EU. The relatively higher proportion among men relegated to temporary work is in line with the severe degradation of working conditions among men over recent years. It is worth mentioning that in Portugal, such proportions are much higher among younger generations, adding another wrinkle to considerations of extending working lives or what can reasonably be expected about patterns of work over the life course in the future.

Table 7.2: Patterns of vulnerability in the labour market in Portugal and the EU28 (2014)

	Portugal		EU28	
	Women	Men	Women	Men
Unemployment rates (15–64 years old)	14.8%	14.2%	10.4%	10.2%
Unemployment rates (55–64 years old)	11.4%	15.2%	6.7%	7.9%
Temporary work (15–64 years old)	21.1%	21.6%	14.4%	13.6%
Temporary work (55–64 years old)	9.3%	11.8%	6.6%	6.4%

Source: Eurostat: Labour Force Survey.

The sharp growth of unemployment, coupled with the deterioration in working conditions, has led to increased emigration in recent years, especially among young and highly qualified men and women (Perista and Carrilho, 2016). The intensification of emigration flows will certainly impact on the profile and the dynamics regarding potential caring in Portugal.

Matrilineal intergenerational support has been a key element in the employment of Portuguese women with small children as older women usually take care of their grandchildren, thereby supporting the full-time employment of their own daughters (Albuquerque and Passos, 2010). Such a pattern may explain the sharp decline in female employment rates from the age cohort 50–55 (76.7% in 2013) to the 55–59 age cohort (59.1%) and particularly to the 60–64 one (34%). However, the low wages and poor pensions may also explain why

Portugal has one of the highest employment rates for women aged 65–74 in the EU – 12.1%, while the EU28 average was 6.1%, in 2013 (Eurostat, no date). It should be stressed, however, that looking at labour force participation is not enough to accurately analyse employment patterns. Recent data on the actual weekly working hours and the preferred working hours for those aged 50 and over among the EU28 show that Portugal – immediately after Greece – is the EU country where these workers are putting in the longest weekly working hours: 46 hours, while preferring to work 38 hours per week (Eurofound, 2014).

Age discrimination at the workplace is the most widespread form of discrimination on the grounds of age in the EU. According to data provided by the Eurobarometer, one out of five individuals reported having personally experienced or witnessed it (European Commission, 2012). In Portugal, the self-reported proportion of witnessing or experiencing age discrimination in employment is lower (14%), followed by those who experienced it in health care (12%), financial products and services (10%), education and training (6%), and leisure (5%) (European Commission, 2012). However, at the same time, 84% of Portuguese citizens consider that older people (55 and over) are more likely to be excluded from training in the workplace, and age combined with lack of training is seen as the main reason why people stop working. This perception of ageism in Portugal is the largest proportion in the EU, after that registered by the Greek population (European Commission, 2012). Such a finding is in line with previous research, demonstrating that training and upskilling opportunities are more limited for older workers as employers are less committed to investing in the qualifications of those who are going to retire soon, and learning opportunities provided by most European governments (by public bodies) are also scarce, short-term-oriented and tend to leave out older and non-skilled workers (Gallie, 2002). In Portugal, this is experienced particularly by older women (Pestana, 2004). The Eurobarometer data also show that only half of the Portuguese respondents (52%) say that in Portugal, workplaces are age-friendly, meaning that they are adaptable to the needs of older people (European Commission, 2012). In response to the statement 'the official retirement age should be higher for women than for men to compensate for career breaks', among Portuguese respondents, 42% tend to disagree and 28% totally disagree with it, but 22% totally agree with the statement. Meanwhile, 82% agree that people who give up their careers to raise a family should be entitled to receive part of their partner's pension after their death, and 71% agree that men and women who have a career break in order to have children should have the same pension rights as people who do not (European Commission, 2012).

Work–family life articulation: policy context

Not only is part-time work relatively rare in Portugal, but flexible working-time arrangements are not common either. Most Portuguese workers still have fixed working-time schedules. According to the European Working Conditions Survey 2010, carried out by Eurofound, fewer than one out of three workers (28.3%) in Portugal reported that they did not work at fixed starting and finishing times. The Labour Law enacted in 2009 aimed at promoting greater flexibility in the Portuguese labour market, including the organisation of working time. The introduction of the 'compressed working week' and the 'hours bank/working-time bank' are examples of new legal measures that might be used by Portuguese workers; nonetheless, the available data show that their use has been low.

A new legal framework for parental leave was enacted in 2009. An initial parental leave may be extended to 180 calendar days if shared by both parents. The mother has to take six weeks after the birth, but the remaining period may be shared upon mutual agreement: a total of 120 days fully paid at 100% of earnings; 150 days paid at either 80% or 100%, depending on whether the leave is or is not shared between both parents; or 180 days at 83% if the leave is shared ('sharing bonus' of 30 days). There is also a parental leave available for fathers: a total of 20 working days, 15 of which are mandatory and have to be taken during the first 30 days after birth (fully paid – 100% of earnings). A complementary parental leave up to three months may be taken up by both parents until the child is six years old. It is paid at 25% of average earnings if taken immediately after the initial leave (for one parent at a time). After this leave, one of the parents may take up to two years of 'childcare leave' (unpaid) on a full-time basis (up to three years when there is a third or subsequent child) (see Wall and Leitão, 2015). The new law (120/2015) has also made it possible for both parents to share the parental leave between the 120 and the 150 days. Employees with children under 12 years old, or regardless of their age if disabled or chronically ill, may opt to work on a part-time basis or on a flexible working-time arrangement without any penalty in their career progression. Parents with children up to three years old may request to work from home (telework) in the event of compatibility with job content and tasks and if the employer can implement this. However, the dual-earner model in Portugal has not eroded the asymmetries in the uptake of parental leaves, despite the increase in the proportion of men taking up the mandatory and optional parental leave for fathers.

Gender asymmetries still prevail in the distribution of unpaid care work, which comprises a wide range of time-consuming activities that still remain on women's shoulders (Perista, 2002, 2010, 2014; Rodrigues et al, 2015; Perista et al, 2016). Such disparities are particularly prominent in Portugal. Going beyond a narrow conception of work as referring only to paid employment is thus especially relevant in Portugal when discussing extended working life policies. In the older ages, women provide essential care for ageing parents (and parents-in-law), as well as adult children or grandchildren (Casaca and Bould, 2012), therefore providing care on 'two fronts' (Kröger et al, 2003). As in other Southern European countries, the gender regime in Portugal is still based on 'familialism' and traditional gender ideologies, therefore meaning that the onus for family care is mainly centred on women's work in the family and that an extended working life is not the same for men and women. The significant amount of time devoted to unpaid care work may limit women's availability to remain in the labour market and influences their present and future living conditions (Addis, 2006; Kauppinen, 2010; Perista, 2010, 2014; Bould and Casaca, 2012).

The provision of formal childcare covers 41.8% of Portuguese under the age of three, and 90.9% of those children aged between three and the minimum compulsory school age (data refer to 2012). That is well above the Barcelona target (33%) for 2011, and has more than doubled since the turn of the century (19.8% in 2000) (Wall and Leitão, 2015). Despite the increasing trend, coverage rates are still below families' needs, thereby reinforcing the need for matrilineal intergenerational support mentioned earlier in the chapter.

However, the coverage rate regarding care for older people remained particularly low in Portugal. In 2013 (the latest year available), the coverage rates were 4.3% regarding nursing homes, 3.2% regarding day care centres and 5% regarding home-care services. This is but a small increase from 2000, when the coverage rates were 3.3%, 3.2% and 3%, respectively (Wall and Leitão, 2015).

The primary role filled by older women in both formal and informal care provision in Portugal reflects a highly asymmetric gender division of unpaid caring responsibilities within the family. This is one of the most serious constraints in terms of their labour market participation and accounts for the persistence of low wages and their eventual lower pensions (Bould and Casaca, 2012). Research on gender and ageing in Portugal to date is still rather partial and segmented, underlining the urgent need for a more systematic, comprehensive and intersectional approach to the implications over the life course of extended working lives.

The current debate and future directions for policy and research: extended working life and gender

In Portugal, the policy debate on extended working life has been guided by concerns about reducing the costs of pensions, health care and social protection systems in general, as well as increasing the labour supply and promoting economic growth (Bould and Casaca, 2012). Moreover, a comprehensive national strategy has never been fully developed in terms of measures to implement an extended working life. Policies have been designed in a fragmented and ad hoc way and the concern with retaining older workers in the labour market tends to be gender-blind, ignoring the fact that gender roles in paid work and unpaid care work are not equal. Therefore, older men and women do not have the same opportunities or resources for organising their lives (Bould and Casaca, 2012). In fact, despite the vague reference in the 2012 National Action Programme to gender equality as an intersectional criterion for accomplishing active ageing and solidarity between generations, no specific debate was included regarding the potential differential impact of the planned extended working life measures for women compared to men (Governo de Portugal, 2012). Poverty rates are higher among older women. In Portugal, women have primary responsibility for providing care to older and other family members in need (Perista, 2002, 2010, 2014; Torres et al, 2004; Rodrigues et al, 2015). This gendered pattern of care, on the one hand, limits their participation in employment, their current and future financial resources, and their economic condition, and, on the other hand, may further exacerbate the crisis in care provision for those in need.

Women are much less likely to have participated in formal educational and vocational training activities in employment, which may place serious constraints on the quality of employment and may even compromise continuity in the labour market in later life. The austerity context has exacerbated the lack of formal public care provision. While Portugal has recently been developing a basic care network for children, the provision of in-home care and institutional care for the elderly is still very limited, as discussed earlier in the chapter.

The current context within which pension reforms and extended working life have been debated has intensified the risk of a return to a gender regime based on 'familialism' and traditional gender roles. An extended working life may not be the same for men and women since time devoted to unpaid care work may limit women's availability to upgrade their skills and invest in paid work. Further studies adopting a combination of innovative quantitative and qualitative methodologies are required to shed further light on the gender-differentiated implications of extended working life policies in Portugal. Regardless of the lack of research in this field, it is possible to conclude that a comprehensive gender-sensitive policy framework, combined with a social model based on an equal distribution of paid and unpaid work throughout both women's and men's trajectories, is needed, together with specific incentives to support inclusive models of work organisation and workplace culture that are both age- and gender-friendly.

Note

[1]   These figures differ from the ones provided by Eurostat and are the ones used to monitor the gender pay gap by both national researchers and the official mechanisms for gender equality. They follow the data collected under the survey 'Quadros de Pessoal' (Ministry of Work and Social Security). In this case, the data reflect the payment differentials (presented as percentages) between men and women on a monthly basis, considering not only the basic wage, but also the overall earnings (productivity, performance-related bonuses and other payments – overtime and tenure-related payments).

References

Addis, E. (2006) Unpaid and paid caring work in the reform of welfare states, in A. Picchio (ed) *Unpaid work and the economy, a gender analysis of the standard of living*, London: Routledge, pp 189–223.

Albuquerque, P. and Passos, J. (2010) Grandparents and women's participation in the labour market, WP 16/2010/DE/SOCIUS/CEMAPRE.

Arcanjo, M. (2011) Welfare state regimes and reforms: a classification of ten European countries between 1990 and 2006, *Social Policy and Society*, 10(2), 139–50.

Baptista, I., Perista, P., Cardoso, A., Perista, H., Quaresma, M.L. and Mateus, C. (2015) ESPN country profile Portugal 2015, CESIS/LISER/APPLICA/OSE/DG Employment, Social Affairs and Inclusion, Lisbon.

Bastos, A., Casaca, S., Nunes, F. and Pereirinha, J. (2009) Women and poverty: a gender-sensitive approach, *Journal of Socio-Economics*, 38(5), 764–78.

Bould, S. and Casaca, S.F. (2012) Older women workers and the European Union's employment goals: bringing gender into the debate, *ex aequo*, 26, 27–42.

Casaca, S.F. (2012) Mercado de trabalho, flexibilidade e relações de género: tendências recentes [Labour market, flexibility and gender relations: recent trends], in S.F. Casaca (ed) *Mudanças laborais e relações de género. Novos vetores de desigualdade* [Labour market changes and gender relations. New strands of inequality], Lisboa: Fundação Económicas/ Almedina, pp 9–50.

Casaca, S.F. and Bould, S. (2012) Género, idade e mercado de trabalho [Gender, age and labour market], in S.F. Casaca (ed) *Mudanças laborais e relações de género – novos vetores de desigualdade* [Labour market changes and gender relations. New strands of inequality], Lisboa: Fundação Económicas/Almedina, pp 87–132.

Casaca, S.F. and Damião, S. (2011) Gender (in)equality in the labour market and the Southern European welfare states, in E. Addis, P. de Villota, F. Degavre and J. Eriksen (eds) *Gender and well-being: The role of institutions*, London: Ashgate, pp 183–98.

CITE (Comissão para a Igualdade no Trabalho e no Emprego [Commission for Equality in Labour and Employment]) (2015) Factsheet – 6 de Março: Dia nacional da igualdade salarial [6 March: Equal Wage National Day].

EIGE (European Institute for Gender Equality) (2015) *Gender gap in pensions in the EU. Research note to the Latvian Presidency*, Luxembourg: Publications Office of the European Union.

Estatísticas da Segurança Social [Social Security Statistics] (no date) Estatísticas da Segurança Social. Available at: http://www.seg-social. pt/estatisticas

Eurofound (2014) *Work preferences after 50*, Luxembourg: Publications Office of the European Union.

European Commission (2012) Special Eurobarometer 378 – active ageing report.

Eurostat (no date) Statistics – Population and Social Conditions. Available at: http://ec.europa.eu/eurostat/data/database

Ferreira, V. (1999) Os paradoxos da situação das mulheres em Portugal [The paradoxes of women's situation in Portugal], *Revista Crítica de Ciências Sociais*, 52/53, 199–227.

Gallie, D. (2002) The quality of working like in welfare strategy, in G. Esping-Andersen (ed) *Why we need a new welfare state*, Oxford: Oxford University Press, pp 96–129.

Governo de Portugal (2012) Ano Europeu do Envelhecimento Ativo e da Solidariedade entre Gerações, Programa de ação, 2012/Portugal. Available at: http://www.igfse.pt/upload/docs/2012/Programa%20 A%C3%A7aoAnoEuropeu2012.pdf

INE (Instituto Nacional de Estatística [Statistics Portugal]) (no date) Statistics – Population and Social Conditions. Available at: https://www.ine.pt/xportal/xmain?xpgid=ine_main&xpid=INE

Karamessini, M. and Rubery, J. (2014) Economic crisis and austerity: challenges to gender equality, in M. Karamessini and J. Rubery (eds) *Women and austerity: The economic crisis and the future of gender equality*, New York, NY: Routledge, pp 314–51.

Kauppinen, K. (2010) Who cares when grandmother gets sick?, in T. Addabbo, M.-P. Arrizabalaga, C. Borderias and A. Owens (eds) *Home, work, and family: Gender and well-being in modern Europe*, Farnheim/Burlington: Ashgate Publishing, pp 163–75.

Kröger, T., Sipilä, J., Repo, K., Zechner, M., Martin, C., Debroise, A., Le Bihan, B., Vion, A., Trifiletti, R., Pratesi, A., Simoni, S., Wall, K., Correia, S.V., São José, J., Baldock, J., Hadlow, J. and Larsen, T. (eds) (2003) Families, work and social care in Europe – a qualitative study of care arrangements in Finland, France, Italy, Portugal and the UK, SOCCARE Project Report 6, European Commission.

Naumann, R. (2013) Portugal: the role of governments and social partners in keeping older workers in the labour market, European Observatory of Working Life, Eurofound. Available at: http://www.eurofound.europa.eu/observatories/eurwork/comparative-information/national-contributions/portugal/portugal-the-role-of-governments-and-social-partners-in-keeping-older-workers-in-the-labour-market

OECD (Organisation for Economic Co-operation and Development) (2015) *Pensions at a glance 2015: OECD and G20 indicators*, Paris: OECD Publishing.

Perista, H. (2002) Género e trabalho não pago: os tempos das mulheres e os tempos dos homens [Gender and unpaid work: women's times and men's times], *Análise Social*, 163, 447–74.

Perista, H. (2010) Mulheres, homens e usos do tempo – quinze anos após a Plataforma de Acção de Pequim, onde estamos, em Portugal [Women, men and time use – where are we in Portugal, 15 years after the Beijing Platform for Action], *Revista de Estudos Demográficos*, 47, 47–63.

Perista, H. (2014) Um olhar feminista sobre os usos do tempo [A feminist approach on time use], in E. Ferreira, I. Ventura, L. Rego, M. Tavares and M.A.P. Almeida (eds) *Percursos feministas: desafiar os tempos* [*Feminist paths: Challenging times*], Lisbon: UMAR/Universidade Feminista.

Perista, H. and Carrilho, P. (2016) High, and growing, emigration in a context of high, but slightly decreasing, unemployment: the Portuguese case, European Observatory of Working Life, Eurofound. Available at: http://www.eurofound.europa.eu/observatories/eurwork/articles/working-conditions-labour-market/portugal-high-and-rising-emigration-in-a-context-of-high-but-decreasing-unemployment

Perista, H. and Perista, P. (2012a) *Género e envelhecimento, planear o futuro começa agora – Estudo de diagnóstico [Gender and ageing, planning the future must begin today! Diagnosis study]*, Lisbon: CIG/PCM.

Perista, H. and Perista, P. (2012b) *Género e envelhecimento, planear o futuro começa agora – Recomendações [Gender and ageing, planning the future must begin today! Recommendations]*, Lisbon: CIG/PCM.

Perista, H., Gomes, M.E. and Silva, M. (1993) *A pobreza no feminino na cidade de Lisboa [Women and poverty in the city of Lisbon]*, Lisboa: ONG'S do Conselho Consultivo da CIDM.

Perista, H., Cardoso, A., Brázia, A., Abrantes, M. and Perista, P. (2016) *Os Usos do Tempo de Homens e de Mulheres em Portugal [Time use of men and women in Portugal]*, Lisboa: CESIS, CITE.

Pestana, N. (2004) Os desafios do envelhecimento activo [The challenges of active ageing], *Sociedade e Trabalho*, 21, 71–87.

Pordata (no date) Database – Contemporary Portugal. Available at: http://www.pordata.pt/

Rodrigues, C.F. (2011) Minimum income in Portugal: changing the rules in times of crisis, Host country independent expert paper for the Peer Review on Improving the efficiency of social protection, Lisbon 29–30 November. Available at: http://ec.europa.eu/social/BlobServlet?docId=8043&langId=en

Rodrigues, L., Cunha, V. and Wall, K. (2015) Policy brief I – homens, papéis masculinos e igualdade de género [Men, male roles and gender equality], Instituto de Ciências Sociais da Universidade de Lisboa/Comissão para a Igualdade no Trabalho e no Emprego.

Torres, A., Silva, F., Monteiro, T. and Cabrita, M. (2004) *Homens e mulheres, entre família e trabalho [Men and women between family and work]*, Lisbon: DEEP/CITE.

Wall, K. and Amâncio, L. (2007) *Família e género em Portugal e na Europa [Family and gender in Portugal and in Europe]*, Lisbon: Imprensa de Ciências Sociais.

Wall, K. and Leitão, M. (2015) Portugal country note, in P. Moss (ed) *International review of leave policies and research 2014*. Available at: http://www.leavenetwork.org/lp_and_r_reports/

EIGHT

Sweden: an extended working life policy that overlooks gender considerations

Clary Krekula, Lars-Gunnar Engström and Aida Alvinius

Introduction

When the Swedish debate on raising the retirement age began in the early 1990s, the country was in deep financial crisis and joint efforts were being made across the political parties to stabilise the economy. In the same spirit, a broad political collaboration sought to create a reformed pension system, where the question of retirement age was central. The problem was said to be increasing life expectancy and a pension system that was dependent on economic growth. The goal was therefore to lower the costs of the national pension system and to reduce the financial burden for workers (Government Bill, 1992/93). In 1994, the parliamentary collaboration created a new old-age pension system (Ds, 2009: 53) that included the implementation of a flexible retirement age between 61 and 67 years.

In the autumn of 2015, the government, in collaboration with the multiparty pensions group, which has existed since the 1990s, stated its intent to propose raising the minimum retirement age within the near future, in accordance with international recommendations (see European Commission, 2009; OECD, 2006). Increasing life expectancy and the financing of the pension system surfaced again as arguments for reform. However, policymakers also emphasised that many people do not have the physical ability to work until the age of 65, in light of sick-leave statistics for women in the public sector, and that it is therefore important to highlight the occupational health and safety issues before raising the retirement age (SVT Nyheter, 2015).

Two decades of unanimous arguments convey the impression that raising the retirement age is a unique rational solution to an objective and unambiguous problem. However, in line with Bacchi (1999, 2009), we argue that political proposals are flawed in that they are based on limited articulations of the problem to be solved and on a simultaneous exclusion of other possible perspectives. Policy documents on retirement age are, thus, not objective solutions to problems; rather, they are proactive actions that focus on some aspects and play down others (Bacchi, 2009).

From this starting point, the Swedish labour market from a gender and age perspective is considered, looking at the Swedish pension system and the perceived obstacles to an extended working life. Analysis of the assumptions made about the older workforce in the government inquiry challenges the starting point for the current negotiations on a raised retirement age, the Government Commission for Longer Working Life and Retirement Age (SOU, 2013). The chapter concludes with an in-depth gender analysis and an argument addressing which socio-political changes have been central in the development of the approach to retirement age.

A gender-segregated labour market and an age-blind gender policy

Sweden is a country with one of the highest proportions of older people in its population. In 2015, 19.8% of the Swedish population was over the age of 65 (Statistics Sweden, 2016). Sweden is frequently described as 'one of the world's most gender equal countries' and as the country with the highest amount of feminists (SOU, 2005). The reconciliation of family life and work is a central topic in national gender-equality goals, where older people are only referred to as old-age pension and older care recipients, that is, defined with respect to being older, and not as citizens in a wider sense. This description of the family life–work balance, with its focus on a fertile and working woman, tends to become 'age-blind' in that it renders older women's experiences invisible (Krekula, 2007, 2012).

A total of 83% of Swedish women are in gainful employment, compared to 89% of men (Statistics Sweden, 2014). Within the age group 55–64, 71.5% of the women and 76.3% of the men worked in 2014 (Eurostat, 2016), which is high from an international perspective and clearly exceeds the 50% recommended by the European Union (EU) (European Commission, 2009). During the past 10 years, the labour force participation rate has also gradually increased in the older age groups: among men aged 65–69, between 2006 and 2015, it has risen from 17% to 27%, and among women in this age group from 10% to 18%. One explanation given for this increase is that the birth cohorts now reaching retirement age are in better health and have higher educational levels; another is that recent political decisions have made it financially beneficial to postpone retirement (SOU, 2010). Despite high levels of employment, working hours decrease with age. Among the gainfully employed between ages 65 and 69, men work, on average, 29.8 hours/week and women 24.8 hours/week (Swedish Pensions Agency, 2016).

In 2013, 30% of all women worked part time (Statistics Sweden, 2014). Within female-dominated health-care professions, part-time and temporary employment has become almost a norm (Wall, 2014). In the female-dominated professions of the Swedish Municipal Workers' Union (Kommunal), 57% of women and 53% of men work part time, compared to the union's male-dominated professions, where 84% of the men and 67% of the women work full time. Part-time work is mostly explained by a lack of suitable full-time jobs. Women are, thus, affected by involuntary part-time unemployment to a greater extent than men. This could lead to a weaker connection with the labour market and greater difficulties remaining in working life in the long term (Wall, 2014).

Swedish women, on average, earn 86% of men's wages. Women over the age of 65 in 2012 received 66% of the men's pension (Adolphson, 2015), an even wider gap. These economic differences between women and men are due to the fact that women generally have lower wages, are more likely to work part time than men and still carry a significantly heavier load in terms of housework and childcare than men do, for example, through longer parental leave (Wall, 2014). Parental leave is, however, included when calculating pension entitlements.

The Swedish pension system

In 1913, the state pension was implemented for people at the age of 67. This retirement age has remained mostly unchanged despite two large pension reforms. The first of these reforms was introduced in 1959, when the Swedish Parliament decided to implement the *Allmän Tilläggspension* (Supplementary Pension) (ATP) system. This meant that the previous old-age pension from 1913, which was based on a flat rate, was complemented by income-related benefits. The benefits were now based on a worker's 15 best income years, but to receive a full pension, one had to have been working for 30 years. This led to a pension system where an average worker received 65% of their former gross income. The pension system was mainly financed by payroll taxes and was based on pay-as-you-go principles (Sundén, 2006). Intermediate-level white-collar workers with an income unevenly distributed over life are usually described as winners in this pension system, whereas lower-level white-collar and blue-collar workers with flatter lifecycle incomes were less favoured by the pension model (Ståhlberg et al, 2006).

During the 1970s, the political debate around pensions focused on differences between those who were included in retirement schemes, for example, occupational pension, and those who received pensions in accordance with the national pension insurance (SOU, 1974, 1975). Most employees of the time with a collective agreement had already been ensured a lower retirement age than 67 through pension schemes outside of national insurance. Housewives and individual entrepreneurs, including farmers, were among those who still could not retire until age 67. Lowering the retirement age within the national pension system was thus seen as a matter of fairness (SOU, 1974). The outcome of the debate resulted in a lower retirement age of 65 years and a concurrent expansion of the flexible retirement age to a period between 60 and 70 years, with individual assessment of early retirement, that is, greater flexibility than today. Housewives made up one of the central target groups for the reform.

During the 1980s and early 1990s, there were new debates on reforming the pension system. Demographic developments, with greater life expectancy in combination with a younger workforce that started employment later, led to concern about financial sustainability problems with the benefit-based pension schemes. This led to the second large pension reform, where a new system was implemented in 2001. The recent system is based on contribution-based schemes with a pay-as-you-go principle. For those with low lifetime earnings, the pensions system also includes a minimum guaranteed benefit as a poverty safety net.

Whereas the individual's pension in the old ATP system was based on the 15 best income years, after the 2001 reforms, the public pension was based on the total income of a person's working life. The so-called lifelong earnings principle was described as perhaps the most important change to achieve better financial sustainability in the system through a strong connection between contributions and benefits. However, the new system also contained many other components that aimed to create incentives to continue working into old age, for example, a lower gross replacement rate for unchanged retirement behaviour in relation to the old system and a raised age limit for the earliest pension (SOU, 2012).

Simulations of the new pension system outcomes forecasted that women would be able to receive higher replacement rates than men

(Ståhlberg et al, 2006). However, studies based on actual pension outcomes show that women receive a relatively lower pension in relation to final income than men, even when taking into account income levels as well as in which sector they have been working. This is explained by the fact that for many women, their professional careers have to a large extent consisted of part-time work (Öjemark, 2016).

There is also a large difference between how much women and men are affected by the basic insurance in the pension system, that is, the guaranteed minimum pension. In 2014, 56% of women with pensions received a full or part-guaranteed pension; the corresponding number among men was 16% (Swedish Pensions Agency, 2016). These differences reflect women's generally lower wages and greater extent of part-time work.

Retirement patterns

The average retirement age in Sweden has continued to increase in recent years (SOU, 2010). In 1998, the retirement age was 61.8 for women and 62.7 for men; in 2008, it had risen to 62.7 and 63.7. By 2015, it had further increased and is now at 64.6 for women and somewhat less for men, at 64.4 (Swedish Pensions Agency, 2016).

Gender, level of education, marital status and income are described as central factors that determine whether or not a person continues to work after the age of 65 (SOU, 2010). Overall, current retirement patterns imply that more men than women stay gainfully employed after the age of 65, even though the average level of education among women is increasing at a higher rate than among men.

Married or cohabiting people tend to retire earlier than single people; high demands on employees in terms of working efficiently, as well as poor health, also contribute to early exits and economic incentives such as the existence of collective agreement pensions create an increased tendency to leave working life early. The same can be seen among individuals with an average income level above the ceiling in the public old-age pension system (The Swedish National Audit Office, 2001). Family, leisure time and the opportunities that come with the collective agreement pension also contribute to early retirement, while the profitability of continued employment and opportunities for part-time and flexible working hours may contribute to postponed retirement, as well as the fact that a lot of people continue to work longer because they find it enjoyable and stimulating (Arnek, 2012). Work satisfaction and perceived health/poor health is more important for a lot of people than income (Nilsson, 2013).

There has been a slight change in terms of which factors contribute to the will to retire. More time with family and friends and more leisure time are less important today than earlier. The same applies to negative working conditions and little appreciation for the competence held by older workers. However, the feeling of being forced to retire seems to be an increasingly important factor (SOU, 2012). This illustrates that local organisational discourses and practices can diverge from the hegemonic political imperative on extended working life.

Identified obstacles against an extended working life

Ageism and age discrimination are described as an obstacle to older people's participation in the labour market (European Commission, 2009). In 2009, a law against age discrimination was introduced in Sweden. This was not based on the phenomenon having been identified as a problem; rather, it was based on age as a ground of discrimination as part of the EU labour market directives (2000/78/EG), which state that it should be possible to implement the principle of equal treatment in the member states (Article 1). Consequently, in the current Government Commission for Longer Working Life and Retirement Age (SOU, 2013), age discrimination is for the first time related to the question of an extended working life. The document emphasises the need for continuous measures against age discrimination, for example, through tougher legislation. Swedish studies show that discrimination against older people in working life might be widespread (Stålhammar, 2009; Krekula, 2011; Arnek, 2012). A survey of 1053 Swedes between the ages of 18 and 65 shows that a third of those applying for jobs experienced that their age was an issue – applying primarily to the youngest and oldest age categories, and to those who are unemployed (Mild Nygren and Sjöberg, 2012). A focus group study presents recruitment as particularly critical and also identifies discrimination against older people in terms of not being allowed access to training resources. It also sheds light on the fact that age codings, that is, the assumption that age groups are more or less suitable for different work tasks, are used as a basis to organise workplaces, which, in turn, results in horizontally age-segregated workplaces (Krekula, 2010, 2011). There is, however, a lack of knowledge on how age discrimination and other types of ageism relate to retirement behaviour among older workers.

Voices in the European debate on an extended working life have emphasised adult education as a central concern. For example, the European Commission's (2010) *Agenda for new skills and jobs* identified the need to address upskilling in the older workforce as a priority.

Sweden has long had a well-developed system of adult education compared to other European countries (EAEA, 2011). Nearly 72% of persons aged 20–64 years participated in some form of either formal or informal education or training during a 12-month period (Statistics Sweden, 2014). However, in the age group 55–64, Sweden ranks low in terms of the number of people who raise their formal education level, which can partly be explained by the fact that many people are denied further training after the age of 50 (Halvorsen and Tägtström, 2013). Adult education only contributes towards increased income to a limited extent, but it may threaten wage development and employment security (SOU, 2013). Men and highly educated people participate to a greater extent in formal as well as informal training (Krekula and Engström, 2015). The absence of directed initiatives that empower older people's participation in labour market training indicates that Swedish adult education has not had as its main objective to create conditions for an extended working life; rather, the ambition has been to empower low-skilled groups – it has been based on a justice perspective focusing on class (Krekula and Engström, 2015).

The working environment is frequently presented as a central factor that affects possibilities for an extended working life (SOU, 2013). Studies on women who work within, for example, health care show that precarious conditions with uncertain contracts of employment and less control and stability have a negative effect on the length of their working life. One cause could be that those with uncertain and temporary employment are called in when the workload is at its heaviest and that they often work for more than one employer in order to obtain a sufficient income, leading to physical and psychosocial strain (Anxo et al, 2014).

Women run a higher risk of being forced into sick leave (Ryderheim, 2015). The highest amount of sick leave caused by poor mental health can be found within the female-dominated workplaces of school, health and geriatric care (Granlund, 2015). Among women in municipalities and county council organisations, the psychosocial working environment is described as the primary cause behind sick leave (Leppänen et al, 2006). Female sectors such as nursing and social services have been described as having a work situation where there is not enough time, which leads to stress and, in turn, may cause anxiety and depression among employees (Eriksson, 2009). This ties in well with the comprehensive research that has illustrated the presence of a leaner work organisation and how this creates stress among staff (see, eg, Chatterjee and Hambrick, 2007). Female-dominated professions often include heavier demands, less control, more temporary employment and lower wages, and workplace-related violence also tends to be higher for women than for men (Ryderheim, 2015).

As has also been pointed out by feminist scholars (Lewis, 2006; OECD, 2011; Dewilde, 2012), the possibility to keep on working is related to whether an individual is caring for close family members. In a Swedish study, 4.5% of women and 1.5% of men in the age group 55–74 stated that they worked part time or had left work to care for an elderly family member. Out of these carers, 9% of women and 6% of men stated that they had cut their working hours to do so (Szebehely, 2014). Therefore, women risk being in a situation in the later part of their working life where caring for a family member has significant consequences for their gainful employment, to a greater extent than men. This is related to cuts in publically funded elderly care at the same time as the elderly population is growing. As an example, there has been a 25% cut in the number of places in nursing homes during the 21st century, which has increased need for family care (Ulmanen, 2015). Between 1994 and 2000, the amount of care provided by family members rose from 60% to 70% out of the total care given to elderly people living at home (Sundström et al, 2002). This illustrates that the question of an extended working life cannot be limited to work organisations, but needs to be seen from a wider perspective (see Chapter Two).

Starting point of the debate: a homogenisation of older people as a group

In this section, the policy document that forms the basis for today's political debate on an extended working life are discussed by problematising the assumptions about the older workforce that are applied regarding a raised retirement age. The Government Commission for Longer Working Life and Retirement Age (SOU, 2013) was based on many smaller research and commission reports and had broad parliamentary support. The commission presented about 50 proposals, with different measures to achieve an extended working life. For example, it proposed raising the earliest retirement age from 61 to 62, and raising it by another year in the future. Further, it was proposed that the protection of employment should be raised from age 67 to age 69, and that the age limits for the earliest draw of occupational pension should be raised.

The explicit goal: increased labour supply

In the policy document, the need for extended working life is
presented as inevitable and necessary to achieve an increased number
of older workers. Examples of this abound in the arguments, where
the ageing population and the stagnating older workforce are
described as challenges that:

> have been known for some time. A number of reforms
> have thus been implemented which *contribute to an increased
> labour supply*, such as pension reform, in–work tax credit and
> reduced social security contributions for older people....
> The inquiry has, however, reached the conclusion that *the
> improvements are not enough*. (SOU, 2013: 124, emphases
> added)

The quote presents examples of efforts that have been implemented to
make older people retire later in life, but that have only limited success
when it comes to increasing labour supply.

The goal to increase the labour supply can be viewed against the
statistics which show that the number of long-term unemployed
people increases significantly between the age groups 45–54 and 55–64
(Statistics Sweden, 2014). The reasoning of the document regarding
the goal of increased labour supply – a goal that is not backed up
by arguments – can be seen in relation to Standing's (2011; see also
Chapter Two) argument that an ageing population makes up a driving
force for the growth of the precariat since older workers can be used
as a growing source of cheap labour.

A focus on those who are willing to continue working

The current policy report on raised retirement age (SOU, 2013) is
mainly based on a relatively homogeneous categorisation of older
people. It is not that the document ignores differences among older
people entirely; there are some arguments that are based on an
awareness that older people differ. For example, it states that not
everyone can continue to work later in life, that many retire early due
to illness and that people with lower education have poorer working
conditions and lower wages and also retire early. The document states
that: 'Even though many people are unable to continue to work it is
important that those who are able, willing and have the energy to do
so, are given the right to work for a couple more years' (SOU, 2013:
129). The discussion considers an improved working environment to

counteract illness later in life and to avoid repetitive strain injuries via efforts aimed at younger people as well. Starting from the idea that extended working life may lead to bigger health problems for those who are already worn out from heavy labour, the document also underscores the importance of financial stability for those who, for health reasons, are not able to work anymore.

However, when identifying the obstacles to extending working life, this more refined understanding of heterogeneity among older people seems to disappear. In fact, the problems that many older workers face are simply turned into a non-question in relation to an extended working life. This is evident, for example, in the following quote:

> The older workforce is a heterogeneous group and the differences between individuals increase with age. Efforts for a longer working life need to be adapted to these variations. It is not reasonable to keep obstacles for a longer working life when more and more people are able and willing to continue working, *simply because there are still people who cannot work throughout an entire working life.* (SOU, 2013: 145, emphasis added)

That there are groups for whom an extended working life is not possible is not defined, as stated in the quote, as an obstacle to an extended working life more generally. Instead, a categorisation based on *those who are able and willing to continue working* is constructed. It is the obstacles that *this able and willing group* faces to an extended working life that the inquiry focuses on. This delimitation gets its logic in the formulations of what is needed to increase the number of working hours among older people:

> The inquiry has reached the conclusion that the weak employment development and the unchanged retirement patterns are, to a great extent, due to different obstacles for those who are willing and able to continue working into old age or even an entire working life. (SOU, 2013: 127)

Thus, it is by creating longer working lives for those who are able and willing to continue working that the inquiry argues that employment rates among older people will increase.

A homogenisation of older people for changed retirement behaviour

In the document, there are recurrent arguments stating that '*current retirement behaviour is outdated and therefore needs to change*'; this transpires, for example, in statements that it is 'anachronistic that so many still consider it acceptable that well-educated and healthy people in their 60s leave the labour market permanently' (SOU, 2013: 130). In statements like this, older people are again treated as a homogeneous group with presumed good health and high skill levels. Such a one-sided description represents an oversimplification in relation to the huge body of research that illustrates the variations that exist among groups of older people in terms of health improvements. One obvious example is that women, despite having a higher life expectancy than men, in many respects also have poorer health. Such gender differences in poor health persist to the oldest age groups and are described as a gender paradox in health (Schön, 2011). The one-sided description is an example of the type of ageism that Tornstam (2006) refers to as 'consistently positive'. In the inquiry, the homogeneous descriptions of older people's health and education as improved are an essential starting point in order to create the assumption that the time for retirement can be *either* up to *or* out of date. This downplays differences in health among the older workforce.

An unproblematic assertion that the pension system is out of date can also be found in descriptions of anachronistic age rules, values and attitudes in society. Again, homogeneous descriptions of older people are applied to bolster claims that these have not kept up with changes, 'where older people are getting more and more healthy, clever and skilled' (SOU, 2013: 128) and where a growing number of older people are able and willing to continue working. By connecting the arguments on improved health and education to a homogeneous framing of older people, those who do not live up to this, that is, people with poorer health and lower skill levels, are excluded. Thus, the homogenisation is not a broad and inclusive approach to meeting the needs of all Swedish elders. It can, however, be seen as a well-adapted building block in the inquiry's arguments that there must be new, more up-to-date retirement behaviour among older people, shifting responsibility for extending working life to the implied appropriate willingness and behaviour of individuals to continue in employment.

That the policy document aims to change retirement behaviour is clear from the fact that further arguments are used to this end. This can be seen in the statement that:

> An unchanged retirement behaviour would mean that the pension system would, over time, serve a different purpose than what it was designed for. The pensions would turn into a type of leisure insurance which provides older people with more and more work-free years during their lifetime. (SOU, 2013: 176)

The description of life as a pensioner – and thus also of the time that workers do not spend in working life – as a time free of responsibilities and obligations is to disregard the comprehensive research, which is discussed earlier in the chapter, which shows that a big part of the so-called leisure time is work, by many, spent caring for family members. This idea that hours outside of an employment relationship – and thus also the time as a pensioner – are free from responsibilities also neglects the fact that large groups of women today already leave the labour force before the current normative retirement age of 65 because they must work to care for older family members. The statements in the inquiry that an unchanged retirement age risks pensions developing into a leisure insurance illustrates a lack of knowledge about the reality that applies to large groups of older people, primarily older women (see also Lewis, 2006; Dewilde, 2012). Put differently, the older people who have been used as a starting point for the analysis are not only expected to be healthy and well educated, they are also expected to live a life without any broader obligations or care commitments in relation to others.

Concluding discussion

In this chapter, the assumptions about older people that have been used as a benchmark in the Swedish government inquiry that makes up the basis for the current political ambitions to raise the retirement age have been problematised. It has been shown that the debate on extending working life does not just regulate the retirement age; it also institutionalises notions of older people and upholds central social discourses, for example, a neoliberal view of the older individual (see also Chapter Two).

The homogeneous description of the older workforce that has been illustrated in this chapter stands in stark contrast with the explicitly heterogeneous description that was used in the debate in the 1970s on a reduced retirement age. In the earlier debate, the heterogenisation of the older labour force was aimed to improve the retirement and pension conditions for disadvantaged groups. Put differently, during the 1970s, the pension change was a reform to develop the welfare system, while contemporary debates are about a change that aims to strengthen the national economy, a transition in focus that has also been described as a shift from rights to responsibility (Lewis and Giuillari, 2005). Despite an awareness that groups of older people already leave working life before the current minimum retirement age of 61, the change has led to less and less flexibility over time; the pension range in the 1970s of 60–70 has today turned into 61–67.

Although the policy document discussed here has been analysed to discern the consequences of the proposals from a gender-equality perspective, this is carried out without problematising the factors outside of working life that lead to early retirement, for example, greater care responsibilities for older family members (for a further discussion, see Chapter Two). This is in sharp contrast to the rich research which has illustrated that women's participation in working life depends on surrounding social factors and structural conditions, such as a well-developed childcare system (Leitner and Wroblewski, 2006). This leads to a narrow understanding of gender equality, which deviates from the view of other national political documents on gender equality (Krekula, 2015). By treating issues of gender equality and the relation between women and men using other starting points than those applied in the prevalent national understanding of gender equality, the debate on extending working life contributes to excluding older women and men from the Swedish gender-equality project. In light of the central position that the gender-equality ambitions hold in Swedish politics, as well as the fact that they are described as part of Swedish national identity, the debate on extending working life thereby contributes to excluding older people from a fundamental national political discourse and practice (Krekula, 2015).

In the ambition to change older people's retirement behaviour, the policy document analysed here (SOU, 2013) claims, as shown earlier in this chapter, that behaviour must change to avoid the risk of turning the pension into a leisure insurance. This view on employment-free time is not new. A big debate was sparked in Sweden in 1983 when the then chairman of the Swedish Trade Union Confederation, in a debate about six-hour working days, stated that a shortened work day would create problems because it would lead to more people spending more time in front of the TV. The statement caused a big stir at the time and the chairman of the union was criticised for his lack of knowledge about the reality that his women members were living in, with stress and difficulties in managing both work and family responsibilities (Axelsson, 1983). Now, as the same line of argumentation is being used as a basis in the debate on retirement age, the insinuation of 'too much' leisure has been met with silence. This can be seen as an illustration that the question of retirement age is not framed as a gender-equality issue in the same way as the previous debate on shorter working days was.

An overall point in the preceding argument is that the current debate on an extended working life uses arguments that enable a proposal that is adapted to those who are willing and able to continue working later in life. Those who are not able to keep on working due to repetitive strain injuries, heavy jobs or informal care are instead referred to the social security scheme or to the prospect that a gradually improved working environment will make it possible for them to cope. Despite the starting point of the Government Commission for Longer Working Life and Retirement Age that an extended working life is needed to ensure the value of pensions, this does not apply to those who are *not able* to continue working. To them, it is not a matter of getting the pension to last throughout the rest of their lives; instead, they are expected to rely on the social security scheme. With this, two different future scenarios are presented for the older workforce: on the on hand, for those who are able and willing to work, there are promises of a secure economic situation; while, on the other hand, there is an acceptance that those who are not able to work anymore are excluded from the labour market, and thus also placed in a situation of financial insecurity. The focus on those who are able and willing to continue working seems reasonable on its face, but from a more comprehensive social perspective, it means that change that is equitable and broad based is put at a low level. If the pension debate had been based on those who struggle the most to continue working instead, it would have forced a more profound change in terms of the organisation both of working life and of obstacles in society in general, and paid far more attention to women's experiences. By settling for the removal of the obstacles that, in this respect, the most privileged groups of older people face in working life, it seems likely to result in greater inequalities and injustices among older people.

References
Adolphson, D. (2015) Pensionsrapport [Pension report], AMF. Available at: http://mb.cision.com/Public/1040/9915053/9a7424 97e9757528.pdf

Anxo, D., Månsson, J. and Ivarsson, E. (2014) *Sambandet mellan arbetsmiljö och beslutet att lämna arbetskraften* [*The connection between working environment and the decision to leave the labour force*], Stockholm: The Swedish Work Environment Authority.

Arnek, M. (2012) *Skäl till att gå i pension eller inte* [*Reasons to retire or not*], Pensionsmyndigheten analyserar 2012:1, Stockholm: The Swedish Pensions Agency.

Axelsson, P. (1983) Nye LO-chefen: 6-timmars arbetsdag, Javisst, men ... Vad ska vi göra med all fritid? [The new president of the Swedish Trade Union Confederation: 6-hour working day, sure, but ... what are we going to do with all our leisure time?], *Vi mänskor*, 3, 12–15.

Bacchi, C. (1999) *Women, policy and politics: The construction of policy problems*, London: SAGE.

Bacchi, C. (2009) *Analysing policy: What's the problem represented to be?*, Frenchs Forest, NSW: Pearson.

Chatterjee, A. and Hambrick, D. (2007) It's all about me: narcissistic CEOs and their effects on company strategy and performance, *Administrative Science Quarterly*, 52(3), 351–86.

Dewilde, C. (2012) Life course determinants and incomes in retirement: Belgium and the United Kingdom compared, *Ageing and Society*, 32, 587–615.

Ds (2009) *Detta* är *pensionsöverenskommelsen* [*This is the pension agreement*], Official Reports of the Swedish Government, 2009:53, Stockholm: Fritzes.

EAEA (European Association for the Education of Adults) (2011) *Country report on adult education in Sweden*, Helsinki: EAEA.

Eriksson, U.-B. (2009) *'Man är ju inte mer än människa': Långtidssjukskrivning ur ett emotionellt, relationellt och strukturellt perspektiv* [*'One is only human': Long-term sick leave from an emotional, relational and structural perspective*], Karlstad: Karlstad University Studies 2009:2.

European Commission (2009) *Dealing with the impact of an ageing population in the EU*, Brussels: European Commission.

European Commission (2010) *An agenda for new skills and jobs: a European contribution towards full employment*, Brussels: European Commission.

Eurostat (2016) Employment statistics. Available at: http://ec.europa.eu/eurostat/statistics-explained/index.php/Employment_statistics

Government Bill (1992/93) *Om höjd pensionsålder* [*On raised retirement age*], 1992/93:155, Stockholm: Swedish Riksdag.

Granlund, L. (2015) Friskt liv i sikte? En rapport om sjuknärvaron i välfärdstjänstesektorn [A healthy life in sight? A report on sick attendance in the welfare service sector], The Swedish Municipal Workers' Union.

Halvorsen, B. and Tägtström, J. (2013) Det dreier seg om helse og arbeidsglede: Om seniorer, arbeid og pensjonering i Norden [A matter of health and job satisfaction: on seniors, work and retirement in the Nordic countries], *TemaNord 2013:519*. Available at: http://norden. diva-portal.org/smash/get/diva2:700971/FULLTEXT01.pdf

Krekula, C. (2007) The intersection of age and gender: reworking gender theory and social gerontology, *Current Sociology*, 55(2), 155–71.

Krekula, C. (2010) Age coding: on age-based practices of distinction, *International Journal of Ageing and Later Life*, 4(2), 7–31.

Krekula, C. (2011) Åldersdiskriminering *i svenskt arbetsliv: Om ålderskodningar och myter som skapar ojämlikhet* [*Age discrimination in Swedish working life: On age codings and myths which create inequality*], Stockholm: Official report from the Ombudsman for Discrimination.

Krekula, C. (2012) With equality on the agenda: an age perspective on Swedish gender mainstreaming, in M. Jansdotter Samuelsson, C. Krekula and M. Åberg (eds) *Gender and change: Power, politics and everyday practices*, Karlstad: Karlstad University Press, 165–77. Available at: http://jamda.ub.gu.se/bitstream/1/864/1/gender_change.pdf

Krekula, C. (2015) Extending working lives in the context of gender equality mainstreaming, Paper presented at the 12th Conference of the European Sociological Association, Prague.

Krekula, C. and Engström, L.-G. (2015) Swedish adult education: an undeveloped road towards an extended working life, *Public Policy & Aging Report*, 25, 4, 125–8.

Leitner, A. and Wroblewski, A. (2006) Welfare states and work–life balance. Can good practices be transferred from the Nordic countries to conservative welfare states?, *European Societies*, 8(2), 295–317.

Leppänen, V., Jönsson, S., Peterson, H. and Tranquist, J. (2006) Villkor i arbete med människor – en inledning [Conditions when working with people – an introduction], in H. Peterson, V. Leppänen, S. Jönsson and J. Tranquist (eds) *Villkor i arbete med människor – en antologi om human servicearbete* [*Conditions when working with people – an anthology on human service work*], Stockholm: Arbetsliv i omvandling, 2006:4, pp 1–18.

Lewis, J. (2006) Work/family reconciliation, equal opportunities and social policies: the interpretation of policy trajectories at the EU level and the meaning of gender equality, *Journal of European Public Policy*, 13(3), 420–37.

Lewis, J. and Giullari, S. (2005) The adult worker model family, gender equality and care: the search for new policy principles and the possibilities and problems of a capabilities approach, *Economy and Society*, 34(1), 76–104.

Mild Nygren, G. and Sjöberg, A.-S. (2012) *Du har fel ålder: Om åldersnojan på arbetsmarknaden* [*You have the wrong age: On age anxiety on the labour market*], Stockholm: Trygghetsrådet. Available at: https://www.trr.se/globalassets/dokument/material/du-har-fel-alder.pdf

Nilsson, K. (2013) *To work or not to work in an extended working life? Factors in working and retirement decisions*, Lund: Lund University.

OECD (Organisation for Economic Co-operation and Development) (2006) *Live longer, work longer*, Paris: OECD.

OECD (2011) *Help wanted? Providing and paying for long-term care*, Paris: OECD.

Öjemark, F (2016) *Hur stor blir pensionen?* [*How much pension will I get?*], Stockholm: Min Pension. Available at: http://mb.cision.com/Publi c/1011/9964990/976c3e7e3feb1cd3.pdf

Ryderheim, M. (2015) *Kvinnors arbetsmiljö 2011–2014* [*Women's working environment 2011–2014*], Stockholm: The Swedish Work Environment Authority.

Schön, P. (2011) *Gender matters: Differences and change in disability and health among our oldest women and men*, Stockholm: Stockholm University.

SOU (Statens Offentliga Utredningar. [Official Reports of the Swedish Government]) (1974) *Sänkt pensionsålder m.m.: Betänkande av pensionsålderskommitten* [*Lowered retirement age etc.: Report by the Retirement Age Committee*], 1974:15, Stockholm: Ministry of Health and Social Affairs.

SOU (1975) *Rörlig pensionsålder: Betänkande av pensionsålderskommittén* [*Flexible retirement age: Report by the Retirement Age Committee*], 1975:10, Stockholm: Ministry of Health and Social Affairs.

SOU (2005) *Makt att forma samhället och sitt eget liv – jämställdhetspolitiken mot nya mål* [*Power to shape society and one's own life – new objectives in the gender equality policy*], 2005:66, Stockholm: Fritzes.

SOU (2010) *Vem arbetar efter 65 års ålder? En statistisk analys* [*Who works after the age of 65? A statistical analysis*], 2010:85, Stockholm: Fritzes.

SOU (2012) *Längre liv, längre arbetsliv, förutsättningar och hinder för äldre att arbeta längre* [*Longer life, longer working life, conditions and obstacles for older people to work longer*], 2012:28, Stockholm: Fritzes.

SOU (2013) *Åtgärder för ett längre arbetsliv. Slutbetänkande av Pensionsåldersutredningen* [Measures for an extended working life. Final report by the Government Commission for Longer Working Life and Retirement Age], 2013:25.

Ståhlberg, A.-C., Cohen Birman, M., Kruse, A. and Sundén, A. (2006) Pension reforms and gender: the case of Sweden, *Gender Issues*, 23(1), 90–118.

Stålhammar, J. (2009) Sweden, in N. ten Bokum, T. Flanagan, R. Sands and R. von Steinau-Steinrück (eds) *Age discrimination law in Europe*, New York, NY: Wolter Kluwer Law & Business, pp 347–52.

Standing, G. (2011) *The precariat: The new dangerous class*, New York, NY: A & C Black.

Statistics Sweden (2014) Vuxnas deltagande i utbildning 2011/2012 [Adults' participation in education 2011/2012], Theme report 2014:3, education, Statistics Sweden.

Statistics Sweden (2016) Äldre i befolkningen [Older people in the population]. Available at: http://www.scb.se/sv_/Hitta-statistik/Statistik-efter-amne/Befolkning/Befolkningens-sammansattning/Befolkningsstatistik/#c_li_120253

Sundén, A. (2006) The Swedish experience with pension reform, *Oxford Review of Economic Policy*, 22(1), 133–48.

Sundström, G., Johansson, L. and Hassing, L.B. (2002) The shifting balance of long-term care in Sweden, *Gerontologist*, 42(3), 347–52.

SVT Nyheter (2015) Regeringen: Pensionsåldern bör höjas [The Swedish Government: The retirement age should be raised], 20 October. Available at: http://www.svt.se/nyheter/inrikes/regeringen-snart-hojs-pensionsaldern

Swedish Pensions Agency (2016) *Medelpensioneringsålder och utträdesålder* [*Expected effective retirement age and retirement age*], 2016:3, Stockholm: The Swedish Pensions Agency.

Szebehely, M. (2014) Anhörigomsorg, förvärvsarbete och försörjning [Family care, gainful employment and livelihood], in Swedish Delegation for Gender Equality in Working Life (ed) *Lönsamt arbete – familjeansvarets fördelning och konsekvenser* [*Gainful work – the division and consequences of family responsibilities*], SOU 2014:28, Stockholm: Fritzes.

The Swedish National Audit Office (2001) Män och sjukfrånvaro, om könsskillnader i sjukskrivning, förtidspensionering och rehabilitering [Men and sick leave, on gender differences in relation to sick-listing, early retirement and rehabilitation], *RFV Reports*, 2001: 5.

Tornstam, L. (2006) The complexity of ageism: a proposed typology, *International Journal of Ageing and Later Life*, 1, 43–68.

Ulmanen, P. (2015) *Omsorgens pris i åstramningstid: Anhörigomsorg för äldre ur ett könsperspektiv* [*The cost of caring in the Swedish welfare state: Feminist perspectives on family care for older people*], Stockholm: Stockholm University.

Wall, A. (2014) *Halva arbetstiden, hela ansvaret: En rapport om kvinnors deltidsarbete* [*Half the working hours, all the responsibility: A report on women's part-time employment*], Stockholm: The Swedish Municipal Workers' Union.

NINE

The United Kingdom – a new moral imperative: live longer, work longer

Sarah Vickerstaff and Wendy Loretto

Introduction

The UK's focus very much encapsulates the economic and moral imperatives to extend working lives outlined in Chapters One to Three. Against a background of population ageing and concerns over the funding of state pensions and elder-care costs, successive UK governments have clearly voiced an expectation of working longer. The discourse has changed over time, from reversing early retirement, to extending working lives, to, most recently, encouraging fuller working lives (DWP, 2014a; Altmann, 2015). However, the intention remains firmly focused on delaying permanent withdrawal from paid work. In the last 15 years, policy changes with impacts on later working lives have multiplied, but as Phillipson, Vickerstaff and Lain (2016) note: 'Apart from the general expression of the desirability of encouraging people to delay retirement and extend their working lives, the many initiatives ... cannot be said to have been part of a coordinated strategy.' Gaining momentum, however, is the 'common-sense' view that as we live longer, we should work longer, coupled with increasing talk of intergenerational inequality. As a result, there is a growing tendency for public discussion of extending working lives to take a strong moral tone, placing an emphasis on the responsibility of older age groups to carry on in paid work to pay for their retirement.

There has been legislation prohibiting discrimination on grounds of age since 2006, followed by the subsequent abolition of a default retirement age in April 2011. The age of eligibility for the state old-age pension is rising to 67 and is set to increase further to 68 or possibly beyond while changes to benefit and pension regimes (to be discussed in detail later) have moved to discouraging early retirement or access to ill-health or disability pathways out of work. At the same time, there has also been some emphasis on active, supply-side, labour market policies that encourage or subsidise long-term economically inactive people back into work, such as making work pay through tax incentives. These policies are firmly situated in the neoliberal discourse of helping individuals to help themselves. Emphasis is placed on individuals' responsibility, planning and choice:

> These measures help everyone to take responsibility for their retirement income, to move away from the idea of a cliff-edge retirement that is inevitable at a given age, and ensure they plan for a retirement that is based on personal circumstance and choice. (DWP, 2014a: 3)

This is set against a general background of a move away from mass fixed-age retirement (Rees Jones et al, 2010) to a more diverse set of individual experiences and pathways. The stress in government documents is couched in terms of offering or extending the choice of individuals to work longer by removing barriers that have hitherto prevented them from doing so. Very little is typically said about the differential capacity of people to work or the vitally neglected question of whether there is sufficient labour market demand to absorb extended working lives.

Official labour market statistics show that employment rates for men and, especially, women have increased in the 2000s, with particular rises seen for the over 60s. However, although much lauded in media coverage of labour market trends, such rises are modest and steady (Lain and Loretto, 2016), and as Table 9.1 demonstrates, the majority of men and, especially, women aged 60+ are *not* in paid work.

As can be seen from Table 9.1, women tend to leave the workforce at a younger age, explained by a combination of a historically earlier state pension age of 60 and a propensity for women to retire at a similar time to their husbands. This prompts the government to consider them

Table 9.1: Percentage of men and women age 50+ in employment in the UK, by age band (2004–16)

		50–54	55–59	60–64	65–69	70+
Men	2004	84.0	75.0	54.0	18.0	4.0
	2016	85.8	77.7	59.3	26.5	7.6
Women	2004	75.0	61.0	30.0	10.0	2.0
	2016	78.1	69.5	43.0	16.5	3.4

Source: Authors' analysis of UK Labour Force Survey (GB figures), 2004 and 2016.

as 'untapped potential' in the labour market, with Altmann (2015) observing that encouraging 0.6 million more women over 50 (back) into the labour market on a full-time basis would add £20 billion to gross domestic product (GDP), while adding the same number working part-time would contribute an extra £9 billion to GDP, although little is said about whether jobs are available for this untapped resource. As this chapter will show, recent changes around the eligibility to the state pension for women are designed to promote the 'older women as a resource' perspective, despite the stated intention of pensions policy to be gender-neutral (Grady, 2015: 446). The chapter will also argue that there is very little recognition in policy or practice of the ways in which attitudes, expectations and plans around later-life working and retirement may differ between men and women.

The discussion here will review developments under six headings, stressing the point Taylor and Earl (2016: 120) make that a range of policies that is not necessarily age-related has impacts on the opportunities for later-life working. The areas for consideration are: women in the labour market; age-related policy; benefit changes around ill health and disability; pensions; family and caring-related policies; and flexible working policies. The chapter ends with a concluding discussion that references back to the theoretical framework outlined in Chapter Two.

Women in the labour market

Any consideration of the impact of gender on the extending working lives agenda has to begin with an understanding of the way in which gender structures labour market participation and domestic life. Taking a life-course perspective, the availability of options to continue working at later ages is heavily conditioned by a lifetime's accumulation of advantages and disadvantages.

Access to paid employment in the UK remains heavily gendered, with women and men concentrated in different sectors. Although women's labour market participation has increased markedly (from 53% in 1971 to 69% in 2015), this has not resulted in equal pay or career prospects. The overall gender pay gap is 19.1%, reflecting a wide range of underpinning factors, including the fact that much of the increased female employment is part time and in low-paid jobs and sectors, as well as the impact of intense financial pressures on the public sector, where many women are employed. There is also a widening pay disparity between those at the top and those at the bottom of organisational hierarchies, while we also see a decline in trade union membership and the coverage of collective bargaining (for a full discussion, see Moore and Tailby, 2015).

Women in the UK have been entitled to paid maternity leave since 1975, with men receiving statutory paternity entitlement since 2003. A new innovation, applying to babies born or adopted after 1 April 2015, is shared parental leave and pay. Each parent must satisfy the eligibility criteria in order to take a share of leave and should agree the blocks of leave with their respective employers. While the government expects a take-up of between 2% and 8% of eligible males, recent research suggests a take-up of only 1% (CIPD, no date). It would seem that only a minority of employers is promoting shared leave. Moreover, almost half of organisations paid only the statutory minimum, which would not go far in compensating the loss of salary where the male is the higher income earner. Nevertheless, it is notable that this policy is at least acknowledging that, for the most part, parenthood is not an individual activity and that the caring, financial and career implications are most likely to be considered as a family unit.

In the domestic sphere, a modified male breadwinner model predominates, with men working full time and women working part time, which means that men's wages and pensions are typically the dominant element in domestic finances. Decisions about later-life working are refracted through these gender relations at home and at work (Loretto and Vickerstaff, 2013). By the age of 50, women and men will typically have had very different work histories. For those people aged between 50 and state pension age who are economically inactive, women are more likely than men to report that they are inactive due to home or family commitments and men are more likely to report that they are retired (DWP, 2014b).

Age-related policy changes

In the latter decades of the 20th century, the predominant focus in the UK was on early retirement, against a background of downsizing and restructuring. Early retirement deals that encouraged people to exit from employment in their 50s were seen as an uncontentious way to reduce the workforce. This approach also rested on the belief that early retirement would reduce official unemployment rates and create jobs for younger workers (Duncan et al, 2000: 281). However, increasingly, the costs of such human resource strategies were criticised (Audit Commission, 1997, 2000) and a growing recognition of demographic changes, coupled with concerns that early retirement was often a mask for age prejudice and could constitute age discrimination, led to a complete change of emphasis. UK governments became increasingly concerned about the pressures arising from population ageing on the public purse in terms of state pensions and health service costs on a diminishing tax base.

Age discrimination legislation

In comparison to the US and some other European countries, the UK was late in enacting legislation to prohibit age discrimination (for a broad comparison of legislation in different countries, see Lahey, 2010). The motor for legislation came from the European Union (EU) and was in response to the European Employment Directive on Equal Treatment (Sargeant, 2006). Unlike earlier legislation on gender, race and disability, the move to legislate against age discrimination was not urged by social movements, although it later became more of a social cause.

The Employment Equality (Age) Regulations, enacted in 2006, banned direct and indirect age discrimination in employment and outlawed unjustified compulsory retirement ages below the age of 65, effectively making 65 a default retirement age (Parry and Tyson, 2009; Sargeant, 2010; Lain and Vickerstaff, 2015). This was the first time that individuals up to the age of 65 had protection and they were also given the right to request (but not the entitlement to have) continued employment past the age of 65. This put a focus on age discrimination issues that had largely been absent hitherto and age advocacy groups such as AgeUK campaigned for the removal of the default retirement age of 65. Somewhat surprisingly, and in the face of employer opposition, the Employment Equality (Repeal of Retirement Age Provisions) Regulations 2011 abolished the default retirement age, with the effect that employers can no longer retire people on the basis of age unless they have a legally justifiable reason for doing so. So far, relatively few employers have instituted an employer–justified retirement age.

State pension age

The age at which citizens can claim a state pension is a key age marker structuring the life course and signalling a potential change in social status and role. While in many countries in Europe, the majority of people leave the labour market in advance of their state pension age, it is still a very significant way in which public policy seeks to structure expectations and actions. For the UK, like many other countries, raising state pension ages has been irresistible. It is something that governments control, it is comparatively simple to change and it results in immediate cost savings, although it may ultimately simply displace people onto other benefits.

The first set of changes date back to the Pensions Act 1995, which set a timetable between 2010 and 2020 for a phased equalisation of women's pension age, which at that point was 60, with that of men at 65. The Pensions Act 2011 accelerated the harmonisation of women's pension age, bringing it forward to 2018, and also introduced an increase in state pension age for both genders to 66 from December 2018, phased in until October 2020. Another Pensions Act in 2014 introduced a further rise to 67 by 2028 and instituted a review every five years of the implications of increases in average longevity (Lain and Vickerstaff, 2015, Lain, 2016). While these changes are generally unpopular (Macnicol, 2015: 203), governments have been able to change the state pension age fairly rapidly at no obvious electoral cost, although, at the time of writing, there is a growing campaign, Women Against State Pension Inequalities (WASPI), which is challenging the transitional arrangements for harmonising women's and men's pension ages. In comparison to some other countries (eg the US or Finland), the UK does not allow people to take their state pensions early with actuarial reductions, although this is beginning to be discussed as part of the current review of the state pension age, the terms of reference for which include consideration of 'Whether the current system of a universal State Pension age rising in line with life expectancy best supports affordability, fairness, and fuller working lives objectives' (DWP, 2016).

It is premature to conclude what the full impacts of these changes will be, although changing the rules of the state pension age game disrupts retirement planning for everyone. Women in their 50s have so far undoubtedly borne the brunt of changes to the state pension age; Foster (2014b) notes the shortfall between when many women retire and their state pension age. This can also be illustrated in the figures provided in Table 9.1. The accelerated rise of the state pension age for women will have significantly increased the number of women left 'in limbo' – too young to receive a state pension, yet too old, ill or occupied with caring to work as much as they need to (Ginn and MacIntyre, 2013). Furthermore, the rise in the state pension age also affects other, linked, benefits such as the Pensioners' Winter Fuel Allowance, further penalising women (Foster, 2014b).

It is reasonable to predict that rising state pension ages will affect different income groups in different ways. The poorest sections of the population are least likely to be working up to the state pension age because of compromised health and their weak labour market position, so these groups will spend longer on other benefits before transferring to the state pension. High-income groups are much less dependent upon the state pension for later-life income and therefore the delay in reaching state pension age will be of lesser consequence. It is therefore more likely to be middle- to lower-income groups who will be 'nudged' to delay retirement and work for a little longer because of state pension age increases (Weyman et al, 2012).

Benefit changes

The UK has not had a disability pension, nor have individuals had the opportunity to take their state pension early. The means-tested Pension Credit, based solely on an income test, was designed to function as a top-up safety net for poor pensioners over the state pension age whose income falls below a certain threshold. While women's state pension age was earlier than men's, to avoid discrimination, Pension Credit was available to men from the age of 60. The raising of the state pension age for women has had consequences for men's access to Pension Credit, and will eventually delay access for both genders as the state pension age rises. Access to Pension Credit at 60 was seen as providing a disincentive to find work for older unemployed men. As Phillipson et al (2016) argue, there was evidence that government job centres were encouraging older men to take the Pension Credit rather than continue to search for work. Lain (2016) argues that Pension Credit was arguably providing a 'soft landing' for those older men who lost their jobs and had limited prospects of securing new employment.

In addition to these changes, there have been major reforms to the main ill-health or disability pathways out of the labour market. In the 1990s, Incapacity Benefit was provided for those unable to work due to ill health. Research by Beatty and Fothergill (2007) persuasively demonstrates that Incapacity Benefit provided an honourable escape route, especially for male manual workers who had been made redundant from declining industries and found it difficult to find work. Increasing concern over the numbers of people on Incapacity Benefit (always considerably in excess of those registered unemployed) made it a target for reform, and the Welfare Reform Act of 2007 signalled a greater focus on capacity and fitness to work as Incapacity Benefit was to be replaced with the Employment Support Allowance. The profile of those on Incapacity Benefit had been changing: in the 1990s, the typical recipient was a male manual worker with muscular-skeletal problems, diabetes or heart disease (or some combination of these); in the new century, the numbers of women moving onto the benefit had increased and mental health issues had become a significant cause of incapacity to work. Employment Support Allowance is more difficult to obtain than Incapacity Benefit was (Beatty and Fothergill, 2012).

UK pensions system

The UK pensions system has been denoted the most complex in the world (Foster, 2012), designed predominantly for men, with women intended as indirect beneficiaries through the marital bond (Foster, 2014a). It consists of a combination of state provision (with, until recently, two elements – Basic State Pension and State Second Pension), additional means-tested Pension Credit benefits aimed at the poorest pensioners and private – occupational or personal – pensions. By any measure, women are worse off than men. Half a million more women than men claim the means-tested Pension Credit benefits, and while 80% of male pensioners receive the full Basic State Pension, only 46% of female pensioners do so. Department for Work and Pensions (DWP) figures show that in 2013/14, single men received £97 per week on average from occupational pensions, compared to £78 for women (Ali et al, 2015: 29). As illustrated in Chapter One, the UK has one of the highest gender pension gaps of all the countries considered in this book.

In addition to focusing on the importance of giving more people choice, government policy on the need for extending working lives has also signalled the problem of inadequate individual savings. The DWP estimates that that up to 12 million people below state pension age are facing an insufficient retirement income (DWP, 2014b). Women are more likely than men to under-save (only 47% of women save adequately for retirement versus 59% of men) (Budworth, 2009). The focus of policy is to build individual responsibility for saving to secure one's retirement or, put another way, to shift the risk of insufficient income in retirement from the state and occupational pensions to individuals (Vickerstaff and Cox, 2005).

Changes to the state pensions system

In 2016, the two elements of the state pension were replaced by a single-tier pension, which, in theory, would provide a guaranteed pension income for all. The single-tier pension has been heralded as fairer and designed to address women as 'adults in their own right' (Grady, 2015: 449, quoting the then Minister of State for Pensions Steve

Webb). However, this full amount is based on 35 years of National Insurance credits and although it is possible to claim credits for a range of situations such as unemployment, disability or caring, in practice, women with less labour market participation and lower pay may be disproportionately disadvantaged in reaching the full 35 years of credits. While, in principle, a later state pension age allows extra time to build up credits, opportunities to catch up in practice are likely to be curtailed by poor health or caring responsibilities. Moreover, the new system also ends any derived or inherited rights based on spouse's entitlement. These aspects of the policy change clearly illustrate Grady's (2015) observation that a pensions system with claims to be gender-neutral is actually gender-blind, paying little or no attention to the reality of gendered life courses and lived experiences. Still, in the longer term, there is doubt that the single-tier pension will help to improve gender equality. While it may well benefit women on low lifetime earnings in the short term, the overall level is set at 25% of average wages, 'well below the international accepted poverty level' (Foster, 2014b: 34).

Occupational pensions and the introduction of auto-enrolment

The UK's state pension policy has been driven by concerns around under-saving for retirement and a need to limit state intervention. These drivers have also been behind a wide-scale move from defined benefit to defined contribution occupational pension schemes. Surviving defined benefit schemes are mainly found in the public sector, where in 2011, the government downgraded yearly increases in pension values by changing the basis of inflation indexation from the retail price index to the consumer price index, which usually rises less quickly; this is another change that disproportionately affects women, who predominate in public sector employment. Although defined contribution schemes are less beneficial to all workers regardless of gender, women tend to suffer more as career breaks have more of a financial impact on the overall retirement pot (Foster, 2014b: 30). In general, such schemes serve to translate women's labour market disadvantages into low income in later life (Ginn and MacIntyre, 2013; Foster, 2014a).

The worries about under-saving led to a radical turn in policy: legislation passed in 2010 and implemented in 2012 introduced 'auto-enrolment' into occupational pension schemes. Designed to cover all but the smallest employers, auto-enrolment covers all workers over the age of 22 and earning over £10,000 a year, who are automatically signed up to a defined contribution saving scheme for retirement, though with the right to opt out. Women are more likely to be excluded from auto-enrolment because of the earnings threshold and their overrepresentation in part-time work. Figures from the Trades Union Congress (TUC, 2014) suggest that the majority of women aged over 50 who are working part time earn less than £10,000 per annum. Grady (2015: 451) has criticised auto-enrolment as providing 'the allusion of adequate pension provision, rather than the delivery of it'.

Combining pensions and working

There have been a number of reforms designed to make it easier for people to draw pensions but carry on working. In 1989, state pension 'earnings limits' were removed, which meant that workers can take their pension in full while remaining in work. Most people working past 65 take their pension while continuing to work (Lain and Vickerstaff, 2014). There has been the possibility for people to defer receipt of their state pension and accrue higher benefits later but the take-up of this option was limited and qualitative research found widespread cynicism about the government's motives for offering deferral (Vickerstaff et al, 2008). In 2006, the UK also changed occupational pension rules so that, depending on the individual scheme, people may be able to take a pension and continue working for an employer.

Family and caring-related policies

British women undertake the majority of caring roles, with attendant consequences for their work histories, earning power and pension entitlements. The gender-blindness that surrounds changes to pensions also imbues the UK's approach to benefits for carers. The High Court in England ruled in 2015 that the current policy of penalising carers who did not live with the disabled people they cared for is unlawful. If a carer lives with the disabled person they care for, then their Carers Allowance does not count towards their total benefits in terms of the benefits cap (this is a limit in the total amount of benefits a person of working age can receive). However, if the carer looks after a disabled person (often a family member) who does not live with them, then the Carers Allowance is included in the cap. The High Court ruled that this difference constituted direct discrimination to disabled people and was therefore unlawful (*Hurley & Ors v Secretary of State for Work and Pensions* [2015] EWHC 3382). While this judgement is fair and laudable, it is of concern from a gender perspective that the judge in the case decided 'that because he was satisfied that the discrimination against the affected disabled people was unlawful, he did not need to decide whether the carers themselves should be regarded as the subject of discrimination'. In so doing, although the material disadvantage of the reduction of benefits was addressed, the symbolic disadvantage arising from the lack of visibility of older women and the 'work' that they do was reinforced.

Grandparents' leave

Thinking about the family unit more broadly, the current UK government has also announced an intention to allow grandparents to take some of the shared parental leave and pay by 2018. According to the government's official announcement, this policy change recognises the significant contribution to childcare made by some 7 million grandparents to help families who cannot afford childcare costs (HM Treasury, 2015). While undoubtedly a welcome step, it is unclear how helping with childcare in a baby's first year will solve the issue of the (lack of) affordability of childcare costs that most families will need to bear for many further years. What it might mean, however, is more grandparents getting a taste for childcare and then retiring from their own employment or looking to work more flexibly in order to take on this care longer term. Certainly, evidence from Loretto and Vickerstaff (2015) suggests that grandfathers, in particular, might be keen to seize opportunities for childcare that they missed out on when their own children were growing up. Thus, the implications of take-up of the policy for extending working lives policy will be interesting to see.

Flexible employment and later-life working

The UK was the only country to negotiate a voluntary opt-out from the EU Working Time Directive. Critics (eg Rubery, 2015) maintain that this has allowed for the normalisation and proliferation of a long-hours culture. Rubery (2015: 635) notes that the development of flexible working arrangements and flexible contracts in the UK 'is intertwined with the integration of women into employment but has been dominated more by employer demands than by reconciling work and family life'. Flexible careers at the top mean mobility between organisations, while at the bottom, flexible jobs are often low-skill and insecure. The Trades Union Congress, following the Brexit vote in 2016, fears that employee rights, already less than in many other continental European countries, are at risk of diminishing further once the UK has left the EU.

Surveys conducted before the abolition of the default retirement age (see, eg, Smeaton and Vegeris, 2009) routinely showed a demand for the choice to work longer, often involving working more flexibly. Indeed, flexible working has been widely promoted as a way of extending working lives (CIPD and ILC, 2015) and offering a range of opportunities for and widening the pathways into retirement, by down-shifting, providing bridge jobs, gradual returns to employment for those who had been out of work for some time and 'unretirement' (Maestas, 2010). The right to request (rather than guaranteed access to) flexible working was progressively extended from parents to carers and, from 2014, to all employees with at least 26 weeks' service. The expectation was that this extension would be attractive to older workers. There is some evidence with respect to all requests for flexible work (not confined to older workers) that women are more likely to request a change than men and are more likely to have the request accepted; childcare is the dominant reason for such requests (Smeaton et al, 2014: 95–7). Requests related to grand-parenting may well become more common as older women are working in larger numbers than ever before.

However, there is little proof of a wide-scale uptake of more flexible forms of work among the older workforce (Alden, 2012; Loretto and Vickerstaff, 2015). Even part-time working, the most popular form of flexible working, has fallen in popularity over the past 10 years. Taking the 65–69 age group as an illustration: in 2004, 64% of men working in that age group did so on a part-time basis; by 2013, that had fallen to 54%. For women aged 65–69, the proportions of those in work who worked part time fell from 85% to 74% over the same time period. More detailed analysis of people working beyond 65 (Lain and Loretto, 2016) shows that most of these people occupy jobs that they have held for 10 or more years in permanent posts. While access to flexible work options seems theoretically to encourage people to work for longer, the reality is that much flexibility is employer-driven (ie zero-hours contracts and shift systems) and may serve to worsen older workers' already disadvantaged labour market positions (Earl and Taylor, 2015; Loretto and Vickerstaff, 2015).

Discussion

Much of this chapter has analysed the extent to which policy around later-life working and retirement offers choices and opportunities to older workers and the extent to which such opportunities are equal between men and women. This final section aims to examine UK policy and practice through the theoretical positions outlined in Chapter Two and to highlight where more research is needed. One notable gap in the analysis presented in this chapter (reflecting a gap in the state of knowledge more widely) is the extent to which people's choices and opportunities are constrained or enabled by employing organisations. While there is a body of work that celebrates the older worker and champions their continued employment, employers on the ground are more cautious and often confused. Legislation outlawing age discrimination and abolishing default retirement has left some uncertain about what they can and should discuss with employees. Current research being undertaken by the authors indicates that many traditional retirement planning programmes have been abolished (for fear that they may now been viewed as discriminatory) but that nothing else has arrived to fill the gap. Retirement and later-life working may therefore be carried out in an unmanaged and unplanned fashion, with possible negative consequences for all, but especially those who are in the lower-level jobs and who feel less empowered to ask about such things, that is, older women (see also Loretto and Vickerstaff, 2015). Although the government did appoint a Business Champion for Older Workers, the post was vacant for some time when the incumbent was made Pensions Minister. A new champion from the corporate world was appointed in the autumn of 2016. It is too early to judge whether there has been any change of emphasis or method.

The authors here argue that any joined-up approach should also consider the reality of older men's and women's working lives, including both paid and unpaid work and the balance between these. Grady's (2015: 450) analysis of UK pension scheme changes critiques the concept of hetero-patriarchy, and the way it 'privileges an idealised worker who is able to perform an expected, masculinised occupational life course'. She uses the concept to criticise the notion that the new (pensions) system does much to disrupt dominant discourse; instead, it risks rendering gender inequalities ever more invisible. Life-course (and feminist) approaches that embrace a focus on unpaid work (including family and community activities) move away from a narrow productivist approach (Rubery, 2015) and also reject the individual adult-worker notion (Lewis, 2007) to offer a way of increasing the visibility of older women and the differences between men. Echoing Foster and Walker (2013), we would like to see life-course research extended to include an intergenerational perspective, recognising that older men's and women's engagement with the labour market may be affected by and can influence the labour market engagement of their sons and daughters, through grandparents providing childcare. This would be entirely consistent with the World Health Organisation's (WHO, 2002: 12) definition of active ageing, which is much broader in focus than just labour force participation.

Such approaches would also help broaden the focus to consider the diversity of masculinity beyond the current hetero-patriarchy, which limits the ways in which older men's engagement with work is considered. For example, qualitative research by Loretto and Vickerstaff (2015) has indicated the ways in which older men are now engaging more with unpaid work, specifically in relation to grandparent care (see also TUC, 2014), quite consciously reversing the work–life balance and gender-role assumptions that underpinned their own earlier career and life stages. The same research (Loretto and Vickerstaff, 2013) also demonstrated the ways in which older men, as well as older women, can be blown off the 'ideal' (or expected) life–work trajectory, for example, with health crises or job loss prompting a reassessment of retirement plans and roles.

The drift of government policy affecting older workers in the UK has been focused on encouraging individual responsibility for working longer and saving more, often with an idealised 'adult worker' in mind: an individual devoid of family context and family demands and accumulated advantages or disadvantages. There is also an increasingly strong moral undertow to the public debate that as we are living longer, it is only right that we work for longer. The early retirer is being recast as a selfish baby boomer (Willets, 2010), whereas research tells us that those most likely to be unemployed before the state pension age are out of work because of the lack of job opportunities, poor health or caring responsibilities.

References

Alden, E. (2012) *Flexible employment: How employment and the use of flexibility policies through the life course can affect later life occupation and financial outcomes*, London: Age UK.

Ali, R., Bentaleb, M., Gilogjani, S., Hardcasle, R. and Willdig, T. (2015) *The pensioners' incomes series. An analysis of trends in pensioner incomes 1979–2013/14, UK*, London: Department for Work and Pensions.

Altmann, R. (2015) *A new vision for older workers: Retain, retrain and recruit*, London: DWP.

Audit Commission (1997) *Retiring nature: Early retirement in local government*, London: Audit Commission.

Audit Commission (2000) *Update retiring nature: Early retirement in local government*, London: Audit Commission.

Beatty, C. and Fothergill, S. (2007) Moving older people into jobs: Incapacity Benefit, Labour's reforms and the job shortfall in the UK regions, in W. Loretto, S. Vickerstaff and P. White (eds) *The future for older workers*, Bristol: The Policy Press, pp 65–87.

Beatty, C. and Fothergill, S. (2012) The changing profile of incapacity claimants, in S. Vickerstaff, C. Phillipson and R. Wilkie (eds) *Work, health and wellbeing: The challenges of managing health at work*, Bristol: Policy Press, pp 119–34.

Budworth, D. (2009) Pensions gender gap is widening, study finds, *The Times*, 13 October.

CIPD (Chartered Institute of Personnel and Development) (no date) Pay still a barrier to shared parental leave take-up. Available at: http://www.cipd.co.uk/pm/peoplemanagement/b/weblog/archive/2016/04/05/pay-still-a-barrier-to-shared-parental-leave-take-up.aspx

CIPD and ILC (International Longevity Centre) (2015) *Avoiding the demographic crunch: Labour supply and the ageing workforce*, London: CIPD/ILC.

Duncan, C., White, P. and Loretto, W. (2000) Ageism and employment: controversies, ambiguities and younger people's perceptions, *Ageing and Society*, 20, 279–302.

DWP (Department for Work and Pensions) (2014a) *Fuller working lives: A framework for action*, London: DWP.

DWP (2014b) *Fuller working lives: A framework for action: Background evidence*, London: DWP.

DWP (2016) State pension age review: terms of reference. Available at: http://qna.files.parliament.uk/ws-attachments/456278/original/ToR%20-%20SPa%20Independent%20Review.pdf

Earl, C. and Taylor, P. (2015) Is workplace flexibility good policy? Evaluating the efficiency of age management strategies for older women workers, *Work, Ageing and Retirement*, 1(2), 214–26.

Foster, L. (2012) 'I might not live that long!' A study of young women's pension planning in the UK, *Social Policy and Administration*, 46(7), 705–26.

Foster, L. (2014a) Women's pensions in the European Union and the current economic crisis, *Policy and Politics*, 42(4), 565–80.

Foster, L. (2014b) Towards a fairer pension system for women? Assessing the impact of recent pension changes on women, *Social Policy Review*, 26, 21–38.

Foster, L. and Walker, A. (2013) Gender and active ageing in Europe, *European Journal of Ageing*, 10(1), 3–10.

Ginn, J. and MacIntyre K. (2013) UK pension reforms: is gender still an issue?, *Social Policy and Society*, 12(1), 91–103.

Grady, J. (2015) Gendering pensions: making women visible, *Gender, Work and Organization*, 22(5), 445–58.

HM Treasury (2015) Chancellor announces major new extension of shared parental leave and pay to working grandparents. Available at: https://www.gov.uk/government/news/chancellor-announces-major-new-extension-of-shared-parental-leave-and-pay-to-working-grandparents

Lahey, J.N. (2010) International comparison of age discrimination laws, *Research on Aging*, 32(6), 679–97.

Lain, D. (2016) *Reconstructing retirement: Work and welfare in the UK and USA*, Bristol: The Policy Press.

Lain, D. and Loretto, W. (2016) Managing employees beyond age 65: from the margins to the mainstream?, *Employee Relations*, 38(5), 646–64.

Lain, D. and Vickerstaff, S. (2014) Working beyond retirement age: lessons for policy, in S. Harper and K. Hamblin (eds) *International handbook on ageing and public policy*, Cheltenham: Edward Elgar, pp. 242–55.

Lain, D. and Vickerstaff, S. (2015) National report: United Kingdom, Berlin, Federal Ministry of Labour and Social Affairs (BMAS) and Federal Institute for Occupational Safety and Health. Available at: www.jp-demographic.eu

Lewis, J. (2007) Gender, ageing and the 'new social settlement': the importance of delivering a holistic approach to care policies, *Current Sociology*, 55, 271–86.

Loretto, W. and Vickerstaff, S. (2013) The domestic and gendered context for retirement, *Human Relations*, 66(1), 65–86.

Loretto, W. and Vickerstaff, S. (2015) Gender, age and flexible working, *Work, Employment and Society*, 29(2), 233–49.

Macnicol, J. (2015) *Neoliberalising old age*, Cambridge: Cambridge University Press.

Maestas, N. (2010) Back to work expectations and realizations of work after retirement, *The Journal of Human Resources*, 45(3), 718–48.

Moore, S. and Tailby, S. (2015) The changing face of employment relations: equality and diversity, *Employee Relations*, 37(6), 705–19.

Parry, E. and Tyson. S. (2009) Organizational reactions to UK age discrimination legislation, *Employee Relations*, 31(5), 471–88.

Phillipson, C., Vickerstaff, S. and Lain, D. (2016) Achieving fuller working lives: labour market and policy issues in the United Kingdom, *Australian Journal of Social Issues*, 51(2), 187–203.

Rees Jones, I., Leontowitsch, M. and Higgs, P. (2010) The experience of retirement in second modernity: generational habitus among retired senior managers, *Sociology*, 44(1), 103–20.

Rubery, J. (2015) Change at work: feminisation, flexibilisation, fragmentation and financialisation, *Employee Relations*, 37(6), 633–44.

Sargeant, M. (2006) The Employment Equality (Age) Regulations 2006: a legitimisation of age discrimination in employment, *Industrial Law Journal*, 35(3), 209–27.

Sargeant, M. (2010) The default retirement age: legitimate aims and disproportionate means, *Industrial Law Journal*, 39(3), 244–63.

Smeaton, D. and Vegeris, S. (2009) *Older people inside and outside the labour market: A review*, Research Report 22, Manchester: Equality and Human Rights Commission.

Smeaton, D., Ray, K. and Knight, G. (2014) *Costs and benefits to business of adopting work life balance working practices: A literature review*, London: Department for Business, Innovation and Skills.

Taylor, P. and Earle, C. (2016) Bridging the grey divide – an international perspective on the ageing workforce and longer working lives, *Australian Journal of Social Issues*, 51(2), 119–25.

TUC (Trades Union Congress) (2014) *Age immaterial. Women over 50 in the workplace*, London: TUC.

Vickerstaff, S. and Cox, J. (2005) Retirement and risk: the individualisation of retirement experiences?, *Sociological Review*, 53(1), 77–95.

Vickerstaff, S., Loretto, W., Billings, J., Brown, P., Mitton, L., Parkin, T. and White, P. (2008) *Encouraging labour market activity among 60–64 year olds*, Department for Work and Pensions, Research Report No. 531, London: HMSO.

Weyman, A., Wainwright, D., O'Hara, R., Jones, P. and Buckingham, A. (2012) *Extending working life: Behaviour change interventions*, London: Department for Work and Pensions.

Willetts, D. (2010) *The pinch: How the baby boomers took their children's future – and why they should give it back*, London: Atlantic Books.

World Health Organisation (2002) *Active ageing: A policy framework*, Geneva: World Health Organisation.

TEN

Is 70 the new 60? Extending American women's and men's working lives

Debra Street and Joanne Tompkins

Introduction

Perhaps, as one popular Internet meme suggests, 70 is (becoming) the new 60, as Americans live ever longer, healthier lives (Cutler et al, 2013). Since the mid-1990s, older workers' labour force participation rates have crept up, paralleling a phased increase in the Social Security normal retirement age to 67 by 2027. Some older Americans *want* to work longer – finding careers at later ages intrinsically and financially rewarding (AARP, 2014). That is the extending working lives perspective emphasised by academic and policy formulations of 'productive' (Butler, 1985), 'active' (WHO, 2002) and 'successful' (Rowe and Kahn, 1997) ageing, embracing the notion that some individuals value work in its own right, plus continued wages and benefits. Gerontological ideals about active and successful ageing have contributed to neoliberal and entrepreneurial advocacy in both the health and retirement fields (Hamblin, 2010), nourishing positive stances towards work in later life. However, the unquestioned assumption – that 70 *should* be the new 60 where employment is concerned – implies that extended working life is the right policy prescription for all or most older Americans. Yet, for many, employment is not a choice, but rather the only way to maintain health insurance, pay down debt, meet expenses and accumulate retirement savings (Copeland, 2014), with few alternatives to continued low-paid, insecure or physically demanding employment. Increasingly, workers of all ages are engaged in unappreciated/underappreciated, precarious and demoralising jobs (Kalleberg, 2009), but especially older workers post-recession (Hess et al, 2011).

This chapter considers selected policies that shape work (and work exit) at older ages and some implications of extended working life for Americans. Later-life employment patterns and the US retirement income structure are considered since both pensions and labour markets influence decisions about continuing work or whether and when to retire. Selected policies, from work–family initiatives to anti-age discrimination legislation that could support or encourage work to later ages, are explored. Foreseeable challenges linked to current policy prescriptions that ignore the complexities of extended working life are identified. Policy and research interventions are highlighted that could create a better foundation for dignified and satisfying employment for older workers – and retirement income adequacy when paid work ends – should extending working life become widely feasible and socially necessary in the future.

Older workers in the US

Population ageing, economic circumstances and neoliberal political preferences have fed international appetites for extended working life as 'the' solution to demographic and fiscal challenges. In the US, popular and policy commentary on extended working life and fear mongering about the future affordability of Social Security (since at least the 1980s) have often uncritically assumed that people should – indeed, must – work longer. Little attention has focused on the gender, race and social class implications of such extended working life expectations – or on the idea that 'work is good for you', despite evidence that the salutary effects of employment are mixed and highly dependent on both the type of work and the capacities of the workers (Waddell and Burton, 2006; Di Gessa et al, 2016). Unsurprisingly, in a large country with regional differences in employment markets, complexities of federal/ state policy governance, a diverse population with deep pockets of disadvantage and vulnerability, an ageist and age-denying culture, and the leading edge of the baby boom cohort entering retirement, there is little consensus (insofar as policymaking and practice are concerned) about how to extend American working lives.

The conflation of survivorship to older ages and the presumed capacity for all or most to continue in work longer is the logical foundation upon which broad extended working life policy prescriptions depend. Yet, there are huge disconnects in the supply and demand for older American workers. On the supply side, many older workers have health and disability statuses that make continued employment difficult. Other older workers face the challenge of seeking work under conditions of labour oversupply and skill mismatches, while living in parts of the country plagued by high levels of unemployment or dealing with their own outdated skills. On the demand side, with a mere handful of notable exceptions, American businesses have little appetite for older workers, as evidenced by hiring patterns and widespread age discrimination in employment.

Despite remaining employed to later ages (see Figure 10.1) and increasing rates of older women's employment in recent decades, employment prospects for older American workers are not entirely rosy (Copeland, 2014). The 20th-century tripartite life course – an unambiguous trajectory from education to employment to a crisp exit to retirement – is increasingly rare in the 21st century. The boundaries between employment and retirement statuses are fluid, featuring bridge employment, second careers, flexible working and unretirement (Wang and Schultz, 2010). The aftermath of the 'Great Recession' of 2008–09 featured high levels of unemployment, yet simultaneously accelerated a trend towards work at later ages, during a period when good jobs for displaced older workers were very elusive. Men lost jobs at higher rates than women (Folbre, 2010) and women were re-employed somewhat more quickly post-recession than men. However, older women were also more likely to be re-employed in lower-paid positions than older men (Hartmann et al, 2014).

Once unemployed, older workers are the age group at highest risk of remaining long-term unemployed (six months or longer). Although the official older workers' unemployment rate of 6% is relatively low, the more comprehensive 'U-6' unemployment rate (which includes the aforementioned 'officially' unemployed, plus discouraged workers, part-time workers who would prefer full time and workers underemployed in jobs that do not fully use their skills and qualifications) (BLS, 2016) is nearly double 'official' unemployment figures (GAO, 2012). Long-term unemployment (LTU) increases with age; older women's LTU rate more than tripled in the aftermath of the Great Recession (Federal Reserve Bank of St. Louis, 2015). Even after recovery from the immediate aftermath of the Great Recession, there is little evidence of future US labour market demand for older workers. Rather than needing workers, the American labour market cannot fully absorb the workers it already has. Older workers' actual labour market experiences, combined with high rates of youth/young adult unemployment (BLS, 2015), undermine claims of inevitable future demand for extended working lives.

Figure 10.1: Annual labour force participation rate of Americans aged 55 and older, by age (1975–2015)

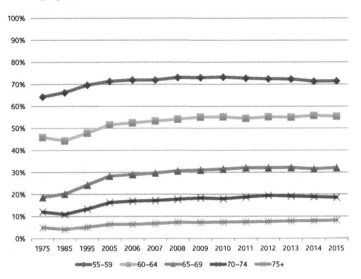

Source: US Department of Labor, Bureau of Labor Statistics, 'Labor force statistics from the current population survey – civilian labor force participation rate'. Available at: http://bls.gov/data/home.htm

Unemployment accelerates retirement. Older individuals who want or need jobs often self-identify as retired, either because they can afford to retire or to avoid the stigma of being unemployed. When older jobseekers do find work, job quality is often poorer – with fewer hours of work or lower pay, or both (GAO, 2012; Lain, 2012; Carrington and Fallick, 2015). Skills–job mismatches make re-employment especially difficult. In the US labour market, such mismatch occurs at both ends of the adult life course, plaguing both older and younger potential workers. Older workers made redundant from, say, manufacturing jobs may lack the cutting-edge technical skills needed for many knowledge economy jobs, while workplace stereotypes and ageism means that they also have fewer training opportunities to enable them to compete (Charness, 2013). Some younger workers face job-seeking challenges because they are 'overeducated', while minority ethnic, working-class and immigrant youth are 'undereducated' for the jobs that are available (Means, 2015; Cappelli, 2015). Consequently, whether sufficient jobs – private or public – can be created to enable extended working life, how they could be distributed throughout the US, what skills would be needed and what pay would be offered are all missing pieces in the extended working life puzzle. Demand-side issues receive scant attention in extended working life debates. Nor have policymakers addressed the paradox that later-life unemployment accelerates retirement while simultaneously consuming the financial resources people need to retire.

Enduring gender gaps in wages and longer life expectancies contribute to non-retired older working women (41%) being more likely than men (29%) to say that they will have to continue working due to financial necessity (Hess et al, 2011). The cause of the gender gap in wages is complex: some of the gap reflects the kinds of jobs women must take to enable them to fulfil normative caring roles; some is attributed to gender discrimination. The gender pay gap is least in the early post-education years but expands soon thereafter, referred to as the 'motherhood penalty' (Correll et al, 2007; Ridgeway, 2011; see also Figure 10.2). Persistent carers tend to be older women, and the associated income, health and well-being disadvantages accumulate over time (Carmichael and Ercolani, 2016). When women juggle paid and unpaid work, they may be unable to work the longer hours that men can tolerate to earn a raise, overtime pay or promotion (Macpherson and Hirsch, 1995; O'Neill and O'Neill, 2005). The gender gap in wages – estimated to range, on average, from 76 to about 85 cents on the dollar, depending on the source of the estimate (Pew Research Center, 2013) – translates into a lifetime of disadvantage for women, the precursor to gender gaps in retirement income (Ginn et al, 2001). This systemic gap may be especially serious for some single women – particularly those working in jobs versus careers – who cannot share a partner's income or receive survivor or dependant benefits in retirement. Nearly half of older American women (47%), compared to about a third of older men (35%), have little to no confidence that their assets will last their lifetimes (Hess et al, 2011).

The US retirement income system

The US retirement income system has traditionally been described as a 'three-legged stool' comprised of Social Security, occupational pensions and individual assets/personal savings. Entitlement to, sources of and amounts of retirement income received differ across population groups in the US and are systematically lower for women and minority groups (Women's Bureau, US Department of Labor, 2015), evidence of the multiplier effects of intersectionality – the conjoined outcomes of being simultaneously an older woman and from a minority group. Feminist political economists point to lesser pension entitlement and fewer potential sources of retirement income as outcomes that reflect life courses shaped by episodes of unpaid employment in lower-quality

Figure 10.2: Median weekly earnings for full-time work, by age and gender (2014)

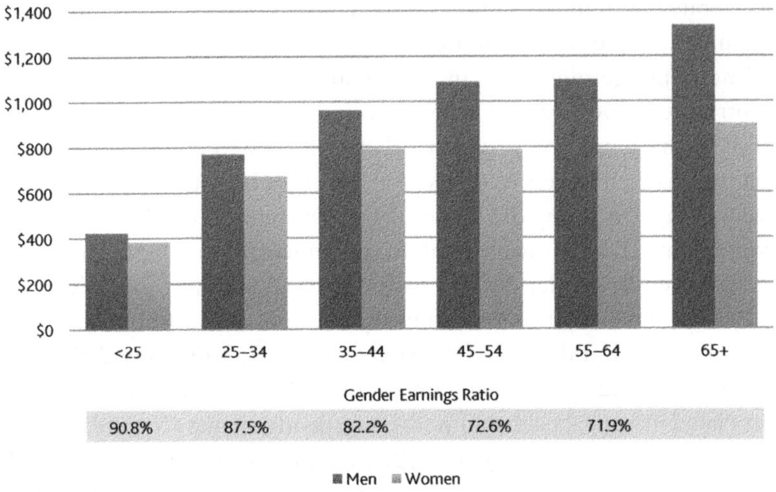

Source: US Census Bureau, Current Population Survey.

jobs that offer few occupational benefits, or are sometimes due to self-employment. Women and minority groups tend to be concentrated in small businesses, part-time or seasonal employment, service work, or contingent (contract or agency) jobs. As Figure 10.3 shows, women's retirement income is lower than men's for all sources and within all race groups. The greatest gendered differences are in earnings from employment and occupational pensions. Further, Figure 10.4 shows that women are much less likely than men to receive retirement income from any source other than Social Security. Data from both figures underscore the overwhelming importance of Social Security income for older women and minority groups, who are less likely than men to have multiple sources of retirement income and, on average, receive less from every source. The combined consequences of the gendered earnings and pension gaps underscore the inadequacy of 'extended working life for all' policies for ensuring income sufficiency in older women's lives. With a public pension system based on the male breadwinner model, and private pensions transformed by neoliberal reforms since the 1980s, it is unsurprising that many older workers, particularly women, worry about whether they will ever be able to retire.

Figure 10.3: Access to retirement income for men and women aged 65 years and older, for largest race and ethnic groups (2011)

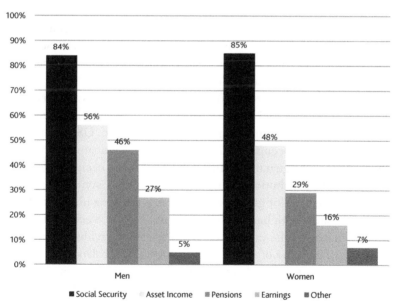

Source: Fischer and Hayes (2013), based on 2012 Current Population Survey, Annual Social and Economic (ASEC) Survey.

Figure 10.4: Percentage of men and women aged 65 and older receiving income from each source

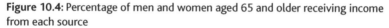

Source: Fischer and Hayes (2013), based on 2012 Current Population Survey, Annual Social and Economic (ASEC) Survey.

Changes to Social Security, pension structures and retirement ages

Since the 1980s, benefit and entitlement distribution across the three legs of the US retirement income – Social Security, occupational pensions and individual savings – have been transformed into a very wobbly stool, contributing to many Americans' perception of the need to extend working lives (Copeland, 2014). The first leg of the stool, Social Security, has undergone decades of sustained political attacks, intended to change its structure and value. However, its resilience is a testament to its financial and social importance: over 90% of Americans aged 65 and older receive Social Security benefits, comprising nearly 40% of American elders' income. Among older Americans, about one quarter of married couples and nearly half of unmarried individuals rely on Social Security for at least 90% of their income. Social Security benefits are at least 50% of income for over half of married couples and three quarters of unmarried people (SSA, 2015). Amendments to Social Security removed an earnings test on wages for recipients who work past the normal retirement age, although earnings tests still reduce Social Security benefits when individuals earn wages but claim benefits before the normal retirement age occurs. The normal retirement age is also increasing gradually, from 65 to 67 (for those born in 1960 or later). Increasing the normal retirement age and eliminating the earnings test after the normal retirement age are Social Security changes that also constitute extended working life policies since both were enacted to encourage longer work.

Social Security provides benefits to workers, dependants and survivors, with the dependant and survivor entitlements especially important to women's later-life income security (Women's Bureau, US Department of Labor, 2015). Occupational pensions once dominated by defined benefit plans that guaranteed income for life have been transformed into defined contribution plans that are individual savings accounts, with no shared risk or guarantee that savings will provide dependable income in later life or benefits for survivors. The 2008 economic crisis wreaked havoc on the value of older Americans' individual retirement resources. The value of defined contribution plan balances shrunk as the stock market dropped, and equity in housing plummeted. Many older Americans dealt with the aftermath of the Great Recession by postponing retirement. Transformations in the second and third legs of the pension stool have contributed to older Americans' decisions to retire or to try to remain employed, by-products of economic trends rather than purposive policies to extend working lives. However, the sheer size and scope of Social Security may make it a singular influence on extending working lives.

Social Security and extending working lives

Social Security is by far the largest social transfer programme in the US, with outlays exceeding US$840 billion in 2014 (CBO, 2014). All but 2–3% of older Americans receive monthly income as beneficiaries. Social Security is a pay-as-you-go defined benefit public pension, financed through payroll taxes levied on wages up to US$118,500 (SSA, 2016). The earnings ceiling on Social Security contributions makes funding Social Security regressive, but there are some progressive elements in payouts. Social Security's retirement benefit formula replaces a smaller percentage of higher earners' pre-retirement earnings (around 28%) and a higher rate for low-wage earners' pre-retirement earnings (about 78%) (Herd, 2009c). Workers earn entitlement to Social Security retirement benefit through at least 40 quarters of contributions (10 years of Social Security-covered employment). The retirement benefit is then calculated based on lifetime earnings, using the highest 35 years. Workers can retire and claim benefits as early as age 62, but the monthly benefit is permanently reduced to account for the presumed longer receipt of benefits. From age 62 to the normal retirement age, wages earned above the annual limit (US$15,720 in 2016) reduce Social Security retirement benefits by US$1 for every US$2 earned. The normal retirement age ranges from 65 to 67, depending on year of birth (current normal retirement age is 66). After the normal retirement age is reached, beneficiaries receive no reduction in retirement benefits associated with wages earned from employment. This policy incentivises continued employment for early beneficiaries of Social Security, at least up to the earnings limit. Finally, postponing benefits past the normal retirement age increases the value of eventual monthly benefit until age 70, given the shorter period for receiving benefits (Munnell, 2013). This supports the interpretation that the normal retirement age is not actually 66 or 67, but that 70 has become the de facto age of 'full benefits' for Social Security retirement (Munnell, 2013). The consequences of continued employment and changes in Social Security benefit accrual at different ages is one way in which Social Security is, arguably, a major extended working life policy.

Spouses of eligible retired workers may receive 50% of that worker's benefit amount as a dependant if that is higher than the value of their own retirement benefit earned through employment. Spousal dependant benefits can go to husbands or wives, but men rarely receive them. Ninety-seven percent of spousal benefits go to women (Harrington Meyer et al, 2005). Surviving spouses receive 100% of the deceased worker's retirement benefits. Lower lifetime earnings and 'missing quarters' of Social Security contributions due to time out of work for motherhood and caring mean that two thirds of older American women receive dependant or widow benefits rather than worker benefits in their own right (Harrington Meyer et al, 2005). Such gender differences in types of benefits received reflect Social Security's male breadwinner foundations.

Social Security financials

The affordability of Social Security has been a political issue since at least the 1980s. Beginning in 2010, current year outlays (benefit payments and administrative costs) exceeded revenues collected. Under current law, Social Security is projected to take in less payroll tax revenue than it pays out in benefits into the foreseeable future, with the gap growing from 9% in 2013 to over 30% by the late 2020s (CBO, 2014). Even without reforms (because payroll taxes would still be collected from workers), there would be current revenue to provide a large fraction of benefits to future beneficiaries. However, reforms will likely increase payroll taxes and the covered earnings income ceiling, and benefits will likely decrease, either through raising the retirement age again, changing benefit calculation formulas or both. Both types of benefit decreases are expected to discourage 'early' retirement among future workers, or, put differently, to encourage them to retire later/extend working lives. Policymakers most often discuss raising the normal retirement age to 69 or 70, meaning that future Social Security recipients would need to work longer before receiving full benefits. This would disproportionately affect low-paid workers in physically demanding jobs. As Street and Desai (2016: 89–90) observed, employment conditions are very different 'for a minimum-wage retail worker who is on his feet all day, a nursing home aide providing personal care to a frail resident, a construction worker in a physically demanding job, or a college professor working in her office'.

Social location and Social Security

Although Social Security is the single most effective anti-poverty policy in the US (Herd, 2009a), pockets of elder poverty and near-poverty persist. Older black, Hispanic and unmarried people all entered the 21st century with poverty rates over 20% (Harrington Meyer et al, 2005). Although the male breadwinner model ensures that, on average, men with typical employment histories fare best in terms of the value of their Social Security benefits, it is also the case that not all women are disadvantaged by the structure of Social Security (Street and Wilmoth, 2001; Herd, 2005; Harrington Meyer and Herd, 2007; Carr, 2010). However, when income inadequacies occur, it is usually because the Social Security programme structure insufficiently compensates for disadvantages that occur at the intersections of gender, class and race (Calasanti and Slevin, 2001) or due to lifetimes of low wages and expectations that women will do most unpaid care work (Street and Wilmoth, 2001; Sayer, 2005). Poor outcomes arise for the very reasons discussed in Chapters Two and Three. As benefits are based on a long work history (35 years) and lifetime wages, Social Security retirement benefits are permanently undercut by time out of paid work or by many years in low-wage jobs. Although the Social Security benefit formula partly adjusts by providing higher rates of return to low-income earners, it does not completely remedy the impact of a lifetime of low wages or gaps in paid work. Even when employed consistently, the gender wage gap leaves average women with considerably lower earnings than their male counterparts. That yields a Social Security benefit gap, where retired women receive about 76 cents on the dollar when compared to similar retired men (Herd, 2009a). The impact on individual women carers in terms of lost wages and Social Security benefits is substantial. Over a lifetime, those losses are estimated to equal, on average, US$142,693 in lost wages and an additional US$131,351 in lost Social Security benefits. On top of that is an estimated US$50,000 in lost pension income from other sources (MetLife 2012 Study of Caregiving Costs to Working Caregivers).

Private sector pensions

The second leg of American retirement income is occupational pensions. Unlike the secure defined benefit monthly pensions (and survivor benefits) of the industrial era, since the 1980s, neoliberal reforms have largely replaced the pooled risk embodied in defined benefit pensions with individualised defined contribution savings plans (Russell, 2014). Most private sector US employers now offer only defined contribution retirement plans, providing the mechanism for savings and even making contributions to individual accounts. However, eventual retirement income depends entirely on the accrued value of individual contributions and investment returns, rather than any pooled risks. Payouts can be lump sums, annuity purchases or the withdrawal of savings. Unlike the guaranteed monthly amount of traditional defined benefit pensions, retirees can, and often do, outlive their defined contribution savings. Many others have no employer-facilitated retirement savings at all (Russell, 2014; Weller, 2016). The shrinking numbers of defined benefit plans still operating are mainly in the public sector, where they are being phased out and replaced with defined contribution plans for new hires.

The transformation of occupational plans from defined benefit pensions to defined contribution savings plans encourages extended work (or later retirement) for two main reasons. First, incentives to retire as soon as the defined benefit pension formulas had been optimised (a combination of years of service and income) disappear once defined benefit pensions are unavailable. Second, under defined contribution retirement plans, amassing savings while enjoying the associated preferential tax treatment is substantially more generous at older ages, likely encouraging workers earning enough to save to remain employed in order to build a larger defined contribution retirement income nest egg.

The third leg of US retirement income is individual savings and income from assets and investments. Like defined contribution occupational plans, Individual Retirement Accounts receive preferential tax treatment, both in terms of savings and returns on investment. Home equity, the most valuable asset that most Americans own, is often regarded as a potential component of individual retirement income, despite the challenges of monetising one's home. This individual leg of the retirement income stool has always been the wobbliest of all since many low-income Americans earn too little to purchase homes or to save individually for retirement. Although it is not an extended working life policy *per se*, low levels of individual savings and wealth among many older Americans is surely an impetus to extending work for the economically insecure.

Most recent retirement system transformations have jeopardised rather than buttressed income security for older Americans and are implicated in extending working lives, whether individuals want to work or not. Currently, 51% of American workers have no private pension coverage and 34% have no savings for retirement (SSA, 2014). Many contemporary middle-income retirees or near-retirees saw huge reductions in the value of their individual retirement accounts and housing assets in the Great Recession. In previous recessions, older workers often left employment in favour of full retirement with Social Security and occupational pension benefits, opening up jobs for younger workers. However, because retirement risk is now so individualised, this is not an option for many older workers, and the recession instead motivated many to continue in employment (Herd, 2009b; GAO, 2012). Through all of the turmoil created by the 2008–09 recession, Social Security has proven the most stable and secure source of income for older people, demonstrating the importance of collectivising risk and providing at least some of the resources that older workers need to make appropriate decisions about extending working life.

Policies associated with work–family balance and anti-age discrimination

The US has been an archetype of neoliberal policies, characterised by the lack of broad-based high-quality work–family policies. There is no federal entitlement to parental leave, although the Family and Medical Leave Act (FMLA) does have provisions for leave due to parenthood or needing to care for immediate family members. Its provisions cover only employees at large organisations (50+ workers), for limited periods (up to six months, regardless of the duration of need), and with no requirement that workers on leave be paid. While some employers offer discretionary benefits that accommodate parenthood, illness or care for a frail or disabled family member, such perquisites are occupational benefits associated with high-quality jobs and not American workers' rights. Childcare for American working families is mainly a private matter; subsidised day care is generally time-limited, rare and focused on getting single mothers off welfare benefits and into employment. Furthermore, while the 35 years used in Social Security benefit formula calculations for retirement benefits may give workers some leeway in maximising public pension benefits despite shorter periods of employment, there is no deliberate policy mechanism within Social Security to compensate employed family carers for essential but unpaid work (Ní Léime and Street, forthcoming).

In terms of workplace policies explicitly linked to employment prospects, the Workforce Investment Act of 1998 established local 'one-stop centers' to provide access to employment and training services for displaced workers (including older workers) under a number of federal and state programmes. Through grants to the states, 'one-stop centers' provided services to terminated or laid-off workers who had exhausted or were ineligible for unemployment benefits, and who were unlikely to return to work in their previous industry or occupation. Such dislocations also included self-employed individuals who became unemployed as a result of general economic conditions or natural disasters. Although not directed exclusively at older workers; it was one mechanism through which many unemployed elder workers sought new employment (GAO, 2012).

The Senior Community Service Employment Program (SCSEP) is the only federal programme specifically targeted at older workers, and provides subsidised, community service-based on-the-job training for individuals age 55 and over who are unemployed, have poor prospects for re-employment and have incomes no more than 125% of federal poverty guidelines (GAO, 2012). Approximately 70% of all SCSEP participants in 2009 were women, 48% were from minority groups and 89% had family incomes at or below the federal poverty level (Senior Service America, no date). The largest federal programme devoted to employing older Americans, it serves approximately 70,000 workers nationwide each year, with an average age of 64 (DOL, 2015). Offering training and paid part-time employment, SCSEP offers important opportunities, but only to relatively few low-income unemployed older Americans. SCSEP jobs and training are part time with low wages, in many ways, the opposite of the types of good jobs that would be available under ideal extended working life conditions.

In 2006, the US Department of Labor convened the Taskforce on the Aging of the American Workforce (the Taskforce), involving several other federal agencies. Its 2008 report recommended that the federal agencies work together to implement strategies that it had identified, from coordinating research and demonstrations, to inventorying legal and regulatory barriers that could limit older workers' employment. While there were some concerns about displaced older workers, in the pre-recession booming economy that preceded the Taskforce's work, strategising how to encourage talented baby boomers to embark on meaningful second careers, rather than retiring completely, was a central theme of the work. Despite identifying potential actions that could help older Americans remain in or re-enter the labour market or pursue self-employment or gratifying second careers, the timing of the Great Recession guaranteed that unemployment took centre stage, and few Taskforce recommendations were ever pursued (GAO, 2012).

In one of the toughest job markets in recent history after the last recession, the unavailability of jobs was a major problem for extending working lives (GAO, 2012). However, even when jobs are relatively abundant, employers often prefer to hire younger rather than older workers. While the US was a world leader in enacting anti-age discrimination legislation – its *de facto* impact has been, at best, limited to only isolated cases, despite the widespread perception that age discrimination is pervasive in the American workplace (GAO, 2012;

AARP, 2014; Ghilarducci, 2015). On the demand side of the extended working life equation, employers appear to have few jobs for which the skills of most older workers in are high demand, job creation has been relatively slack in the aftermath of the Great Recession – sometimes referred to as a jobless recovery – and structural ageism is a feature of the modern American workplace. None of the demand-side conditions offer fertile ground for expansive extended working life policies.

Discussion

Compared to many other countries, where recoveries from the 2008 recession have been slower, or the extent of population ageing has been greater or more accelerated, the US has experienced *relatively* positive macro-level labour market opportunities for some older workers. Higher proportions of older Americans are currently in work, and extending working life would mean that Americans (who already work to older ages than counterparts in many other countries) would work even longer. However, that general characterisation can be quite misleading, as it masks work-related insecurity and hardship (especially for women and minority groups) and the realities of labour markets and prospects for many older workers. One unique component of the American political economy that encourages older workers to remain employed is the structure of its health-care system, and the linkage of health insurance to employment. Most Americans younger than 65 depend on employers to be eligible for affordable group health insurance, which is a source of 'job lock' that keeps many Americans in full-time employment until they become eligible for state-provided Medicare at age 65. That may change as the provisions of the Patient Protection and Affordable Care Act 2010 are more widely implemented over a longer period, but only if health insurance is truly affordable for older workers in non-standard employment in the pre-Medicare eligibility years. It is too soon to tell whether health insurance reform will be sufficient to change older workers' employment behaviour.

There is little indication that there is any 'joined-up' thinking or coordinated US policy initiatives to help older workers extend working lives. Rather, policies tend to be piecemeal, underfunded and unevenly implemented and experienced across the country, despite the intentions for more integrated efforts to extend working life of the Taskforce mentioned in the previous section. There is no single, well-integrated suite of federal policies or mechanisms to coordinate the actions of multiple agencies that could ensure cohesive extended working life policies. Further, in a federal system like the US, even the fragmented policies that exist (such as 'one-stop centers' and SCSEP) are unevenly implemented geographically and variously effective across the states. The predominant trajectory for most US social policies in recent decades has been driven by the demands of its neoliberal agenda to minimise the role of government in citizens' lives and to increase dependence – already high – on the market for social welfare (Harvey, 2005). The current US policy climate gives little reason to expect that work–life balance policies that could better support extended working lives – such as extra quarters of Social Security credit for lost earnings for parents and carers who must leave work or work part time, or better support for flexible work arrangements or mechanisms for phased retirement – will become available to all Americans.

For some older Americans, there are a few bright spots in terms of extended working life policies and retirement prospects. Despite difficulties in finding jobs once an older American becomes unemployed, their overall rates of official unemployment are somewhat lower than for younger Americans. As many contemporary older Americans have higher levels of education than previous cohorts, prospects for continued employment in rewarding jobs seems feasible for some. Individuals who are able to delay retirement until age 70 continue acquiring credits towards Social Security retirement benefits, and for some working women, extended working life could mean that their public pensions will be calculated based on a full 35 years of employment earnings, with fewer missing quarters (unless benefit formulas change). Raising the normal retirement age and leaving the calculation formula intact at 35 years will likely create a larger cohort of women eligible for retirement benefits in their own right as workers, rather than dependant benefits derived from marital status. However, it will be based on lower lifetime wages due to the enduring gender wage gap. For many conventionally married women, the dependant and survivor benefits of Social Security provide secure incomes for those who had low incomes and/or spells out of the labour force for motherhood and care work (regulations for benefits for same-sex couples have not yet been finalised) (Street and Desai, 2016).

Politicians, academics, think tanks as diverse as the leftish Economic Policy Institute and the right-leaning Cato Institute, and advocacy organisations ranging from the American Association of Retired Persons, the National Committee to Preserve Social Security and Medicare, and the Institute for Women's Policy Research, to name a few, have weighed in on the merits and risks of extending working life – or perhaps, more accurately, postponing retirement by raising the retirement age – but not with a single voice. The fragmented nature of policymaking in the US, the disparate interests of advocacy groups and an increasingly strident political discourse have stymied integrated discussion of what extending working life means for Americans with different life circumstances.

Feminist political economists highlight the fact that older women in the US are often more likely to be poor than older women in many other affluent countries due to the absence of family-friendly policies to support women's employment during spells of caring, and due to the way in which public and private pensions were designed (Ginn et al, 2001; Herd, 2009c; Harrington Meyer, 2013). Life-course scholars underscore the accumulation of advantages and disadvantages over entire life courses that feed into outcomes in later life. Adequate retirement income that is less tightly linked to lifetime earnings and marital status, and that is delivered through public pensions, is essential for reducing income insecurity and inequality in old age. Older women fare better in countries where public pensions make up a larger proportion of retirement income as long as the public pension provides an adequate benefit, and especially when there are compensatory policies for women's caring built in (Ginn et al, 2001). Yet, in the US, such improvements are difficult to imagine because Social Security reform is so difficult to accomplish. The sheer volume of stakeholders and beneficiaries makes for a complex and slow-moving political process (Hudson, 2014). The interactions among family, caring, employment and pension policies are sometimes mutually reinforcing and regressive, and occasionally create perverse incentives, yet, at other times, they yield progressive outcomes. This adds another layer of complexity to understanding the opportunities and constraints for older workers. Extended working life policies, unsurprisingly, are prone to similar complex and slow-moving political processes, particularly in the aftermath of the recession (GAO, 2012).

Future directions for research and policy include reformulating the idea of extended working life, fully comprehending the roles of age, gender and other social statuses intersecting with employment structures (as called for in Chapter Two), and acknowledging (and accommodating) the unequal life chances that structure individual life courses through carefully refined policies (an argument underscored in Chapter Three). For example, the many individual Americans whose working years commenced immediately after high school have already extended their working lives compared to their more highly educated contemporaries because they started younger. This extension of working life through employment at earlier ages tends to be overlooked in extended working life policy discussions. Such circumstances typically add three to five, or even 10, years of extra employment in low-paid and (for many) unappealing work at the early end of the employment life-course trajectory, compared to age contemporaries who spend more years in higher education and who start employment later. In the increasingly bifurcated world of employment, the 'job-rich' older worker may 'extend work' in the later phase of their professional, satisfying, highly compensated careers and feel empowered while being enriched. However, for 'job-poor' workers with a lifetime of low wages and unfulfilling and often precarious or insecure employment, the unelaborated demand for extended working life ignores many insights that a life-course approach can offer because it frames the discussion of extended working life as a matter only for older workers and ignores the extension of working lives while young. Policy initiatives could remedy more of the risks embedded in current policies and practices by compensating both tails of the working life course through policy initiatives that compensate early extended work, say, with extra Social Security credits or higher rates of return on pre-retirement earnings, and which reward later extended work by more generous progressive adjustments to Social Security benefits (similar to the continued accrual of Social Security quarters to age 70). Similar policies could adjust Social Security-credited earnings by adequately taking the demands of motherhood and caring into account, making extended work more palatable or possible by compensating for socially necessary unpaid work, and acknowledging the realities of differently experienced life courses, both between women and men, and among Americans in differing social circumstances. Finally, proponents of extending working lives must also confront the challenges of adequately remunerative employment given other bifurcations that occur for older workers, what Theresa Ghilarducci (2015) characterises as the contrasts between 'elders who must work, and those who can afford not to', and the widening gaps in the last quarter of life. Gender is heavily implicated in the gap embodied by the difference between 'must work' and 'can afford to stop', and between 'need the money' and 'love to work'.

Most neoliberal extended work policy initiatives in the US are less about empowering individuals' choices to pursue satisfying careers and more about disempowering older workers by pinching pennies in public pension systems. That requires discouraging retirement for as many as possible and for as long as possible, regardless of life circumstances. Workers in high-quality jobs may well perceive their continued choice to remain employed as evidence that 70 is the new 60. However, 70 is an unreasonably advanced age to expect some individuals to work in affluent countries. For disadvantaged and vulnerable workers – too often women – 70 is not the new 60. After lifetimes of work, paid or not, the 60s are the very same 60s that pension systems were designed to protect in old age in order to acknowledge lifetimes of social contributions and hard work.

References

AARP (American Association of Retired Persons) (2014) *Staying ahead of the curve 2013: The AARP work and career study, older workers in an uneasy job market*, Washington, DC: AARP.

BLS (Bureau of Labor Statistics, US Department of Labor) (2015) Employment and unemployment among youth – summer 2015. Available at: http://www.bls.gov/news.release/pdf/youth.pdf

BLS (2016) Local area unemployment statistics. Available at: http://www.bls.gov/lau/stalt.htm

Butler, R. (1985) *Productive aging: Enhancing vitality in later life*, New York, NY: Springer Publishing.

Calasanti, T. and Slevin, K. (2001) *Gender, social inequalities, and aging*, Walnut Creek, CA: Alta Mira Press.

Cappelli, P.H. (2015) Skill gaps, skill shortages, and skill mismatches: evidence and arguments for the United States, *ILR Review*, 68, 251–90.

Carmichael, F. and Ercolani, M.G. (2016) Unpaid caregiving and paid work over life-courses: different pathways, diverging outcomes, *Social Science and Medicine*, 156, 1–11.

Carr, D. (2010) Golden years? Poverty among older Americans, *Contexts*, 9, 62–3.

Carrington, W. and Fallick, B. (2015) *Do we know why earnings fall with job displacement?*, Working Paper 2015-01, Washington, DC: Congressional Budget Office.

CBO (Congressional Budget Office) (2014) CBO's 2014 long-term projections for social security: additional information. Available at: www.cbo.gov/publication/49795

Charness, N. (2013) Job security in an insecure world: adaptations of older workers in the IT industry, in P. Taylor (ed) *Older workers in an ageing society: Critical topics in research and policy*, Cheltenham: Edward Elgar, pp 109–14.

Copeland, C. (2014) Labor-force participation rates of the population ages 55 and older 2013, *Notes*, 35(4), 2–8.

Correll, S., Benard, S. and In, Y. (2007) Getting a job: is there a motherhood penalty?, *American Journal of Sociology*, 112(5), 1297–338.

Cutler, D., Ghosh, K. and Landrum, M. (2013) *Evidence for significant compression of morbidity in the elderly U.S. population*, Working Paper 19268, Cambridge, MA: National Bureau of Economic Research.

Di Gessa, G., Corna, L., Platts, L., Worts, D., McDonough, P., Price, D. and Glaser, K. (2016) Are there health benefits to working beyond state pension age?, paper presented to the Pensions Policy Institute Policy Seminar, Wellbeing, Health, Retirement and the Lifecourse (WHERL), London, 13 April.

DOL (US Department of Labor) (2015) FY 2015 congressional budget justification, Employment and Training Administration, Community Service Employment for Older Americans. Available at: https://www.dol.gov/dol/budget/2015/PDF/CBJ-2015-V1-07.pdf

Federal Reserve Bank of St. Louis (2015) Age and gender differences in long-term unemployment: before and after the Great Recession, Economic Synopses 26. Available at: https://research.stlouisfed.org/publications/economic-synopses/2015-11-10/age-and-gender-differences-in-long-term-unemployment-before-and-after-the-great-recession.pdf

Fischer, J. and Hayes, J. (2013) The importance of social security in the incomes of older Americans: differences by gender, age, race/ethnicity, and marital status, Institute for Women's Research, Briefing Paper IWPR # D503. Available at: http://www.iwpr.org/publications/pubs/the-importance-of-social-security-in-the-incomes-of-older-americans-differences-by-gender-age-race-ethnicity-and-marital-status

Folbre, N. (2010) The declining demand for men, *The New York Times*, 13 December.

GAO (2012) *Unemployed older workers: Many experience challenges regaining employment and face reduced retirement security*, GAO 12-445, Washington, DC: GAO.

Ghilarducci, T. (2015) Senior class: America's unequal retirement, *American Prospect*, 25th Anniversary Special Edition, Spring.

Ginn, J., Street, D. and Arber, S. (eds) (2001) *Women, work, and pensions: International issues and prospects*, Buckingham: Open University Press.

Hamblin, K. (2010) Changes to policies for work and retirement in EU15 nations (1995–2005): an exploration of policy packages for the 50-plus cohort, *International Journal of Ageing and Later Life*, 5(1), 13–43.

Harrington Meyer, M. (2013) Changing social security in the US: rising insecurity?, *Social Policy and Society*, 12(1), 135–46. Available at: http://doi.org/10.1017/S1474746412000486

Harrington Meyer, M. and Herd, P. (2007) *Market friendly or family friendly? The state and gender inequality in old age*, New York, NY: Russell Sage Foundation.

Harrington Meyer, M., Wolf, D. and Himes, C. (2005) Linking benefits to marital status: race and social security in the US, *Feminist Economics*, 11(2), 145–62.

Hartmann, H., Shaw, E. and O'Connor, R. (2014) *Women and men in the recovery: Where the jobs are*, Briefing Paper, IWPR #C426, Washington, DC: Institute for Women's Policy Research.

Harvey, D. (2005) *A brief history of neoliberalism*, New York, NY: Oxford University Press.

Herd, P. (2005) Reforming a breadwinner welfare state: gender, race, class and social security reform, *Social Forces*, 83(4), 1365–93.

Herd, P. (2009a) The problem of poverty among older people in America: options for reform, *Benefits*, 17(2), 125–35.

Herd, P. (2009b) The two-legged stool: the reconfiguration of risk in retirement income security, *Generations*, 33(3), 12–18.

Herd, P. (2009c) Women, public pensions, and poverty: what can the United States learn from other countries?, *Journal of Women, Politics & Policy*, 30(2/3), 301–34.

Hess, C., Hayes, J. and Hartmann, H. (2011) *Retirement on the edge: Women, men, and economic insecurity after the Great Recession*, Washington, DC: Institute for Women's Policy Research. Available at: http://www.iwpr.org/publications/pubs/retirement-on-the-edge-women-men-and-economic-insecurity-after-the-great-recession

Hudson, R.B. (ed) (2014) *The new politics of old age policy* (3rd edn), Baltimore, MD: Johns Hopkins University Press.

Kalleberg, A. (2009) Precarious work, insecure workers: employment relations in transition, *American Sociological Review*, 74, 1–22.

Lain, D. (2012) Working past 65 in the UK and the USA: segregation into 'lopaq' occupations?, *Work, Employment & Society*, 26(1), 78–94. Available at: http://doi.org/10.1177/0950017011426312

Macpherson, D. and Hirsch, B. (1995) Wages and gender composition: why do women's jobs pay less?, *Journal of Labour Economics*, 13(3), 426–71.

Means, A.J. (2015) Generational precarity, education, and the crisis of capitalism: conventional, neo-Keynesian, and Marxian perspectives, *Critical Sociology*, DOI: 10.1177/0896920514564088.

Munnell, A. (2013) *Social security's real retirement age is 70*, Issue Brief 13-15, Boston, MA: Center for Retirement Research at Boston College.

Ní Léime, A. and Street, D. (forthcoming) Gender and age implications of extended working life policies in the US and Ireland, *Critical Social Policy*.

O'Neill, J. and O'Neill, D. (2005) What do wage differentials tell us about labor market discrimination?, Working Paper 11240, National Bureau of Economic Research.

Pew Research Center (2013) On pay gap, millennial women near parity – for now. Available at: http://www.pewsocialtrends. org/2013/12/11/on-pay-gap-millennial-women-near-parity-for-now/

Ridgeway, C. (2011) *Framed by gender: How gender inequality persists in the modern world*, New York, NY: Oxford University Press.

Rowe, J. and Kahn, R. (1997) Successful aging, *The Gerontologist*, 37(4), 433–40.

Russell, J. (2014) *Social insecurity 401(k)s and the retirement crisis*, Boston, MA: Beacon Press.

Sayer, L. (2005) Gender, time and inequality: trends in women's and men's paid work, unpaid work and free time, *Social Forces*, 84, 285–304.

Senior Service America (no date) The Senior Community Service Employment Program. Available at: http://www. seniorserviceamerica.org/our-programs/the-senior-community-service-employment-program/

SSA (Social Security Administration) (2014) Social Security Administration fact sheet. Available at: https://www.ssa.gov/policy/docs/chartbooks/fast_facts/2014/fast_facts14.pdf

SSA (2015) OASDI and social security program rates & limits. Available at: http://www.ssa.gov/policy/docs/quickfacts/prog_highlights/index.html

SSA (2016) Social Security program fact sheet. Available at: https://www.ssa.gov/oact/FACTS/

Street, D. and Desai, S. (2016) The US old age welfare state: social security, Supplemental Security Income, Medicare, Medicaid, in M. Harrington Meyer and E. Daniele (eds) *Gerontology: Changes, challenges, and solutions*, Santa Barbara, CA: Praeger, pp 83–110.

Street, D. and Wilmoth, J. (2001) Social insecurity: women and pensions in the US, in J. Ginn, D. Street and S. Arber (eds) *Women, work and pensions: International issues and prospects*, Buckingham: Open University Press, pp 120–41.

Waddell, G. and Burton, A. (2006) *Is work good for your health and well-being?*, London: TSO.

Wang, M. and Schultz, K. (2010) Employee retirement: a review and recommendations for future investigation, *Journal of Management*, 36(1), 172–206.

Weller, C.E. (2016) *Retirement on the rocks: Why Americans can't get ahead and how new savings plans can help*, New York, NY: Palgrave Macmillan.

WHO (World Health Organization) (2002) *Active ageing: A policy framework*, Geneva: World Health Organization.

Women's Bureau, US Department of Labor (2015) *Older women workers and economic security*, Issue Brief, February, Washington, DC: DOL.

Part Three:
Conclusion

ELEVEN

Gendered and extended work: research and policy needs for work in later life

Sarah Vickerstaff, Debra Street, Áine Ní Léime
and Clary Krekula

Introduction

Extended working life is but one component of the larger global political project of neoliberalisation, in this case centred on contextual issues associated with post-industrial economies and population ageing. In this book, we have refocused the issue by using a gendered lens, highlighting the failure of policy imagination associated with current approaches to extended working lives. One aim has been to point the way forward to a new theoretical and hence a new empirical and policy agenda for research in what everyone agrees will be continuing political, policy and private concerns for the next few generations. We have argued for a widening of the approach to studying older workers that more firmly situates them in their turbulent social, political and economic contexts, and have suggested the ways in which interlocking theoretical perspectives can provide a framework for understanding the complex reality in which older members of society approach employment in the later stages of their adult working lives.

All of the individual countries considered here share the dynamic of ageing populations in the context of global economic pressures that are diminishing national governments' room for manoeuvre. Despite their very different political and economic backgrounds, all of the countries have, more or less, bought into the argument that ageing populations are a major problem unless more people delay retirement and work longer. Street (in Chapter One) uses a range of international data to underscore the problem of using such a simplified stance because it masks an incredibly complex set of multi-level interactions within country-specific labour markets. As Krekula and Vickerstaff argue (in Chapter Two), more people are expected to make the 'right' decision and continue working. Ní Léime and Loretto (in Chapter Three) provide a critical overview and analysis of the current policy landscape that bears on extending working lives.

This brief postscript fulfils several objectives: to briefly summarise the contributions of each of the individual country chapters; to highlight major cross-national similarities and differences; to emphasise topics where more research is needed to better understand the myriad implications of extended working lives; and to consider some policy directions that could improve prospects for extended working life by countering the increasing polarisation of later-life opportunities that current policy trajectories will create.

Countries' experiences of extended working life

Comparing the countries discussed in this volume, while not denying the materially better conditions in Sweden or the US than, say, Portugal or Ireland, there is not as much variation as might otherwise have been expected when extended working life is considered through a gendered lens. This compression of difference is the likely outcome of at least three intersecting processes: the taken-for-grantedness of calls for extended working life; the neoliberalising tendencies of affluent governments nearly everywhere; and persistent gender disadvantage. The taken-for-grantedness of extended working lives has been treated extensively in earlier chapters of this volume. Traditional welfare state literatures have emphasised the differences across regime types in terms of social welfare outcomes, which would logically suggest significant differences in nearly all policy areas and outcomes, including those associated with extended working lives. Yet, women are disadvantaged everywhere, with lower pay, greater likelihoods of working part time and caring for other family members, facing lower pensions, and, in many countries, a considerable and growing risk of poverty in older age. Diminished prospects in later life are shared or compounded in all cases by low skill, poor health and being single. The twin pressures of rising state pension ages and weak demand for less-skilled older labour are everywhere increasing the gap between the (pension) haves and have-nots, with the trend towards a higher proportion of jobs in labour markets being precarious further entrenching intra-cohort differences in risk. The global neoliberalising project of the past several decades has doubtless contributed to a narrowing or homogenisation in the early 21st century of what otherwise could have been very different later-life outcomes arising from the traditional 20th-century structure of social-democratic, conservative and liberal welfare state regimes.

In Australia, government initiatives to encourage working lives have been characterised as a 'repair strategy', intended to fix a perceived problem with intergenerational equity and to ensure the sustainability of pension spending for its ageing population. In Australia (as in other countries), government policies to extend working lives focus exclusively on the productionist components of life courses, ignoring almost completely the essential reproduction of the labour force. Although women's labour force participation has increased in recent decades, the government focuses attention on increasing women's employment as one component of the repair strategy it is pursuing. Among the countries in this volume, Australia's plans to increase the retirement age to 70 by 2035 is the highest retirement age, a policy initiative accompanied by freezing benefit ceilings and changing the indexation of public pensions, with women bearing a disproportionate burden of such neoliberal policies. At the same time as public pension generosity is contracting and reliance on individualised private pensions is increasing, other family-friendly policies are also being retrenched, including disability benefits and income supports. Similar to extended working life policies elsewhere, Australian policies associated with extended work are often associated with tax-subsidised savings for retirement income, which disproportionately benefit well-employed high-income older workers, who are most likely to be men. Brooke (in Chapter Four) argues that the neoliberal project in Australia has yielded a political agenda of downward mobility in the context of globalised labour markets, and that women's typical life courses systematically disadvantage them in terms of the kinds of jobs available to them and the amounts of retirement income that they are able to acquire, rendering the scope and variation in women's working experiences invisible in the Australian initiatives for extended working life.

The employment rates of older people in Germany have increased the most of the countries covered in the volume and, for this reason, it has been heralded as successful in trying to reverse the tide of early retirement and encourage people to work for longer. Chapter Five by Hokema demonstrates that these changes not only cannot be taken at face value, but also signal worrying trends for the future. The liberalisation of the labour market, in particular, the creation of so-called 'mini-jobs', which get around the collectively agreed labour contracts that used to characterise the German model, distorts the picture as many older workers, and especially women, are working part time and/or in mini-jobs, with low pay and contract insecurity. This development of more marginal employment coupled with reforms to the state pension age and the closing of some pathways to early retirement is serving to shift the risk of income insecurity in old age from the state to the individual, with the attendant dualisation of the labour market and growing inequality in retirement chances and incomes. Women are disproportionately affected by these developments because with the persistence of a modified male breadwinner model of the family (male full-time, female part-time employment), they continue to shoulder the main responsibility for family care and hence do not reap the benefits of secure full-time employment, which is still rewarded by the state pension system. It is not only women who find themselves in this position, but also men in some regions with less buoyant labour markets and those with health and skills deficits. Of all the countries discussed in this volume, the neoliberal turn in policy is perhaps most stark (although changes in Sweden make it another contender for the starkest changes), beginning to chip away, as it does, the post Second World War conservative social-democratic model.

In Ireland, extended working life policies were introduced without much debate about the gender implications. The rhetoric used to promote extended working life was initially aligned with the European Union's (EU's) 'Active Ageing' agenda, but, for the most part and increasingly, it echoed the Organisation for Economic Co-operation and Development's (OECD's) exhortation for the need for the sustainability of the state pension system. This argument gained traction during the severe economic recession experienced in Ireland, which started in 2008 and peaked in 2012. In common with other countries analysed in this volume, the typical extended working life policies of raising the state pension age, closer links between paid employment and pension outcomes, and the individualisation and privatisation of pensions were introduced. As Ní Léime explains, while extended working life policies were originally proposed prior to the global economic crisis, the many shortcomings of extended working life policies in Ireland were amplified because many of the policies were implemented at the height of the recession, while other austerity policies were also being imposed. Similar to other countries, the state pension age was raised despite Ireland's relatively young population, from 65 pre-2012 to 68 in 2028, disrupting the pension expectations of many older workers; the negative impacts of this were only very recently (September 2016) addressed somewhat by the removal of mandatory retirement. The gender regime in Ireland has changed quite rapidly from being a strong male breadwinner state with very low proportions of older (particularly married) women in employment to one that is more facilitating of women in the workforce. EU membership initially tempered some of the most unfriendly aspects of

Irish social policy for women via initiatives like removing the marriage bar, the implementation of the Home-maker's Scheme (allowing some credit for caring for children) and enhanced maternity and paternity leave. However, the countervailing influence of austerity, which ushered in closer links between work and contributory pensions, is likely to result in lower state pensions for women, increasing gender pension gaps. Similar to Portugal, although not in such a stark fashion, the global recession, with its high levels of unemployment, challenges the assumption of demand for older workers. The chapter highlights the increasing precarity of employment in Ireland, which makes it more difficult to contribute to state and/or private pensions, under the new policies.

Portugal, too, has introduced extended working life policies without considering their gender implications. The main rationale offered has been a reduction in pension costs, and while there are references made to gender equality in some policy discussions, there has been no specific debate or measures implemented to ensure that women are not adversely affected by extended working life policies. In particular, there has been little consideration of how unpaid work will continue to be done if older women workers must work longer, as is demanded by the increase in state pension age. Casaca and Perista (in Chapter Seven) highlight Portugal's unusually high female employment rate for a Mediterranean country, but it is accompanied by traditional gender ideologies. Despite relatively generous paternity/maternity and parental leave policies, there is very little public provision of elder care and there are no pension credits for caring. Since the pension system has recently been dramatically changed to reward greater attachment to the labour market, with early retirement penalised, older women who are expected to carry out unpaid care work for older family members are likely to end up with lower pensions and be even more vulnerable to poverty in the future. Similar to Ireland, where extended working life policies were already being introduced pre-recession, the global financial crisis and its accompanying austerity policies affected Portugal more severely than the other countries considered. Pensions were reduced and frozen temporarily, resulting in financial hardship. Even now, high levels of unemployment reduce the prospect of employment for workers of all ages. High female employment is characterised by concentration in precarious, low-paid employment and limited availability of flexible employment. Of all the countries in this volume, Portugal was hardest hit by the recession and provides a stark empirical example that problematises one of the underlying assumptions of extended working life policies – the availability of employment opportunities for older workers. High levels of female employment coupled with Portuguese older women's greater poverty demonstrate that without policy measures to reward unpaid care work, women are likely to be even more disadvantaged under extended working life policies.

The development towards extended working life in Sweden is based one-sidedly on economic arguments, and constitutes a substantial transformation of its welfare model. The number of older people in working life, already high from an international perspective, continues to gradually increase. As Krekula and colleagues argue in Chapter Eight, political initiatives have, to a great extent, aimed to make late retirement less costly to the state despite processes like widespread age discrimination in Sweden. Economic inequality between Swedish women and men increases with age, and the gender pension gap is larger than the gender pay gap. This is mostly due to the fact that women have lower incomes, that they are forced into part-time employment to a greater extent and that they still carry a significantly heavier load in terms of housework than men. Whether women and men have equal opportunities to work is influenced by changes in the national elderly care system, which have not been included in the debate on extended working life. Due to substantial cuts in public elder care, older women, in particular, risk ending up in a position where the care they provide for older family members negatively affects their work situations. This illustrates that consideration of extended working life cannot be limited only to work organisations, but must also be seen from a wider social perspective. Older women's participation in working life is also under threat by the fact that female-dominated professions often include greater demands, less influence, more temporary employment, lower wages and more frequent workplace-related violence. The Swedish political debate on extended working life is based on arguments that are adapted to those who are *willing and able* to continue working later in life. Despite the argument that an extended working life is needed to ensure the value of pensions, this does not apply to those who are not able to continue working – they are instead expected to rely on the social security scheme. Thus, the Swedish transformation towards an extended working life contributes to increased gaps between groups of older people.

In the UK, as Vickerstaff and Loretto (in Chapter Nine) demonstrate, the new orthodoxy that if individuals live longer, they should expect to work longer is widely accepted, as is the accompanying belief that it is an individual's responsibility to secure their retirement income. The context of austerity has only served to sharpen the idea that older people – baby boomers – are somehow responsible for some of the current economic ills. While there have been some positive policy developments, such as age discrimination legislation, the end to mandatory retirement ages for the most part and the extension of the right to request flexible working to all employees, there is very little recognition in public discussion or policy documents of the different circumstances in which people reach their early 60s and hence the very different impacts that the need to extend paid working lives will have. Access to disability benefits has become more difficult and British women, in particular, have seen a dramatic rise in their state pension age, disrupting expectations and planning for retirement. There is little or no discussion of the role of unpaid labour, especially caring, on individuals' ability to extend their paid working lives. Changes to the state pension, though positive in some respects, still prejudice women and others who have interrupted employment histories. The net effect of these policy developments, which have largely emerged in an uncoordinated way, is that the traditional two nations in retirement (the well-off versus the less well-off) is being further entrenched, with potentially more middle-income people finding themselves in the less well-off category and the traditional risk of poverty for older women becoming further ingrained.

It is never a surprise when the US appears to be somewhat exceptional in terms of the contours of its social policy experiences. In terms of extended working life, the US was among the earliest countries to enact a gradual change to the state pension age, from 65 to 67. The neoliberal agenda of the Reagan years (1980s) provided the catalyst to the replacement of traditional defined benefit pensions with defined contribution savings plans, a pension innovation of privatisation and individualisation that was mimicked throughout the affluent world. Together, as Street and Tompkins show in Chapter Ten, privatising and individualising the risk in private occupational pensions while gradually increasing the normal retirement age ensured that extended working life in the US was as much a function of delaying retirement as of individuals choosing to extend work. The lack of national policies for paid maternity leave, parental leave or carer credits for unpaid care disadvantage American women in terms of how appropriately their paid and unpaid work are valued. Yet, compared to women in most other countries, American women have worked full time over longer periods and at higher rates than elsewhere, despite the lack of public childcare provision or much in the way of policy supports for unpaid family carers or any other family-friendly policies. What often sets the US apart from other countries, beyond the stinginess of most of its welfare state (Social Security is the rare exception), is the sheer size and strength of the US economy, which seems to offer better or more opportunities for many workers, including older ones, than in other countries. Still, older American women share with their counterparts in other countries the interlinked disadvantages of gender-normative expectations for providing unpaid care, a gender gap in wages that is larger than many other countries and increasing precarity in employment. There are no coordinated policies for private sector organisations to enable or compel working conditions that would appeal to older workers, nor has anti-age discrimination legislation been particularly effective in counteracting ageism in employment. The absence of mandatory retirement permits older Americans who choose to or must work to remain employed, but robust employer preferences for younger workers are a countervailing pressure. As the US pursued liberal, and then neoliberal, policies much earlier than many other countries, it is perhaps unsurprising how apparently stable, underdeveloped, yet relatively empty of meaningful content its extended working life policies are.

Insights from a comparative assessment of extended working life

As the foregoing summaries and the individual country chapters indicate, the countries discussed in this volume contrast significantly with respect to the scope and coverage of welfare state policies and the degree to which the social partners coordinate labour market policy. The literature on welfare state regimes or varieties of capitalism would classify them as a social-democratic coordinated regime (Sweden) at one end, through corporatist conservative regimes (Germany), to liberal uncoordinated (the US) at the other (Esping-Andersen, 1990; Hall and Soskice, 2001), with the attendant assumptions that responses to an ageing workforce might be expected to differ markedly across the spectrum. Ebbinghaus (2006), in his comparative analysis, used these categories to explain different patterns of early retirement. The contributions here, however, viewed from a contemporary vantage point and through a gendered lens, show a remarkable convergence towards a neoliberal turn with respect to pensions, disability and unemployment benefits, with measures to individualise or privatise the risk of income sufficiency in retirement. Perhaps the most unexpected patterns observed from the country chapters is the distance that Sweden and Germany have travelled down the neoliberal path, while the US, the 'vanguard' neoliberal country in this volume, has had decades of stable extended working life expectations and fewer disruptive recent changes to the structure of its employment and pension systems (the late 20th-century conversion to defined contribution occupational pensions notwithstanding) than several other countries, like Australia, Ireland and Portugal. While the impact of extended working life is much sharper in countries with less generous state pension systems to begin with, the direction of travel is similar across the countries. This seeming convergence to the individualisation of risk, retrenchment in public policies and increasing precarity in employment are hallmarks of the neoliberal global project.

This is coupled in all cases (though to different degrees) with an increasing bifurcation or polarisation of job opportunities between good, often reasonably well-paid occupations with career possibilities, and low-skill, poorly paid and often precarious jobs (for a discussion, see Rubery, 2015). These twin developments, as has been discussed in the individual chapters, sharpen up the differences between older workers and the risks that they face, typically worsening the position of many women but also of other vulnerable groups, such as those in ill health or with few marketable skills.

In this macroeconomic context, and taking into consideration the agenda of the neoliberal project, the behaviour of employers towards older workers (like the policy initiatives of states) is bounded by the rigours of economic competition and the urge to spend less but get more out of employees. In all of the countries studied here, the older unemployed find it more difficult to get back into paid employment than prime-age workers. For example, older Americans took longer to be re-employed and were substantially more likely to be among the long-term unemployed than were younger workers. This is consistent with the typical hiring practices of most private sector organisations, which favour the younger over the old, though, in some cases, age discrimination legislation and the ending of mandatory retirement ages (eg in the UK, the US, Ireland and Australia) have made it easier for older workers to stay in work at older ages (Lain and Loretto, 2016). There are also issues around the labour costs of older workers, who may attract seniority-based pay and higher employee benefit packages. We see in the German case the creation of 'mini-jobs' as a way of avoiding the relatively good collectively bargained conditions of permanent workers. Women are overrepresented in this more precarious employment.

Public policy and employer policy operate in the context of prevailing cultural attitudes and assumptions about age. While age discrimination may be progressively outlawed, all of the societies privilege youth culture, with increasing age and the signs of ageing being negatively evaluated (Clarke and Bennett, 2015). The impact of age stereotypes and 'lookism' on employment opportunities is well documented, as is their particular impact on women, who are 'never the right age' (Duncan and Loretto, 2004; Calasanti, 2005; Warhurst et al, 2009; Jyrkinen and Mckie, 2012).

The focus in all countries has thus been primarily productionist, with extended working life being seen as the 'solution' to the welfare state crisis. The common responses are: raising state pension ages; the retrenchment of state pensions; reduced scope for early retirement; and a general pulling back on disability/ill-health retirements and unemployment benefits as a bridge to retirement for unemployed older workers. In all cases, the policies are not joined up, with issues affecting older workers crossing different ministries, agencies and jurisdictions (for a similar conclusion, see Taylor and Earl, 2016: 120). Sweden, of all the countries, has had the most comprehensive and joined-up policy discussions about extended working life, but even there, the implications of the growing need for care in an ageing population is not adequately brought together with extending working lives initiatives.

None of the countries has done particularly well at redesigning the range of policies that would need adjustment for extended working to appeal to a broad range of older workers. All of the countries have enacted policies that fail to recognise the heterogeneity of the older population. Where the value of public pensions diminishes, given women's greater dependence upon state pensions, this means that the gender gap in retirement incomes will likely increase. The productionist focus of policies also neglects the connections between paid and unpaid labour and the effects of women's different life courses on their paid work histories. In all cases, women's relative disadvantage in the labour market is carried through into gendered pension gaps. Even in those countries with more dual-earner model families, those where more women work full time (Sweden, Portugal and the US), this has not eroded gender pay gaps or significantly altered the disproportionate burden of unpaid care that women perform.

How the issue of extended work is discussed does have particular national flavours. For example, in Australia, the central focus is on intergenerational issues and the seemingly logical extension of those intergenerational concerns into the rationale for later-life work, while in the UK, the rhetorical frame has been dominated by austerity, which has been discussed in terms of what the state cannot afford and that individuals must. That austerity trope has fed into all areas of British social life, including into the expectation that older people should work longer for their keep. In the US, the initial political rationale for working longer was characterised as a matter of 'intergenerational equity' (Street and Quadagno, 1993), a perspective recently used in Australian debates about extended working life. However, more recently in the US, debate has been most strongly associated with claims that Social Security for future retirees is not fiscally sustainable. In the popular media, the need to work at older ages is variously characterised as good for workers and necessary for the private sector, which will presumably suffer when baby boomers retire and employers lose a significant fraction of their skilled and experienced workforce. In Sweden, there is a more nuanced consideration of the gender and health differences in individuals' ability to carry on working but there is still a strong moral undertow that people should carry on working if possible.

Discussion around raising pension ages occurs in all countries, with Australia considering the highest age for retirement – 70 years – among the countries considered in this volume. The countries also differ in whether it is possible to take the state pension early, with an actuarial reduction. The US, Portugal, Australia, Germany and Sweden have flexible policies associated with the state pension, in that individuals can choose to retire at different ages (from 62 to the normal retirement age in the US, from 61 to 67 in Sweden, from 55 for superannuation in Australia, from age 63 in Germany), with actuarially reduced benefits for early retirement. It is not possible to take the state pension early in Ireland or the UK. All countries share the common policy of progressively raising the age for receipt of full state pensions. This has had the most dramatic impact in countries, like the UK, where women historically had a lower state pension age than men. While the ability to take a pension early may soften exit for people struggling to find or maintain work, the US example amply demonstrates that the majority taking a pension early are the poorest and most disadvantaged (Munnell et al, 2016) and hence those most dependent on the state pension for their income.

Research agenda

The contributions to this volume have demonstrated the importance of viewing the extended working life issue through a gendered lens. They have built on the long-established literature on how pension systems ignore women's realities to explore what the impact of ageing populations and welfare state retrenchment is likely to be in the coming period. Further than this, the approach taken in this volume has tried to demonstrate the complexity of factors that condition older workers' experiences and the interconnections between economic, political, social and personal factors that need to be examined to capture the opportunities and constraints that the extended working life agenda raises. Although this book has used gender as its central focus, in every country, other characteristics of individuals, such as race/ethnicity, social class, health and marital status, magnify the vulnerabilities that some older workers face. Intersectionalities across multiple statuses introduce further complexities into the promises and pitfalls of pursuing extended working life as an effective intervention into the challenges confronting national pension systems and, at least as importantly, the capacity for most individuals to experience economic security in later life.

Taking a life-course perspective, the time and place at which the experiences of extending working life occur are shaped both by period (historical) and cohort (the experiences of particular generations of older workers) within national and global economies. For example, current older workers in Ireland had little time to prepare for radical changes in public and private pension structures after a period of economic turmoil and austerity in the aftermath of the Great Recession. During the same period, in a much larger and more stable economy that recovered more quickly, older workers in the US had to adapt to the vagaries of private pensions, but within the context of stable and secure Social Security arrangements. In all countries in this volume, the loss of traditional sources of employment to cheaper labour markets represented a shared experience that seems to undermine the widespread potential for extending working lives in high-quality employment. Yet, in all countries, current older workers are better educated than prior generations, a trend that seems likely to continue and that may mitigate some of the challenges of widespread policies to extend working life, in that such highly educated workforces may be more adaptable. Despite gender gaps in pay and pensions, some women's employment experiences are becoming more like men's, which may mean that for securely employed women who have good jobs, work at the end of life may be less precarious in the future.

Life-course researchers emphasise the accumulation of inequalities over lifetimes, and the country-specific chapters provide ample evidence that recent policy and economic experiences contribute to the magnitude of inequalities, which are logically greater in later life, at the time when conventional policies suggest that work would need to be extended. Sometimes, the accumulation of inequalities is expressed as an accumulation of advantages – good health, high levels of education and income, and rewarding careers, experiences that may make current anaemic extended working life policies palatable for the well-employed. In other instances, the weight of poor health, disabilities, heavy caring burdens and low-paid, precarious or unfulfilling work contribute to the accumulation of disadvantage for the same cohorts of workers, but with very different employment circumstances. The accumulation of inequalities creates status differentials that are both intra- and trans-generational, but that tend to be left out entirely in policy discussions of extending working life. Life-course researchers know that it is not enough to say that people must work into their 60s; they recognise that individuals experience lives that link together families, organisations and institutions. Successful policies to extend work must take into account linked lives, which means understanding what families need (in terms of reproductive and caring work, and income to sustain them), what organisations can and must do for working lives to be extended, and institutional arrangements that are up to the task of creating the opportunity structures for adequately compensated and appropriately distributed employment opportunities for workers of all ages. This amplifies the need for research to resist the homogenisation of 'older workers' into an age-stratified group and the necessity of locating individuals in their social, family and community contexts (Vickerstaff, 2015). Moen (2011: 87) points to:

> the tendency of societies, states, employers, and scholars to think about, develop policies around, and study workers as individuals, not as family members. And yet most workers are married (or partnered), and most in the USA and Europe are part of dual-earner households.

To understand the likely impact of extended working life, the work presented in this book demonstrates the need to employ a feminist comprehension of work which acknowledges that paid and unpaid work are inextricably linked. Such an appreciation supports the identification of a number of research gaps in current understanding, not least that family forms are changing in all of the countries studied here, with increases in divorce, remarriage, singlehood and, almost entirely absent from research, same-sex couples, which will all have an impact on the urge to extend people's working lives. As a recent Norwegian research paper concludes:

> As the joint effect of spouses' work exit is likely to be ignored in studies where work disengagement is considered

as an individual and not a household behavior, further research ought to include household data whenever possible. Further, the suggested presence of a household effect on work exits provides policy makers and planners with a better understanding of how they may encourage postponement of retirement. (Syse et al, 2014)

Situating older workers more firmly in their social context also reminds us to consider intergenerational dynamics and, in particular, to focus on transfers between generations, that is, the role of grand-parenting in supporting younger generations' employment (see, eg, Harrington Meyer, 2014). This also brings back onto the research agenda the link between the care needs of an ageing population being combined with the policy push to delay retirement and work for longer. The hitherto separate research agendas of acquiring childcare where it is scarce, financing care in ageing societies and extended working life need to be brought together to more fully understand the medium- to long-term implications of current policy trends and initiatives.

The preceding chapters also suggest that there has been inadequate consideration of how ill health affects the possibility of extending working life and that workers in physically demanding occupations tend to face health challenges earlier, often resulting in inability to work past the state pension age (see, especially, Chapter Five). One fairly constant refrain, from research, media accounts and policy pronouncements, is that access to greater flexibility at work, in terms of hours and/or levels of responsibility, would encourage older workers to stay in employment by allowing them better to meet health, caring or preference needs (Loretto et al, 2005, 2007; DWP, 2006). There is also considerable evidence to suggest that at least some older workers would value opportunities to downshift or retire gradually (Pitt-Catsouphes and Matz-Costa, 2008, Smeaton et al, 2009), although there is less evidence that they actually do it (Loretto and Vickerstaff, 2015). The lesson from the approach taken in this volume is that the value of flexibility cannot be taken at face value. Rather, flexibility needs to be much more critically considered in light of the burgeoning literature on the problems of precarious employment (Standing, 2011; Vosko, 2008). The part-time penalty that many women face should challenge optimism about the prospects for access to work flexibility mitigating the inequalities between older workers.

In the US, a rich body of literature since Doeringer (1990) popularised the concept and heralded a proliferation of so-called 'bridge jobs' as a means to extend working lives. However, bridge jobs are conceptually difficult to precisely quantify and define. According to Cahill et al (2007):

> bridge jobs are closely related to other aspects of labour force transitions later in life, such as phased retirement, part-time work, and self-employment. Bridge jobs can be part-time or seasonal, they can entail a change in occupation or industry, and they can even involve a switch in job type altogether, such as from wage- and salary work to self-employment or the reverse.

Thus, a full-time autoworker who chooses to retire from a career of shift work and who can find part-time work in a florist is one example of a possible bridge job. Hosting paying guests in a spare bedroom through Airbnb or choosing to 'downshift' from a career by driving on some weekends or evenings for Uber could be other examples of bridge jobs. So, too, could a transition from a demanding, highly compensated corporate career to fulfilling a lifetime passion to teach reading to disadvantaged children. However, *choosing*, as in these examples, compared to *settling* for or *needing* one or two part-time jobs to pay bills when laid off or made redundant, even in the period immediately prior to retirement, does not seem like much of a bridge. Rather, the latter circumstances are most consistent with the notion of spreading precarity, another of the globalising trends in neoliberalism (Harvey, 2005; Kalleberg, 2009; Standing, 2011). While contemporary research acknowledges the difficulties of agreeing what constitutes a bridge job (Cahill et al, 2016), the whole notion is perhaps ripe for a thoroughgoing critique of how we conceptualise later working life transitions.

Among older workers in the US, where the terminology of bridge jobs is most widely used to signal flexibility in later-life work, recent data show that while many older Americans choose to continue to work, a substantial percentage feel that they have no alternative to working to pay the bills. Trends documented in the chapter on Germany also challenge the idea of high-quality 'bridge' employment in later life there, where mini-jobs are proliferating. A critical assessment of the kinds of job transitions people make at the ends of their paid working lives is overdue.

Policy agenda

One message that can be taken away from all of the country-specific chapters is the extent of fragmentation across policy areas that bear on extended working lives. There is little evidence of joined-up thinking or joined-up policy about extending working life. The most glaringly obvious issue is a need to link policy about caring for an ageing population with policies to extend working lives, especially those of women. One of many obvious mismatches in the contemporary policy landscape of ageing populations and work is between the need to care for an increasing number of older people in all of the countries considered and the expectation that older people must/should be employed. Current extended working life policies simply ignore this issue.

Evidence from the countries analysed here suggests that policymakers in most countries could benefit from insights gleaned from gender audits of employment, pension and extended working life policies, both existing and prospective, if such enterprises were taken seriously and their implications folded into extended working life policies. Of course, this should ideally have been done when extended working life policies were initially being designed. However, auditing policy and outcomes currently in place and understanding the effects of linkages across policy domains, the strengths and weaknesses of alternative policy approaches, and the particular advantages and disadvantages of extended working life policies that account for life-course realities can help inform what modifications of existing policies need to be put in place.

Totalising policies, like across-the-board increases in state pension ages, fail to account for several realities of working lives: that some people, especially among those who have not had tertiary education, may have already been working for more than 45 years in physically demanding work. Their working lives are already extended beyond (and sometimes far beyond) those attending with university degrees and professional qualifications. In terms of the moral pressure to work longer, any equitable policy would necessarily differentiate between different groups of workers (Ghilarducci, 2015). Researchers at Boston College (Pitt-Catsouphes and Matz-Costa, 2008) have documented the rate at which age leads to decrements to skill and performance in many different occupations, providing systematic evidence for the common-sense notion that many occupations place demands on workers that are more difficult to sustain at older ages. It is not just inequitable, but also irrational, to expect some older workers to continue in employment.

Earlier exit without penalties for those who have already worked for many years or in particular employment sectors seems a reasonably low bar for a feasible extended working life policy regime to surmount.

Employment policies are currently underdeveloped and simply encourage rather than require employers to employ, retain and/or train older workers. Evidence from earlier chapters suggests that, in most countries, few older workers have access to training or employment retention initiatives. While there are formal anti-age discrimination policies in most countries, there is strong evidence that age discrimination persists among employers. This legislation needs to be strengthened and enforced for extended working life policies to be meaningful. In a similar vein, extended working life advocates assume that flexible working policies are widely available when, in fact, they are underdeveloped, and are often synonymous with precarious employment. The underlying assumption of extended working life policy – that employment is available to older workers should they choose to engage in it – is simply not empirically accurate. High unemployment levels in many countries (in this volume, Portugal and Ireland especially) due to the global financial crisis, the difficulty that older workers confront in becoming re-employed when they lose jobs through economic restructuring and redundancies, and high levels of youth unemployment nearly everywhere call this assumption into question.

Patterns of unemployment experiences underscore the problematic tendency to rely too much on supply-side policies and private sector pension measures, which place the responsibility for being continuously and completely employable and building their own pensions on to individual women and men. Individuals who have spent many years in physically demanding work may be less likely to be able to find or perform such work when they are older in the future, which disadvantages women in such occupations. Where they are low paid, they are unlikely to be able to contribute to private pensions. Women's involvement in unpaid care and low-paid work, combined with their disproportionate representation in part-time employment, means that women are most likely to be reliant on state pensions/social security for all or most of their income in all the countries in this volume. At the same time, it seems implausible that the intended policy outcome of extended work life policies is to ensure poverty in old age for a substantial proportion of older women. Given the increased level of precarious work, older women and men in this type of work are even more likely to be reliant on state pensions/social security in the future. Compound that with the well-documented and widely known disadvantages that women's normative life courses impose, makes obvious the imperative that state pensions are maintained at current levels, or increased. How such outcomes are likely to be accomplished without a reversal of neoliberalising policy initiatives is hard to imagine.

The current trend in extended working life policies to link contributory state pensions more closely to wages and time spent in paid employment exacerbates women's disadvantage. Yet, the future health of national economies depends on stable populations of workers and consumers. Is it possible within a neoliberal framework to imagine policy initiatives that support the realities of both production and reproduction? More thoughtful policies could reverse or accommodate the neoliberal project to the greater benefit of vulnerable women. Since one of the characteristics of neoliberalism is individualisation, perhaps policies could be devised to account for women's typical, yet individualised, life courses by using the public pension systems to structure credit for socially essential unpaid labour. Introducing and expanding policies such as carer's benefit to give paid leave and pension credits for time spent caring for older people would help to alleviate some of the existing disadvantages that women face and should be adopted by countries (such as the US) that currently do not have such policies in place. More public provision of childcare and elder care, similar to those offered to Swedish families, would reduce the 'double shift' of paid and unpaid work currently faced by women in countries, like the US and Ireland, which lack such arrangements. Policies that encourage men to share the unpaid work of caring more equitably would also help to reduce the disadvantage faced by women and signal that governments recognise the essential character of care work and the need to distribute unpaid care work more fairly.

A more radical alternative would be to introduce income and pensions systems that fully accommodate unpaid labour as both socially necessary and contributing great value to a country's development and well-being. A universal citizen's income or citizen's pension, an entitlement based on citizenship and not linked to paid employment, would be one avenue to recognise the value of both paid and unpaid work. These should be set at a high enough level to preclude poverty. As affluent countries around the world grapple with a similar set of interlocking problems – stagnant economies, few prospects for expanding labour demand, the unavoidably obvious needs for child-rearing and elder care, and ageing populations – a citizen's income is an idea gaining traction in some policymaking circles. Whether such expansive policy ideas take hold, however, is a matter of political choice and may depend on expanding women's influence in policymaking circles to sensitise policymakers to take into account how the real lives of women are implicated in policies intended to extend working lives.

The future of extending working lives, beyond its seeming inevitability, is difficult to discern and tough to be optimistic about. One fact of policymaking is that it nearly always creates sets of winners and losers, and in the current climate of neoliberalism, the winners are most likely to be individuals who are securely employed and who have choices about how to exit employment with enough resources when retirement looms. However, other policy winners are created by extended working life expectations. Employers may enthusiastically support the idea, if not the practice, of extended working life because a labour market with surplus workers holds down wages and, by extension, boosts profits. As occupational pensions everywhere have been largely converted to defined contribution savings plans, decreasing the value of public pensions and simultaneously shifting more responsibility for retirement income to individuals through tax-subsidised private sector defined benefit plans creates other winners. Financial industries in all of these countries profit greatly from managing the transformed private sector individualised 'pension arrangements', with the well-employed and highly paid best positioned to take advantage of tax breaks, and those lacking a surplus to save gaining no benefit at all. Under such neoliberal policies, states simultaneously 'save' on public pension payouts by raising retirement ages and contracting benefits, while reducing state revenue (constraining state fiscal manoeuvres even further) by providing generous tax benefits to the well-heeled and smaller pensions to everyone else. At greatest risk and, we would argue, at increasing risk of disadvantaged outcomes – such as inadequate income through relegation to precarious low-paid employment – are workers who cannot (whether due to ill health, disability, high local levels of unemployment, caring responsibilities, ageism in labour markets or other reasons) be constantly engaged in full-time work over the entire adult life course and whose financial circumstances compel them to work at older ages.

It is difficult to be hopeful that policymakers will craft policies to carefully take into account the realities of gendered working lives, lives that necessarily involve both paid and unpaid work. One take-home message from the front materials and the country-specific chapters in this book points in the direction of increased expectations in all countries for citizens to work to later ages. What is not clear is what form the 20th-century institution of retirement will take for future cohorts of older people. John Myles (1989) characterised retirement as a triumph of welfare states of all types, bestowing a right for most people to stop work before wearing out. Yet, it appears that the moral imperative that national governments now want some of their citizens to follow is to risk 'wearing out' by remaining employed as long as possible and, ideally, to postpone or avoid retirement altogether. Changing the direction of current trends will take both imagination and more thoughtful policymaking than has occurred to date – not impossible tasks, but difficult ones. Finding ways to compensate (mainly) women for socially essential caring work through public income systems is one possible policy intervention – whether through carers' allowances during the times that care is provided or via credits to future pensions, or both – that would be one pathway to improved outcomes associated with extended working life that could help narrow some of the gender gaps in pay and pensions. Another potential avenue to equitable extended working life is via jobs training and programmes that would guarantee enough meaningful and adequately compensated flexible jobs for older workers who are able to work and who need or choose to continue in employment, complemented by sufficient income replacement programmes for those who cannot. Adjustment to disability policies could help create adaptive workplace technologies and create conditions that address some of the health and disability issues that affect some older workers. Rethinking the increasingly tight connections between pay levels and years of contributions for pensions that make full-time work for a full adult lifetime nearly the only way to acquire adequate retirement income could yield adjustments that fit individualised life courses. What is certain going forward is that economies need workers and societies need carers. If older women's disadvantage is to be minimised or addressed, it is also certain that the private sector alone cannot accomplish that. Only governments can redistribute resources and life chances in ways that would give future women (and vulnerable men) a fighting chance at good employment in later life and adequate income in old age.

References

Cahill, K.E., Giandrea, M.D. and Quinn, J.F. (2007) Down shifting: the role of bridge jobs after career employment, Center on Aging and Work, Issue Brief 6, Boston College. Available at: http://www.bc.edu/content/dam/files/research_sites/agingandwork/pdf/publications/IB06_DownShifting.pdf

Cahill, K.E., Giandrea, M.D. and Quin, J.F. (2016) To what extent is gradual retirement a product of financial necessity?, *Work, Aging and Retirement*, online first. Available at: http://workar.oxfordjournals.org/content/early/recent

Calasanti, T. (2005) Ageism, gravity, and gender: experiences of aging bodies, *Generations*, 29(3), 8–12.

Clarke, L.H. and Bennett, E.V. (2015) Gender, ageing and appearance. in J. Twigg and W. Martin (eds) *Routledge handbook of cultural gerontology*, London; Routledge, pp 133–40.

Doeringer, P.B. (ed) (1990) *Bridges to retirement: Older workers in a changing labor market*, Ithaca, NY: Cornell University Press.

Duncan, C. and Loretto, W. (2004) Never the right age? Gender and age-based discrimination in employment, *Gender, Work & Organization*, 11(1), 95–115.

DWP (Department for Work and Pensions) (2006) *A new deal for welfare: Empowering people to work*, Cm 6730, London: The Stationery Office.

Ebbinghaus, B. (2006) *Reforming early retirement in Europe, Japan and the USA*, Oxford: Oxford University Press.

Esping-Andersen, G. (1990) *The three worlds of welfare capitalism*, Princeton, NJ: Princeton University Press.

Ghilarducci, T. (2015) Senior class: America's unequal retirement, *American Prospect*, Spring Issue, http://prospect.org/article/senior-class-americas-unequal-retirement.

Hall, P.A. and Soskice, D.W. (eds) (2001) *Varieties of capitalism: The institutional foundations of comparative advantage*, Oxford: Oxford University Press.

Harrington Meyer, M. (2014) *Grandmothers at work: Juggling families and jobs*, New York, NY: New York University Press.

Harvey, D. (2005) *A brief history of neoliberalism*, New York, NY: Oxford University Press.

Jyrkinen, M. and Mckie, L. (2012) Gender, age and ageism: experiences of women managers in Finland and Scotland, *Work, Employment & Society*, 26(1), 61–77.

Kalleberg, A. (2009) Precarious work, insecure workers: employment relations in transition, *American Sociological Review*, 74, 1–22.

Lain, D. and Loretto, W. (2016) Workers over 65 in the UK: the new 'precariat'?, *Employee Relations*, 38(5), 646–64.

Loretto, W. and Vickerstaff, S. (2015) Gender, age and flexible work in later life, *Work, Employment and Society*, 29(2), 233–49.

Loretto, W., Vickerstaff, S. and White, P. (2005) *Older workers and the options for flexible work*, Working Paper Series no. 31, London: Equal Opportunities Commission.

Loretto, W., Vickerstaff, S. and White, P. (2007) Flexible work and older workers, in W. Loretto, S. Vickerstaff and P. White (eds) *The future for older workers: New perspectives*, Bristol: The Policy Press, pp 139–60.

Moen, P. (2011) From 'work–family' to the 'gendered life course' and 'fit': five challenges to the field, *Community, Work & Family*, 14(1), 81–96.

Munnell, A.H., Webb, A. and Chen, A. (2016) Does socioeconomic status lead people to retire too soon?, Issue Brief #16-14, Center for Retirement Research at Boston College. Available at: http://crr.bc.edu/briefs/does-socioeconomic-status-lead-people-to-retire-too-soon/

Myles, J. (1989) *Old age in the welfare state: The political economy of public pensions*, Lawrence, KS: University Press of Kansas.

Pitt-Catsouphes, M. and Matz-Costa, C. (2008) The multi-generational workforce: workplace flexibility and engagement, *Community, Work and Family*, 11(2), 215–29.

Rubery, J. (2015) Change at work: feminisation, flexibilisation, fragmentation and financialisation, *Employee Relations*, 37(6), 633–44.

Smeaton, D., Vegeris, S. and Sahin-Dikmen, M. (2009) *Older workers; employment preferences, barriers and solutions*, Equality and Human Rights Commission (EHRC) Research Report no. 43, Manchester: EHRC.

Standing, G. (2011) *The Precariat: The new dangerous class*, London: Bloomsbury.

Street, D. and Quadagno, J. (1993) The state, the elderly and the intergenerational contract: toward a new political economy of aging, in K.W. Schaie and W.A. Achenbaum (eds) *Societal impact on aging: Historical perspectives*, New York, NY: Springer, pp 130–50.

Syse, A., Solem, P.E., Ugreninov, E., Mykleton, R. and Furunes, T. (2014) Do spouses coordinate their work exits: a combined survey and register analysis for Norway, *Research on Aging*, 36(5), 625–50.

Taylor, P. and Earl, C. (2016) Bridging the grey divide – an international perspective on the ageing workforce and longer working lives, *Australian Journal of Social Issues*, 51(2), 119–25.

Vickerstaff, S. (2015) Domain: domestic and household factors, in H.M. Hasselhorn and W. Apt (2015) *Understanding employment participation of older workers: Creating a knowledge base for future labour market challenges*, Research Report, Berlin: Federal Ministry of Labour and Social Affairs and Federal Institute for Occupational Safety and Health. Available at: http://www.jp-demographic.eu/about/fast-track-projects/understanding-employment

Vosko, L. (2008) Temporary work in transnational labor regulation: SER-centrism and the risk of exacerbating gendered precariousness, *Social Indicators Research*, 88(1), 131–45.

Warhurst, C., Van den Broek, D., Hall, R. and Nickson, D. (2009) Lookism: the new frontier of employment discrimination, *Journal of Industrial Relations*, 51(1), 131–6.

Index

References to tables and figures are in *italics*

A

Acker, J. 42
active ageing concept 36, 55–6, 80, 91, 118, 138, 140–1
adult worker model 29, 58–9, 100–1, 129
age coding 30–1, 162
age discrimination *see* ageism/age discrimination
age structure of populations 7–9, *8*
Aged Pension (Australia) 82–5
ageism/age discrimination 21, 29–32, 37–9, 227–8
  in Australia 81–2
  gendered 21, 32–3, 38
  in Ireland 119, 124
  in Portugal 140–2, 149
  in Sweden 162
  in United Kingdom 179
  in United States 206–7
Altman, R. 177
Anderson, K.M. 102, 103
Apt, W. 28
Arber, S. 54
Australia 79–94, 221
  ageism/age discrimination 81–2
  care work *16*, 67, *68*, *69*, 83–4
  countervailing policies 92–4
  de-accumulation 91–2
  demographics 7, *8*
  disability pensions 84–5
  employment relations 89–90
  flexible working policies *65*
  gender pay gap *12*, 70, 89, 90
  government policy discourse 79–82, 221
  labour market *15*
  older workers' experiences *15*
  parental leave *69*

part-time work *15*, *17*, *19*, 90
pensions 63, 64, *65*, 82–9
precarious employment 89–90
retirement age *13*, 63, 64, *65*, 80, 81, 221
unemployment *15*, 90–1
women in the labour force *10*, *11*, *15*, 80, 87–8, *88*
auto-enrolment pension schemes 66, 183–4

B

Bastos, A. 143
Beatty, C. 181–2
Beck, U. 79, 87, 89, 91
Berger, E.D. 92
Bestmann, B. 109
Bodily, C.L. 30
Bray, J.R. 86
bridge jobs 232–3
Brussig, M. 107, 109
Butler, J. 93

C

Cahill, K.E. 233
Calasanti, T. 32, 42, 81
care work
  in Australia *16*, 67, *68*, *69*, 83–4
  childcare 36–7, 68–70, *69*, 110, 120, 151, 185, 205
  gendered critique of policies 56–60
  in Germany *16*, 67, 68, *68*, 69, *69*, 100–1, 104–5, 109–10
  and health of carer 84
  in Ireland *16*, 67, *68*, *69*, 119–20, 122, 124, 129, 130, 223

overview of *16*, 14–18, 42, 67–70, *68*, *69*, 236
parental leave 68–9, *69*, 84, 120, 150–1, 178, 205
and pensions 64, 66, 83–4, 104–5, 109–10, 122, 123, 144–5, 149–50, 183
in Portugal *16*, *68*, 69, *69*, 138, 144–5, 148, 150–1, 223–4
in Sweden *16*, 32, 67, 68, *68*, 69, *69*, 164, 168, 224
in United Kingdom *16*, *68*, *69*, 184–5, 187–8
in United States *16*, 67, 68, *68*, *69*, 197, 205, 210, 225
Carers Allowance (UK) 184–5
Carer's Benefit (Ireland) 120
Castells, M. 89, 90
childcare 36–7, 68–70, *69*, 110, 120, 151, 185, 205
parental leave 68–9, *69*, 84, 120, 150–1, 178, 205
citizen's income 236–7
Commission for Citizenship and Gender Equality (CIG) (Portugal) 141
Connell, R.W. 41, 83
Cooke, M. 60
Crenshaw, K. 39
critical age studies 38–9
Crompton, R. 58

D

Davis, K. 40
de-accumulation 87, 91–2
demographics
age structure 7–9, *8*
dependency ratio *8*, 8–9
life expectancy 6–7, 7
population structure *8*, 8–9
dependency ratio *8*, 8–9
Desai, S. 202
Dietz, M. 107–8
disability/invalidity pensions 84–5, 103, 108–9, 181–2
discrimination *see* ageism/age discrimination
Doeringer, P.B. 232

E

Earl, C. 177
early retirement 28, 56–7, 102–3, 104, 108, 128, 178

Ebbinghaus, B. 226
education, adult 162–3
education levels *15*, 145–6
Elder, G.H. 43
employability 13–14, *15*
Employment Equality (Age) Regulations 2006 (UK) 179
employment insecurity *see* precarious employment
employment relations 89–90
Employment Support Allowance (UK) 181–2
Ennals, R. 37
European Union 55, 124, 139, 179
Everingham, C. 57
extended working life policies (general)
and care work 14–18, 67–70
comparative assessment of 61–2, 226–9
complicating factors 5–6, 21–2
feminist perspective on work 41–2
focus on individuals 29–31
gender critique of 56–61
homogeneous narration of older people 31–3
and interactive societal processes 33–6
international policy actors 55–6
intersectionality 39–40
life-course perspective 42–4, 60–1
limitations of current debate 28–31
masculinity perspective 40–1
and narrow conception of work 36–7
and pensions 62–7
policy agenda 234–8
policy dimensions *55*
power perspective 37–9
research agenda 37–44, 229–33
theories and concepts 27–44

F

Fasang, A.E. 110
feminist gerontology 9, 32–3
feminist political economy perspective 41–2, 54, 60–1, 91, 118, 129, 197–8, 209
flexible working policies 64, *65*, 66, 67, *68*, 125, 150, 185–6, 232
Foster, L. 180, 183
Fothergill, S. 181–2
Fröhler, N. 108

G

gender gap in employment 15
gender pay gap 11–12, *12*, 69–70
  in Australia *12*, 70, 89, 90
  in Germany *12*, 70
  in Ireland *12*, 70, 120, 121, 127, *127*
  in Portugal *12*, 70, 147
  in Sweden *12*, 70, 159
  in United Kingdom *12*, 70, 177
  in United States *12*, 70, 197, *198*,
    203
Germany 99–112, 221–2
  care work *16*, 67, 68, *68*, 69, *69*,
    100–1, 104–5, 109–10
  demographics 7, *8*
  disability pensions 103
  early retirement 104, 108
  East v West Germany 107, 110, 111
  family model 100–1
  flexible working policies *65*
  gender pay gap *12*, 70
  impact of reforms 106–11
  invalidity pensions 108–9
  labour market *15*, 104
  mini-jobs 104, 221–2
  older workers' experiences 15
  parental leave 68, *69*
  part-time work *15*, *17*, *19*, 101
  pension gaps *12*, 70, 110
  pensions 63, 64, *65*, 70, 102, 102–10
  retirement age *13*, 63, *65*, 102–3
  unemployment *15*, 101, 104, 107–8
  welfare state 100–2
  welfare state reforms 102–6
  women in the labour force *10*, 11,
    15, 101, *106*, 106–7, 221–2
Ghilarducci, T. 210
Ginn, J. 54, 87
Giullari, S. 58–9
Grady, J. 182, 183, 184, 187
grandparents' leave 185
Great Recession 12–13, 125–6, 195,
    200, 204–5, 222, 223

H

Hagen, C. 108
Hasselhorn, H.M. 28
health *see* ill-health
Heinz, W.R. 43
Hilsen, A.I. 37
Himmelreicher, R.K. 108
Home-maker's Scheme (Ireland) 122,
    130

homogeneous narration of older people
    31–3, 164–9
*Hurley & Ors v Secretary of State for Work
    and Pensions* (2015) 184–5

I

ill-health
  of carers 84
  disability pensions 84–5, 103
  gender differences 167
  improved working environments
    165–6
  inadequate consideration of 232
  incapacity benefit 181–2
  invalidity pensions 108–9
  of older workers 127–8, *128*
  sick leave 163–4
  social gradient of 31
incapacity benefit 181–2
Individual Retirement Accounts (US)
    204–5
intergenerational equity 79–80, 82–3,
    91
international policy actors 55–6
intersectionality 39–40
invalidity pensions 108–9
Ireland 117–30, 222–3
  Active Ageing 118, 124
  ageism/age discrimination 119, 124
  care work *16*, 67, 68, *68*, *69*, 119–20,
    122, 124, 129, 130, 223
  demographics 7, *8*
  employment reforms 124–5
  flexible working policies *65*, 125
  gender pay gap *12*, 70, 120, 121,
    127, *127*
  Great Recession 125–6
  implications of reforms 125–8, 222–3
  labour market 15
  lack of debate 117–18
  older workers' experiences 15
  parental leave *69*, 120
  part-time work *15*, *17*, *19*, 119–20,
    126, 126–7
  pension gaps *12*, 70
  pensions 63, 64, *65*, 66, 70, 121–4,
    129–30
  precarious employment *126*, 126–8,
    129–30
  retirement age *13*, 63, 64, *65*, 123, 222
  state pension age 122–3
  unemployment *15*, 125
  women in the labour force *10*, 11,
    15, 119–21, 124–5, 127

J

Jefferson, T. 83
Johansson, S. 43

K

Keegan, M. 86
Komp, K. 43
Krekula, C. 30–1

L

labour force participation 9–11, *10*,
11, *15*
  in Australia *10*, *11*, *15*, 80, 87–8, *88*,
    90–1
  in Germany *10*, *11*, *15*, 101, *106*,
    106–7, 221–2
  in Ireland *10*, *11*, *15*, 119–21, 124–5,
    127
  in Portugal *10*, *11*, *15*, 141, 146–9,
    147
  in Sweden *10*, *11*, *15*, 158–9
  in United Kingdom *10*, *11*, *15*, *176*,
    176–8
  in United States *10*, *11*, *15*, *196*,
    225–6
labour market *15*
  gender segregation 41–2
  by industry 87–9, *88*
  nature of 18–21, 227
  'new economy' 33–6
  precarious employment *15*, 19, 34–5,
    89–90, *126*, 126–30, 148, *148*,
    221–2, 232–3
  see also part-time work
Lain, D. 175, 181
Lewis, J. 58–9
life-course perspective 31–2, 42–4,
    60–1, 177–8, 187–8, 230–1
life expectancy 6–7, *7*, 137–8
lifelong earnings principle 160
long-term care insurance (Germany)
    105
Loretto, W. 185, 188
Lorey, I. 34
Lyonette, C. 58

M

male breadwinner model 53, 62, 100,
    102, 119, 178, 222
marginal employment 104, 221–2
Martens, R. 110–11
masculinity perspective 40–1, 187, 188
maternity leave *see* parental leave
McDowell, L. 82
McMullin, J.A. 92
Meyer, T. 102
mini-jobs 104, 221–2
Moen, P. 43, 231
Möhring, K. 110
Myles, J. 7, 237–8

N

Naldini, M. 59
Nash, J.C. 40
National Insurance credits (UK) 182–3
'new economy' 33–6
Nordic universal breadwinner model
    147

O

occupational pensions 63, 66, 85–7,
    122, 183–4, 200, 203–4
OECD 55, 59, 60, 62–3, 66
Onyx, J. 57
O'Rand, A. 87
Orloff, A.S. 110
Özbilgin, M. 33

P

parental leave 68–9, *69*, 84, 120,
    150–1, 178, 205
  grandparents' leave 185
part-time work *15*, 17, *17*, *19*, 19–20,
    34–5, 232–3
  in Australia *15*, *17*, *19*, 90
  and care work 67
  in Germany *15*, *17*, *19*, 101
  involuntary *19*, 127, 146–7, *147*, 159
  in Ireland *15*, *17*, *19*, 119–20, *126*,
    126–7
  in Portugal *15*, *17*, *19*, 146–7, *147*
  in Sweden *15*, *17*, *19*, 159
  in United Kingdom *15*, *17*, *19*, 186
  in United States *15*, 17, *17*, *19*
paternity leave *see* parental leave
pay gap *see* gender pay gap
pension credits 122, 181, 182

pension gap 11–12, *12*, 53–4, 70, 110, 144, 198, *199*, 228
pensions
  in Australia 63, 64, *65*, 82–9
  auto-enrolment 66, 183–4
  and care work 64, 66, 83–4, 104–5, 109–10, 122, 123, 144–5, 149–50, 183
  disability/invalidity 84–5, 103, 108–9, 181–2
  and early retirement 28, 56–7, 102–3, 104, 108, 128, 178
  gender gap 10–12, *12*, 53–4, 70, 110, 144, 198, *199*, 228
  gender inequalities 60–7
  in Germany 63, 64, *65*, 70, 102, 102–11
  in Ireland 63, 64, *65*, 66, 70, 121–4, 129–30
  overview of 7–8, 55–6, 61–7, 234–6, 237
  in Portugal 63, 64, *65*, 70, 139–40, 143–5, 223
  private/occupational 62–3, 85–7, 122, 124, 140, 183–4, 200, 203–5
  in Sweden 64, *65*, 70, 159–61
  in United Kingdom 63, 64, *65*, 66, 70, 179–84, 225
  in United States 64, *65*, 66, 197–201, 203–5, 225–6
  see also retirement age; state pension age
Pensions Act 1995 (UK) 180
Pensions Act 2011 (UK) 180
Pensions Act 2014 (UK) 180
Perrons, D. 33–4
Personal Retirement Savings Accounts (Ireland) 122
Pfau-Effinger, B. 102
Phillipson, C. 175, 181
population statistics *see* demographics
Portugal 137–53, 223–4
  ageism/age discrimination 140–2, 149
  care work *16*, *68*, 69, *69*, 138, 144–5, 148, 150–1, 223–4
  current debate 152–3
  demographics 7, *8*, 137–8
  education levels *15*, 145–6
  employment patterns 146–50
  flexible working policies *65*
  intersectionality 141, 142
  labour market *15*, 146–50, *147*, *148*
  Nordic universal breadwinner model *147*
  older workers' experiences *15*

parental leave 69, *69*, 150–1
part-time work *15*, *17*, *19*, 146–7, *147*
pay gaps *12*, 70, 147
pension gaps *12*, 70, 144
pensions 63, 64, *65*, 70, 139–40, 143–5, 223
policy reforms 138–40
poverty 142–4, 145
retirement age *13*, 63, *65*, 139
social security 139–40, 144–5
temporary work *15*, 148, *148*
training *15*, 146
unemployment *15*, 147–8, *148*
women in the labour force *10*, *11*, *15*, 146–9, *147*
poverty 110–11, 142–4, 145, 202–3
power perspective 37–9
precarious employment *15*, 19, 34–5, 89–90, *126*, 126–30, 148, *148*, 221–2, 232–3
Prins, B. 40

R

recession 12–13, 125–6, 195, 200, 204–5, 222, 223
research agenda 229–33
retirement age 12–13, *13*, 28, 63–4, *65*, 229
  in Australia *13*, 63, 64, *65*, 80, 81, 221
  in Germany *13*, 63, *65*, 102–3
  in Ireland *13*, 63, 64, *65*, 123, 222
  in Portugal *13*, 63, *65*, 139
  in Sweden *13*, 28, *65*, 157–8, 160, 161, 164
  in United Kingdom *13*, 28, 63, 64, *65*, 178, 179
  in United States *13*, 63, 64, *65*, 200, 201, 202
Rodrigues, C.F. 144
Romeu Gordo, L. 109
Rosa, H. 35
Roscigno, V.J. 20
Rothgang, H. 109
Rubery, J. 35, 44, 185

S

Sassen, S. 88
Scherger, S. 107
Scheurman, W.E. 35
Schwalbe, M. 30

Senior Community Service Employment Program (US) 206
sick leave 163–4
Simonson, J. 109
skills
  adult education 162–3
  mismatch 20–1, 196
  training 13–14, *15*, 20–1, 125, 146, 162–3, 206
Social Security (US) 198, *199*, 200, 201–3
social trends 33–6
Solidarity Supplement for the Elderly (Portugal) 139–40
Standing, G. 34–5
state pension age 62, 63, 64, *65*, 82, 102–3, 122–3, 175, 179–81, 229
Staunæs, D. 40
Stratigaki, M. 58
Street, D. 54, 202
superannuation (Australia) 85–7
Sweden 157–70, 224
  ageism 162
  care work *16*, 32, 67, 68, *68*, 69, *69*, 164, 168, 224
  demographics 7, *8*
  education *15*, 162–3
  flexible working policies *65*
  gender-equality perspective 169
  homogeneous narration of older people 164–9
  labour market *15*, 158–9
  obstacles to extended working 162–4
  older workers' experiences *15*
  parental leave 68, 69, *69*
  part-time work *15*, 17, *19*, 159
  pay gaps *12*, 70, 159
  pension gaps *12*, 70
  pensions 64, *65*, 70, 159–61
  policies 164–70, 224
  retirement age *13*, 28, *65*, 157–8, 160, 161, 164
  retirement patterns 161–2
  unemployment *15*
  women in the labour force *10*, *11*, *15*, 158–9
Syse, A. 231–2

T

Taskforce on the Aging of the American Workforce 206
Taylor, P. 177
temporary work *15*, *126*, 148, *148*
Tilly, C. 30

training 13–14, *15*, 20–1, 125, 146, 162–3, 206

U

unemployment 13, *15*, 90–1, 101, 104, 107–8, 125, 147–8, *148*, 195–6, 205–6, 227
Unger, R. 109
United Kingdom 175–88, 224–5
  ageism 179
  auto-enrolment pension schemes 183–4
  benefit changes 181–2
  care work *16*, 68, *69*, 184–5, 187–8
  current discourse 175–6
  demographics 7, *8*
  flexible working policies *65*, 185–6
  gender pay gap *12*, 70, 177
  grandparents' leave 185
  labour market *15*
  National Insurance credits 182–3
  occupational pensions 183–4
  older workers' experiences *15*
  parental leave *69*, 177
  part-time work *15*, *17*, *19*, 186
  pension gaps *12*, 70
  pensions 63, 64, *65*, 66, 70, 179–84, 225
  policy changes 178–82, 224–5
  retirement age *13*, 28, 63, 64, *65*, 178, 179
  state pension age 175, 179–81
  unemployment *15*
  women in the labour force *10*, *11*, *15*, *176*, 176–8
United States 193–211, 225–6
  ageism 206–7
  care work *16*, 67, 68, *68*, *69*, 197, 205, 210, 225
  demographics 6, 7, *8*
  employment prospects policies 205–6
  flexible working policies *65*, 66
  future research/policy 209–11
  gender pay gap *12*, 70, 197, *198*, 203
  health insurance 207
  Individual Retirement Accounts 204–5
  labour market *15*, 194–5, 207
  life-course perspective 209–10
  older workers *15*, 194–7
  parental leave 68, *69*, 205
  part-time work *15*, 17, *17*, *19*
  pension gaps *12*, 198, *199*

pensions 64, *65*, 66, 197–201, 203–5, 225–6
piecemeal policies 207–9
poverty 202–3
private sector pensions 203–5
retirement age *13*, 63, 64, *65*, 200, 201, 202
Social Security 198, *199*, 200, 201–3
training *15*, 206
unemployment *15*, 195–6, 205–6
women in the labour force *10*, *11*, *15*, 225–6
universal breadwinner model 147
unmarked age-marked age 38–9
upskilling 162–3

V

Vickerstaff, S. 175, 185, 188

W

wages *see* gender pay gap
Walwei, U. 107–8
Welfare Reform Act 2007 (UK) 181
work-life balance *see* care work
workforce *see* labour force participation
Workforce Investment Act 1998 (US) 205

Y

Yuval-Davis, N. 32, 40

Printed and bound by CPI Group (UK) Ltd, Croydon, CR0 4YY

23/04/2025

14661023-0001